NEW APPROACH TO VIŚIṢṬĀDVAITA

NEW APPROACH TO VIŚIṢṬĀDVAITA

With Special Reference to Svāminārāyaṇa Vedānta

Dr. Suresh Vakil

BKP

BHARATIYA KALA PRAKASHAN
DELHI (INDIA)

First Edition : 2003

ISBN : 81-8090-011-8

Published by : C.P. Gautam
for BHARATIYA KALA PRAKASHAN
3421-A, IInd Floor, Narang Colony,
Tri Nagar, Delhi-110035.
Phone : 7153083 (O), 7177129 (R)

Laser Typesetting by : Twinkle Graphics, Delhi-110085.

Printed at : Santosh Offset Press, Delhi.

Dedicated

with great love to my wife

Freny

FOREWORD

I feel great pleasure in writing a foreword to 'New Approach to Viśiṣṭādvaita', with Special Reference to Svāminārāyaṇa Vedānta' by Dr. Suresh Vakil. I had the occasion to go through this work carefully and certainly it is an erudite and scholarly work.

Dr. Suresh Vakil is well known advocate by profession and scholar of Indian and Western Philosophy. He holds M.A and Ph.D in Philosophy of Gujarat University. He is also president of Tattvadarshana, a philosophical study group since three decades.

Śrī Svāminārāyaṇa (1781-1830 AD) was a great religious and social reformer of Hindu society in the eighteenth century A.D. He was critic of casteist society and accepted people from all walks of life into his Sampradāya (sect) without making any distinction between caste or creed.

His philosophy stands almost similar to Viśiṣṭādvaita of Rāmānuja. Infact Śrī Svāminārāyaṇa himself described his philosophy as Viśiṣṭādvaita only. Still he differs from Rāmānuja in several respects. His philosophy may be called as Neo-Viśiṣṭādvaita School of Vedānta. Rāmānuja accepts three realities, *viz.,* Cit, Acit and Īśvara (Brahman) while according to Svāminārāyaṇa there are five kinds of metaphysical entities, *viz.,* Parabrahman, Akṣarabrahman, Īśvara, Jīva and Māyā. Only Parabrahman or God is independent, all others are dependent on Him.

Svāminārāyaṇa like other Vaiṣṇava philosophers believes that God is personal (Saguṇa) not Nirguṇa. He also emphasizes the intense love for God, which is based on the real understanding of his greatness and glory. According to him, love of God (Bhakti) is the only means of attaining salvation. Complete surrender to God, is the most effective means of securing grace of the God. Just as a devoted wife loves her husband only, similarly the devotee of God should love God and only God (Pativratābhakti). This kind of love of God enables the spiritual aspirant to reach the state of Samādhi and have the mystical experience of God realization. This devotion must be supported and supplemented by Dharma, Jñāna and Vairāgya.

Śrī Svāminārāyaṇa's works are mostly in Gujarati language except Śikṣāpatrī. His followers have written commentary on Brahmasūtra, Upaniṣads and some other philosophical topics. But not much research work has been done to expose Śrī Svāminārāyaṇa's philosophy from all angles.

Dr. Suresh Vakil's work is unique in its own way. He has studied Śrī Svāminārāyaṇa's works thoroughly, which enables him to produce this very good piece of research.

Philosophical ideas are scattered here and there in original works of Śrī Svāminārāyaṇa, so systematic treatment of specific topic is very difficult task. Dr. Suresh Vakil has done it most efficiently and successfully.

This is an exhaustive study on the concept of Self in Svāminārāyaṇism. The author deals with concept of self from various angles, such as metaphysical nature of self, empirical nature of self, self and God, self and Akṣarabrahman, Law of Karma and rebirth, Liberation and Jīvanmukti. In the last chapter, Dr. Suresh Vakil has compared Śrī Svāminārāyaṇa's view with great stalwarts like Śaṅkara, Rāmānuja, Madhva, Vallabha and Plato which is in itself remarkable and first of its kind.

I have no hesitation in recommending this scholarly work to the readers and I am sure it will get the due welcome, which it deserves.

Ahmedabad
23.2.2003

Prof. Dr. Yajneshwar S. Shastri
Professor and Head
Department of Philosophy
Gujarat University
Ahmedabad-380009

PREFACE

The present work embodies my humble but sincere endeavour to understand Svāminārāyaṇa's Philosophy in general and his philosophy of self in particular. From my studies I have felt that Svāminārāyaṇa's philosophy is really a great heritage of mankind of which we can justly be proud. I have tried to grasp the basic principles of Svāminārāyaṇa in respect of the nature of self and to present the same in rational terms. My approach all throughout has been constructive.

I have divided my work into five parts. Each part consists of one or more chapters. Part one contains only one chapter (First Chapter). It purports to provide a general introduction to the subject of this work. Part Two comprises four Chapters (Chapters two to five). It deals with the metaphysical nature of self. Part three consists of six chapters (chapters six to eleven). It is concerned with the empirical nature of the self. Part Four comprises four chapters (chapter twelve to fifteen).

It endeavours to describe the fundamental concepts of Svāminārāyaṇiya Doctrine of Liberation and the means to attain liberation pointed out by Svāminārāyaṇa. Part Five consists of one chapter (Chapter Sixteen). It attempts to compare Svāminārāyaṇa's philosophy of self with that of Śaṅkara, Rāmānuja, Madhva, Vallabha and Plato.

From the studies I have made certain basic principles of Svāminārāyaṇa's philosophy of self emerge. It would be worthwhile to present here a brief statement of Svāminārāyaṇa's philosophy of self. According to Svāminārāyaṇa, self (Jīva) is real. It is one of the five realities accepted by Svāminārāyaṇa. The other four realities are : Parabrahman

(God), Akṣarabrahman (eternal abode and the first servant of God), Māyā (matter) and Īśvara (Cosmic God). Self is never created. It is eternal. It neither before nor after God. It is co-eternal with God. It cannot be destroyed. It is imperishable. There are innumerable selves. Self is neither part of God nor appearance of God. It is different and distinct from God having its own individuality. It is eternally existing in itself. Each self is different and distinct from the other selves. Self is formless. It has no gender. It is atomic in size. But, it pervades the entire body through its consciousness. Self is knower (jñātā). It is also doer (kartā) and enjoyer (bhoktā). It has three material bodies : causal (Karaṇa), subtle (sūkṣma) and gross (sthūla). Its consciousness has three states : waking (jāgrata), dream (svapna) and deep sleep (suṣupti).

God dwells in self as antaryāmī (indweller). God also dwells in it as sākṣin (witness self). God is the self of self, without God self can do nothing. Self is eternally dependent upon God for its existence and activity. Self's metaphysical dependence upon God has been explained by Svāminārāyaṇa in terms of śarīra-śarīri relation. According to Svāminārāyaṇa, souls are of three kinds : Nitya Mukta, Mukta and Baddha. Nitya Mukta souls are eternally liberated, like Nārada. Mukta souls were once bound (baddha), but they attained liberation by spiritual sādhanā and grace of God. Baddha souls are tied to the wheel of birth and death. They have yet to attain their liberation. Due to ignorance the self identifies itself with body. But self is not body. Self is distinct from body. The false identification of Self with body constitutes its bondage. The knowledge that the self is different from body as well as from God constitutes real knowledge which saves from the cycle of births and deaths. When by Sādhanā and by grace of God the self gains this saving knowledge, it attains liberation. On attaining liberation the self does not merge in God. It retains its individuality even in the state of liberation. Devotee of God, on liberation, after leaving the body goes to Akṣaradhāman. God eternally resides in Akṣaradhāman, the devotee of God attains a divine body. Housed in this divine body the self eternally resides there. With this divine body, it eternally worships and serves God and enjoys His blissful communion. For self, having once attained that state, there is no return from it to the mundane existence. Svāminārāyaṇa believes that even in the state of liberation in Akṣ aradhāman the difference between selves continues to exist, and each self attains knowledge and bliss of God in proportion to its receiving capacity. *i.e.* the capacity to understand and appreciate the greatness and glory of God. Of course, Svāminārāyaṇa has admitted the eternal growth of this capacity. But the greatness and glory of God being infinite and unfathomable, the self will never be able to have complete knowledge of God and hence there will be no full stop to its growth.

For the attainment of liberation Svāminārāyaṇa has pointed out different kinds of means of liberation. Dharma, Jñāna, Bhakti and Vairāgya are principle means of liberation. He has also pointed out auxiliary means of liberation. The principle four means are not exclusive of each but they are complementary to each other. In Svāminārāyaṇa's view religion at its highest must express a harmonious synthesis of dharma (morality), Jñāna (understanding of the metaphysical nature of self, world and God), Bhakti (intense love for and devotion to God) and Vairāgya (detachment towards sensuous objects of the world). Such a harmonious synthesis of these four means is found in the life of an Ekāntika Bhakta. In Svāminārāyaṇa's view Ekāntikapaṇuṅ is the highest form of religious life.

According to Svāminārāyaṇa although self is metaphysically dependent upon God, it has freedom to endeavour for its liberation. Self is free to love and worship God and adopt all or any of the means of liberation. All the same Svāminārāyaṇa has clarified that even if the self adopts all the means of liberation and worships God, it cannot attain liberation without the grace of God. Grace of God is sine qua non for the liberation of the self.

Svāminārāyaṇa has accepted the possibility of Jīvanmukti. If a man intensely loves God and it firmly devoted to Him, it is possible for him to attain liberation here and now.

Such a devotee of God attains liberation even while he is embodied.

Svāminārāyaṇa had found out a master principle for his life. This master principle was the stark reality of God. He was absolutely certain about God. The reality of God and his intimate relationship with God occupies the central place in his preaching and discourses. God was much more to Svāminārāyaṇa than a mere object of worship. The intimacy and report of communion with God in Prayer exceeded everything that he experienced in men. For him the ultimate fact giving religious value to everything in his world was God.

The age in which Svāminārāyaṇa lived and worked was an age of belief and universal faith in God. In Vacanāmṛta we do not find a single person asking him whether God existed or not. The assemblies before whom he spoke were constituted of his disciples, his devotees, saints, members of royal families and laity. They never questioned the existence of God. What they desired to know was, what kind of God was He? What is His nature? Where does He reside? What does He do? What are His attributes and powers? On these questions Svāminārāyaṇa spoke with great authority and certitude. What he meant to convey to the persons sitting in assemblies was like this, please listen to me carefully. It is not I who speak. It is God who speaks through me. He spoke with great assurance from his profound and personal experience. In teaching his disciples to love and worship God, he communicated something of his mystic experience to them. But something remained in-communicable. His attempt to communicate the incommunicable caused great awe and wonder in his disciples.

For Svāminārāyaṇa God is sovereign moral personality ruling the universe. In his view God is primarily occupied with human redemption. Man is free to make his decisions. Though God allows men to make their own decisions, he continues to love him throughout the redemptive process in which the consequences of their actions inevitably follow. God of Svāminārāyaṇa does not condemn any man to eternal damnation. God wants that every self must attain final emancipation and get eternal life in Akṣaradhāman. No person is to be excluded from endeavouring to reach Akṣaradhāman. No self is unworthy of Cod's grace or attaining eternal fellowship with God.

These are some of the universal and fundamental elements in Svāminārāyaṇa's philosophy of self and its relationship with God. The conception of liberation and particularly the details of the state of liberation are, perhaps, in my humble opinion, the greatest contribution of Svāminārāyaṇa to world thought. Svāminārāyaṇa gives a daring promise to the suffering humanity that man can be free from all kinds of pains if he lives the life of an Ekāntika. Today science and technology has advanced to a point where possibility of the annihilation of the entire human race cannot be ruled out. The root cause of the possibility and danger of annihilation and suffering of humanity lies in the grim fact that man is ignoring spiritual values. Man has become material minded. Materialist outlook dominates the world. Everywhere the cry of more goods and more comforts is heard. But when man comes in actual possession of the objects of worldly enjoyments, happiness remains away from him. Materialistic approach invariably brings pains and sufferings with it. Endeavours for removing pains and sufferings by acquisition of more and more material objects are just like endeavours to extinguish fire by petrol. And, therefore, the ideal of liberation (Mokṣa) as preached and pointed out by Svāminārāyaṇa become highly relevant and assumes great importance in the present context. An humble attempt, in the following pages, has been made to expound and explain that laudable ideal which is capable of inspiring hope in the hopeless and suffering humanity.

It would be quite in the fitness of things if I record here the points of originality which I have worked out in this thesis.

1. I have found out the interrelations of the scattered utterings of Svāminārāyaṇa in Vacanāmṛta and verses in Śikṣā Patrī and have worked out their epistemolo-

gical, ontological, ethical and religious implications with regard.

2. In determining the aforesaid interrelations and philosophical implications, I have attempted to interpret them in the true spirit of Svāminārāyaṇa. I have taken care to see that the interpretations I place on them are true and faithful to the views of Svāminārāyaṇa. I have tried to justify my interpretations by the actual words uttered by Svāminārāyaṇa in the situation concerned.

3. I have attempted to compare and contrasts the philosophical concepts and positions in regard to self, as interpreted by me, with some of the traditional and modern concepts of Indian and Western philosophy.

4. On the basis of the facts and relations found, I have conceived the nature of self and have attempted to present Svāminārāyaṇa's philosophy of self in as comprehensive a manner as has been possible by me and have also attempted to discover the grounds on which it can be justified.

5. I have attempted to present almost all the important features and aspects of Svāminārāyaṇa's philosophy of self. There are points on which two views are possible. But in such situations I have relied on Svāminārāyaṇa's own assertions and have attempted to interpret them in his true spirit.

6. Whenever I have come across contradictions, I have attempted to reconcile them and bring out the truth in apparently contradictory statements.

I thank Dr. Yajneshwar Shastri, Head of Department of Philosophy, Gujarat University and his wife Dr. Mrs. Sunanda Shastri for going through the manuscript and making valuable suggestions. It should be noted that my wife Freny gave me loving encouragement and great cooperation in this work.

Ahmedabad. **Suresh Vakil**
7th March, 2003

CONTENTS

Part Four

LIBERATION

Part Five

SOME COMPARISONS

LIST OF ABBREVIATIONS

R.	Radhakrishnan
S.P.	Śikṣāpatrī
V.A.S.	Vacanāmṛta Amadāvāda Series
V.G.F.S.	Vacanāmṛta Gaḍhaḍā First Series
V.G.M.S.	Vacanāmṛta Gaḍhaḍā Middle Series
V.G.L.S.	Vacanāmṛta Gaḍhaḍā Last Series
V.J.S.	Vacanāmṛta Jetalpura Series
V.K.S.	Vacanāmṛta Kāriyāṇī Series
V.L.S.	Vacanāmṛta Loyā Series
V.P.S.	Vacanāmṛta Pañcālā Series
V.S.S.	Vacanāmṛta Sāraṅgapura Series
V.V.S.	Vacanāmṛta Varatāla Series.

PART ONE

INTRODUCTION

CHAPTER 1

INTRODUCTION

1. Aim of the Present Work

Men have asked certain questions in all ages. They are asking them even today. These questions demand answers. Unless the answers are obtained, man is not at peace with himself. Philosophy deals with these questions. It tries to answer them.

The greatest question of man is, who am I? This is the question of questions. What is this "I"?

Man is very anxious to know it. Many philosophers have tried to answer this question. Svāminārāyaṇa has also answered the question. It is Svāminārāyaṇa's answer to this question that constitutes the subject of this work. We have made a search of Svāminārāyaṇa's answer and have attempted to reconstruct the same. Vacanāmṛta and Śikṣāpatrī are the field of my search. "The Philosophy of Sri Svāminārāyaṇa" by Dr. J.A. Yajnik, a work of high erudition and penetrating insight, has illumined my path at every step.

The present work aims at fairly complete and comprehensive critical exposition of Svāminārāyaṇa's philosophy of self. To the best of my ability I have tried to lay bare the nature of self as conceived by Svāminārāyaṇa. In my search I have found that although Svāminārāyaṇa has remained open to the ideas of other philosophical systems and thought-patterns, he has made very striking and valuable contributions of his own in many respects. In some respects he is unique. It is this that entitled him to a place of honour in Indian philosophy. His concept of five reals is unique and original.

Though influenced by Madhva, his concepts of Svatantra and Paratantra have many things of their own. Like Śaṅkara and Bradley, and such other philosophers, Svāminārāyaṇa is not interested in the distinction between "appearance" and "reality". He is interested in the distinction between independent Reality and dependent realities. Above all he is interested in reconciling the truths of Monism and Pluralism. As Dr. J.A. Yajnik has very clearly pointed out, Svāminārāyaṇa has achieved the reconciliation in a remarkable manner.[1]

2. Life of Svāminārāyaṇa

Svāmi Sahajānanda, who later became known as Svāminārāyaṇa was born in 1781. At an carly age of eleven, he left his home and went to Himālayas. He wandered all over India in quest of spiritual knowledge and visited almost all the places of religious importance. In the year 1800 he came to Loja, a village in Saurashtra, and accepted Svāmi Rāmānanda as his Guru (religious teacher). Although Rāmānanda had a number of senior disciples, he selected Svāminārāyaṇa and appointed him as the head (ācārya) of his organisation called Satsanga. Immediately after his appointment he started his spiritual work and propagated his philosophical and ethical principles. He exhibited extraordinary qualities of leadership and turned the small fellowship of Svāmi Rāmānanda into a great sampradāya with huge temples over-crowded with devotees, vast literature and well-established traditions. It should be noted that even during his life time he was worshipped as God (Puruṣottama) by thousands of his followers. It is remarkable to see that the bulk of his followers came from the lower strata of society. Even so called untouchables and Muslims, especially khojas, were among his followers.[1] As pointed out by Dr. K.M. Munshi, he made a way for non-Brahmins to become religious teachers.[2]

Svāminārāyaṇa was a mystic. As Dr. J.A. Yajnik has pointed out, he "was neither a metaphysician, nor a methodologist, nor a moral philosopher. He was primarily a great prophet who conceived a philosophy of religion in the light of his own intuitive experience and founded a religious community on the basis of the fundamental principles of this philosophy"[3].

After a serious illness of a few weeks Svāminārāyaṇa left his mortal frame. It was in 1830. He was 49. As James Burgess has pointed out, "At the death of Nārāyaṇa (Svāminārāyaṇa) there were about 5,00,000 heads of families holding his tenets and about 500 Sadhu ascetics"[4]. Appraising life and work of Svāminārāyaṇa Bhai Manilal Parekh says, "In him Hinduism approximates to the perfect form of Religion as in few others, and his life, work and the movement he led have few parallels in the entire range of history".[5] Pointing out a parallel Bhai Manilal says that "it is the life and work of Jesus Christ that offer a most striking resemblance to those of Svāminārāyaṇa."[6]

3. Vacanāmṛta

Vacanāmṛta is a book of discourses, arranged date-wise, delivered by Svāminārāyaṇa in different assemblies of saints and devotees assembled at different places.

These discourses are in the form of dialogues. But they are not debates. They are spiritual dialogues between the teacher and disciples. They have a didactic purpose. The disciples have free faith in the authority and the ability of the teacher to solve their problems and answer their questions. They approach the teacher with a question and receive a satisfactory answer, sometimes the disciples seek solution of the problems and puzzles disturbing them. Sometimes Svāminārāyaṇa himself would raise a question and invite answer from the audience. In most cases the answers that come from the assembly are found inadequate. Svāminārāyaṇa would either correct them or add to them or replace them. Sometimes he would pick up an interesting feature from some scripture and would attempt to elaborate and analyse it.

Vacanāmṛta is scriptural text. It can be said to be the Gospel of Svāminārāyaṇa Sect. It can also be described as

Svāminārāyaṇa Veda. Bhai Manilal has called it "The Book of Books".[1] It contains the essence of Svāminārāyaṇa doctrine. It embodies the religious and spiritual teaching of Svāminārāyaṇa. The book has a flavour of authority arising from the highly personal experience of the Master. It reveals the truth of Svāminārāyaṇa system of philosophy.

The book is in Gujarati language. The language of the discourses is simple and easy. But they are not easy to understand. Even the intellectuals will find the book difficult. The reason of it is this that in the discourses Svāminārāyaṇa has *inter alia* discussed the important questions of epistemology, ontology, religion and ethics. The discussions of these questions are bound to be difficult for the lay intellectual who has no previous acquaintance with philosophical doctrines and principles. It is very surprising to find the highly technical problems and the fundamental questions of epistemology, ontology, ethics and religion expressed and discussed in simple and easy Gujarati language. This makes it a classic in Gujarati literature. It is really a great book. "It can very well take its place among the religious classics of the world."[2] Giving a characteristic description of Vacanāmṛta Dr. J.A. Yajnik has written, "Inspite of the scattered character of the discussions in Vacanāmṛta, the clarity and consistency of Śrī Svāminārāyaṇa's vision pervades the whole collection. This, however, cannot be revealed unless a careful analysis is made. Thus painstaking and profound study of Vacanāmṛta is absolutely necessary for the clear understanding of epistemological, metaphysical, religious and ethical principles of Śrī Svāminārāyaṇa."[3]

4. Śikṣāpatrī

Śikṣāpatrī is in Sanskṛta. It is written by Svāminārāyaṇa himself for his followers scattered throughout the different parts of the country. It contains 212 verses. It is a Code of Moral Conduct. It embodies Moral Rules prescribed by Svāminārāyaṇa. Bhai Manilal calls it "an Epistle of Precepts". He also describes it as a kind of Law Book.[1] Although strewn with metaphysical flashes, Śikṣā-Patrī is primarily a book of ethics. Dr. B.C. Desai calls it "document of ethics"[2]. It lays down duties and virtues pertaining to Gṛhasthāśrama and Tyāgāśrama. It contains regulations of the life of householders as well as ascetics. As observed by Dr. B.G. Desai, "In Śikṣāpatrī Svāminārāyaṇa specifies in a summary manner the duties of one and all. A detailed list of duties is given.[3] Analysing the structure of Śikṣāpatrī, Dr. B.G. Desai has pointed out that, "the first twelve ślokas are by way of general introduction. From the 11th to the 122nd ślokas, he (Svāminārāyaṇa) describes the Sādhāraṇa dharma of men, and gives there directions on numerous points such as Ahimsā, Conduct, Diet & Drinks, Friendship, Suicide, Religious Toleration, Relationship between men and women, Health & Hygiene, Respect, Habit-formation, Etiquette, Work and Aptitude, Dress, Religious marks and symbols, Worship, Treatment to others, Pilgrimage, Varṇāśrama, Penance, Scriptures, Dharma, The twice born etc."[4] It is in this part that we have his views on god, self and world. From the 123rd to the 202nd ślokas Viśeṣa dharmas of Ācārya, of Vahuje, of Male Gṛhasthīs, of Female Gṛhasthīs, of Rulers, of widows of Brahmacāris and Sādhus.[5] In its true spirit Śikṣāpatri is an instrument of command. The whole book is written in the form of a directive. Although the book is very small, it points out a way in which Svāminārāyaṇa's philosophical principles can be made practically applicable to the problems and facts of life. It evinces Svāminārāyaṇa's reformative interest in organising a moral community. It presents Svāminārāyaṇa as a great reformist.

5. State of Philosophical Studies on Svāminārāyaṇism

It would be worthwhile to cast a glance at the state or philosophical studies on Svāminārāyaṇism. Dr. Macnicol, R.G. Bhandarkar, John Mckenzie, Dr. R.D. Ranade and Monier Williams were renowned scholars of Indian religious systems. It is very regrettable that the valuable contribution made to philosophical systems of India by Svāminārāyaṇa escaped their notice. Dr. Macnicol, R.G. Bhandarkar and John Mckenzie have not written a single sentence about the life and philosophy of Svāminārāyaṇa in their scholarly works. Monier Williams, Dr. R.D. Ranade and some others have merely said that he was a great social reformer. They have not taken any note of his philosophy.

Bhai Manilal Parekh has written a book named "Shrī Svāminārāyaṇa" (1936). The book is well written. But it is largely concerned with the life and work of Svāminārāyaṇa. It is not a philosophical work. Nor does it claim to be so.

There is a book entitled "Life and Philosophy of Shree Svāminārāyaṇa (1967) by Shri H.T. Dave. Although this book claims to be an exposition of Svāminārāyaṇa's philosophy, it is, in fact, no more than a biographical narration of Svāminārāyaṇa in an ecclesiastical setting. It gives no idea of the Svāminārāyaṇa system of philosophy. It only gives some information about the life and teaching of Svāminārāyaṇa to non-technical lay readers.

Very recently (1981) on the occasion of the bicentenary commemoration of Svāminārāyaṇa a Bicentenary Commemoration Volume under the title "New Dimensions in Vedānta Philosophy" has been published in two parts. This volume claims to bring out the latent truths and clarifications about Vedāntic teachings of Svāminārāyaṇa and to provide new dimensions to Vedānta philosophy.[1] The volume consists of articles by various authors some of whom are known for their philosophical studies. But most of the authors are not acquainted with Svāminārāyaṇa's philosophy in all its technicalities. Naturally one cannot expect such a volume to provide a coherent and consistent exposition of Svāminārāyaṇa's philosophy. The volume does no more than to provide some social, ethical and religious aspects of his teaching.

In the existing literature on Svāminārāyaṇism Dr. J.A. Yajnik's book "The Philosophy of Srī Svāminārāyaṇa" dominates the field. The book is of an exceptional character. It was a thesis on which the author was awarded Ph.D. Degree. This is the only book wherein we find a consistent and clear-cut exposition of Svāminārāyaṇa system of philosophy. As noted above, the celebrated scholars of India have failed to produce a system of Svāminārāya philosophy. As pointed out by Dalsukh Malvania, "The Credit goes to Dr. Yajnik for reconstructing for the first time a comprehensive philosophical system out of the teaching of Svāminārāyana who was more interested in religion and morality than in Logic and Metaphysics."[2] Shri Malvania has rightly observed that "Svāminārāyaṇa's philosophical ideas which constitute the basis of his moral and religious teachings were never explained in the past in the manner Dr. Yajnik has explained them in this book. He has not only critically expounded the philosophical system of Svāminārāyaṇa but also attempted a comparison between Svāminārāyaṇism and the different school of Indian and Western philosophy."[3] One cannot but feel that in this work Dr. Yajnik has ably brought out the basic principles of Svāminārāyaṇism and has systematically dealt with epistemological, metaphysical, psychological, ethical and religious questions of Svāminārāyaṇa's philosophy. To my knowledge there is no work in any language wherein basic principles of Svāminārāyaṇa's philosophy have been so clearly and consistently explained. Till the advent of Dr. Yajnik's book, there was nothing that could give us the entire system of Svāminārāyaṇa's philosophy.

But, in Dr. Yajnik's work the problem of self has received a general treatment which is received by all other philosophical problems dealt with therein. When the work is of a comprehensive nature, like Dr. Yajnik's book no single problem can be expected to receive special attention. Naturally, therefore, the problem of self could not have been dealt with in details and in all its perspectives. Many aspects are just touched and left to be worked upon in future. Some aspects dealt with therein need fuller consideration and further elucidation. There are certain areas in Svāminārāyaṇa's philosophy of self which have remained completely unexplored and certain points absolutely untouched.

It is under this condition of philosophical literature on Svāminārāyaṇism that I was inspired to take up the problem of self for my studies. It is matter of common knowledge that the problem of self always occupies a central position in all philosophical systems. Therefore, with a keen desire to attempt to do what was left out and what remained to be done, I undertook study of the nature of self in Svāminārāyaṇism. To the best of my ability I have attempted to go in all possible details and thereby tried to work out "A Comprehensive Philosophy of Self" from the standpoint of Svāminārāyaṇism. It is hardly necessary to add that as far as our knowledge goes, there is no work in any language dealing with Svāminārāyaṇist philosophy of self in all its details. Hence the justification of my humble attempt.

6. Method Employed

A word may be said about in method employed in this work. Four words would indicate the method : search, interpretation, reconstruction, logical arrangement. The interpretations made and the positions arrived at are supported by evidence from Vacanāmṛta and Śikṣāpatrī. My approach to Svāminārāyaṇa's philosophy is critical. By "Critical" I do not mean "Controversial". Instead of falling into polemics, I have tried to harmonise contradictory situations. In every system of thought some contradictions are bound to appear. I have attempted to reconcile the contradictions, of course very few, and to derive a synthetic truth from them in the true spirit of Svāminārāyaṇa's philosophy. Besides being "synthetically critical" in the sense explained above I have also tried to be "analytically critical" in the sense that I have tried to take meticulous care to see that Svāminārāyaṇa is not misrepresented on any point in this work.

REFERENCES

1. Aim of the Present Work

1. Dr. J.A. Yajnik, The Philosophy of Śrī Svāminārāyaṇa (1972), p. 131.

2. Life of Śrī Svāminārāyaṇa

1. Dr. J.A. Yajnik, The Philosophy of śrī Svāminārāyaṇa (1972), p. 4.

2. Dr. K.M. Munshi, Preface to First Edition, Life and Philosophy of Shree Svāminārāyaṇa (1974) by Shri H.T. Dave, p. 12.
3. Dr. J.A. Yajnik—The Philosophy of Śrī Svāminārāyaṇa, p. 4.
4. James Burgess, The Svāminārāyaṇ Sect and its Leaders (1887) p. 4, quoted by Dr. J.A. Yajnik in his work The Philosophy of Śrī Svāminārāyaṇa, p. 4.
5. Bhai Manilal Parekh : Preface to Śrī Svāminārāyaṇa, (1936), p. xii.
6. *Ibid.*, xiii.

3. Vacanāmṛta

1. Bhai Manilal Parekh, Śrī Svāminārāyaṇa (1936) p. 260.
2. *Ibid.*, p. 260.
3. Dr. J.A. Yajnik, The Philosophy of Śrī Svāminārāyaṇa, p. 9.

4. Śikṣāpatrī

1. Bhai Manilal Parekh, Śrī Svāminārāyaṇa, p. 282.
2. Dr. B.G. Dasai, Ethics of Śikṣhāpatrī (1970), p. 1.
3. *Ibid.*, p. 4.
4. *Ibid.*, p. 3.
5. *Ibid.*, p. 3.

5. State of Philosophical Studies on Svāminārāyaṇism

1. Preface, New Dimensions in Vedānta Philosophy (1981), p. viii.
2. Dalsukh Malvania, Foreword to Dr. Yajnik's book, The Philosophy of Śrī Svāminārāyaṇa, p. 1.
3. *Ibid.*, p. 1.

PART TWO

METAPHYSICAL NATURE OF SELF

CHAPTER 2

CONCEPT OF SELF

1. Five Reals

How many reals are there? If such a question is asked by someone, different philosophical systems would answer it differently. According to Mādhymika, a school of Buddhism, nothing is real and permanent. Everything is transitory and void. Cārvāka believes that matter is the only reality. According to him, consciousness is the by-product of matter and therefore unreal. As against Cārvāka Śaṅkarācārya believes that the consciousness is the only reality and matter is unreal. According to him, Brahman is the sole reality, one without the second. According to Sāṅkhya, there are two ultimate reals : puruṣa (self) and prakṛti (matter). According to Rāmānuja, Madhva and Vallabha there are three ultimate reals : God, souls and matter. Rāmānuja calls his reals Īśvara (God), Cit (souls) and acit (matter). Madhva calls them Īśvara (God), cetana and Acetana. Vallabha calls them Īśvara, Jīva and Jagat. According to Nyāya-Vaiśeṣika system of philosophy, there are seven reals. They are dravya (substance), guṇa (quality), karma (action), sāmānya (generality), viśeṣa (particularity), samavāya (inherence) and Abhāva (non-existence). In Nyāya-Vaiséṣika philosophy, ātmā (soul) is considered as an eternal substance. There are two kinds of souls Jīvātman (individual souls) and paramātaman or Īśvara (supreme soul). According to Jaina philosophy, there are nine reals. They are Jīva (living), ajīva (non-living matter), āsrava (influx of matter into soul), puṇya (meritorious deeds), pāpa (evil deeds), bandha (bondage), samvara (stopping the influx of new matter into the soul), Nirjara (exhaustion of karmas in soul) and mokṣa (liberation).

Svāminārāyaṇa does not accept any of the above views. According to him, there are five reals. They are Jīva (self), māyā (matter), Īśvara (higher soul), Akṣarabrahman and Parabrahman (God).[1] These five kinds of entities are ultimate ontological reals in the sense that they are eternally existing. They are ontologically different from each other. Their difference is eternal and irremovable.[2]

2. No Distinction Between Jīva, Jīvātman and Ātman.

Any one who reads Vacanāmṛta will find that for the purpose of signifying self or soul Svāminārāyaṇa uses three words. These three words are "Jīva", "Jīvātman", and "Ātman". Largely he uses the word "Jīva" to indicate self or soul. But some times he uses the word "Jīvātman"[1] or "Ātman"[2] for the same purpose. He uses these three words synonymously. He has given no reason why he chooses a particular word instead of the other. This means that the current usage in Gujarati language permitted him to use these three words as synonyms.

3. Svāminārāyaṇa Proves the Existence of Self

On a plain reading of Vacanāmṛta one might have an impression that Svāminārāyaṇa does not make any attempt to prove the existence of self (jīva). One might also have an impression that Svāminārāyaṇa takes it for granted that the existence of self cannot be proved. But a careful scrutiny of the sentences of Vacānāmṛta will disclose that such an impression is not correct. It is not that Svāminārāyaṇa makes no attempt to prove the existence of self. It is true that Svāminārāyaṇa does not advance elaborate and well chiselled arguments to prove the existence of self. But in a simple manner, by simple statements, Svāminārāyaṇa does seek to establish the existence of self. Let us see how he does it. Knowledge is defined by Svāminārāyaṇa as the awareness of something.[1] The knowledge or awareness of something is either produced by sense experience or by reasoning, or by intuitive experience.[2] Thus, sense, reason and intuition have been accepted by Svāminārāyaṇa as three valid methods of knowledge. Out of these three methods Svāminārāyaṇa adopts reason and intuition to establish the existence of self.

Svāminārāyaṇa , in clear terms, says that the existence of self cannot be proved by sense perception, but it can certainly be proved by inference.[3] Inference is a method of reason. Using this method of reason Svāminārāyaṇa argues that when a speaker explains something to the hearer, he is revealing his self. Similarly, when the hearer understands what is explained to him, he also reveals his self. This means that there is some entity which makes possible the activity of speaking and hearing or understanding. This entity is nothing, but the self.[4] This is how, by means of reason Svāminārāyaṇa establishes the existence of self.

Then Svāminārāyaṇa takes to the method of knowledge by intuition. He says that when a person has an intuitive experience, the self becomes evident to him. He feels that "I am the self."[5] In intuitive experience he becomes conscious of his self. He feels "I am". He is certain of his self.[6] Svāminārāyaṇa says that when the limitations of sense organs are overcome and the highest intuitive experience is made possible one realises the self as it is.[7]

This view of Svāminārāyaṇa is supported by many Indian and Western philosophers. According to Śaṅkarācārya self-knowledge is the basis of all knowledge. Radhakrishnan says that, "All experience is always an experience to an "I". An "I" is implicit in all awareness. This "I" is not the body, however intimate the connection of the body with the "I" may be.[8] Radhakrishnan further says that "I" implicit in all knowledge is not something to be inferred from experience, but something immediately lived and known by experience.

According to Dr. J.A. Yagnik, it is not necessary to prove the existence of self as it immediately known in each and every kind of cognition.[10] Instinctive certainty of the self is ascertained by St. Augustine's formula : S Faller sum. Descartes doubted everything. But he could not doubt his own existence. For, he said, I am really doubting. Whateverelse may be doubtful, but the fact that I am doubting is indubitable. I could not doubt if I did not exist. He summed up his argument in his famous formula : I think, therefore, I am. (cogito, ergo sum). According to Kant, all knowledge is contained in judgements. The "I think" must accompany all my judgements. The "I think" is an act of spontaneity. It cannot he regarded as belonging to mere sensibility. It is in all acts of consciousness one and the same, and unaccompanied by it no representation can exist for me.[11] According to Peter Koestenbaun, the self manifests itself in consciousness in a manner altogether different from ordinary objects of experience. Self is experienced as the source of consciousness whenever experiencing takes place. Whenever man is conscious, self is experienced. I experience myself as distinct from the body and our psychological states. I experience my anxiety, my joy and my body. The "I" that does the experiencing is structurally different from that which it experiences.[12]

As shown above, we can see that Svāminārāyaṇa has made some attempt to prove the existence of the self. And therefore, the observation of Dr. J.A. Yajnik that "The attempt to prove the existence of self and its consciousness is not made by Shrī Svāminārāyaṇa"[13] is to be understood only in the light of the above mentioned qualification.

4. What is Self?

There are many theories of self. But there are four theories which can be said to be the main theories of self. They are (1) the theory of soul-substance, (2) the theory of empirical self, (3) the theory of noumenal self and (4) the theory of self as pure consciousness.

The soul substance theory is subscribed by Plato, Aristotle, Augustine, Acquinas, Descartes, Leibnitz, Locke Berkley and others in Western Philosophy. In Indian philosophy this theory is subscribed by Jainas,[1] Vaiśeṣika,[2] Nyāya,[3] Pūrva Mīmāmsā[4] and Rāmānuja[5]. According to this theory, self is a permanent spiritual substance which lies behind and beyond fleeting mental processes. It is a principle of spiritual unity which underlies all thinking, feeling and willing.

In Western philosophy David Hume is the Chief proponent of the theory of empirical self. In Indian Philosophy Nāgasena[6] and Nāgārjuna[7] subscribe to this theory. According to this theory self is an aggregate of mental processes without any underlying principle of unity among them. This theory denies the existence of an abiding spiritual substance behind mental states.

Immenual Kant advances the theory of noumenal self. This theory was anticipated in India by Diṅṅāga in the fifth century.[8] According to this theory self is not a substance. Substance is a category of understanding. The self applies the category of substance to phenomena. Self is the source of categories. It is the permanent and abiding background and support of all mental phenomena. Kant calls it pure or transcendental self.[9]

Śaṅkarācārya, as is very well known, is the chief advocate of the theory of self as pure consciousness. Sāṅkhya[10] and Madhva[11] subscribe to this theory. Of these four theories Svāminārāyaṇa accepts the theory of soul-substance. In very clear terms he has declared that soul is a spiritual substance (caitanya vastu).[12] According to Svāminārāyaṇa the self is a self-luminous spiritual substance possessing consciousness as its essential attribute.[13] Svāminārāyaṇa would not agree with Kantian view which does not regard self as a substance. He would say to Kant that which is the source of categories has to be substantial. So also he would not agree with Hume and all those who maintain that self is nothing more than a bundle of different perceptions which succeed one another with an inconceivable rapidity. Nor would he agree with Śaṅkarācārya who holds that self is mere consciousness without substance. Svāminārāyaṇist argument against both Huminions and Śaṅkarites would be that it is not possible either for fleeting or for pure consciousness to be there without the ontological support of self. Thus according to Svāminārāyaṇa consciousness is a quality of self and not an independent entity.

5. Self is not By-product of Matter

According to Svāminārāyaṇism, soul and consciousness are not the by-product of the conglomeration of physical elements. It is well known that Cārvākas and other materialists regard them as mere by-product of matter. It is a matter of common knowledge the Cārvākas regard matter as the only reality. What is material is real. According to them, ultimate elements are four : earth, water, fire and air.[1] Consciousness is produced when these four elements combine in a certain proportion.[2] Consciousness, according to Cārvākas, is the by-product of these elements. And thought is a function of matter.[3] Just as the combination of betel, areca nut and lime produces the red colour, though the ingredients separately do not possess red colour, in the same way particular combination of the elements produces consciousness. Given these four elements and their particular combination, consciousness manifests itself in the living body.[4] Consciousness is always found associated with the living body and vanishes when the body disintegrates.[5]

It is also said that the consciousness is nothing but an epiphenomenon of the body. According to epiphenomenalism, the relation of consciousness to body is like that of the shadow to the person. The motion of the person cause the motion of his shadow, but motion of the shadow does not cause the motion of the person. Similarly, the physical causes the mental, but mental never in turn causes physical.[6]

So also behaviourism denies that there is any non-material element like mind, consciousness or soul in our make-up. According to behaviourism, human being is all body. There is neither mind nor soul. As for consciousness, it is a by-product of bodily processes which accompany them. It does not cause the processes it accompanies.[7]

The difficulty with these theories is this that they commit us to the belief that the entire course of events in the physical world would have been exactly the same as it is now, even if there had been no minds at all. But how, one might ask, could cities have been built, books and symphonies written, colleges attended and courses tought, if human minds were not causally efficacious in the world ?[8]

Svāminārāyaṇa would not agree with any of these theories which maintain that the Jīva is the by-product of matter. Svāminārāyaṇa has clearly stated in Vacanāmṛta that the soul is in no way like the body.[9] According to him soul is neither matter nor a by-product of matter. It is a spiritual substance completely different (Vilakṣaṇa) from three material bodies.[10] Human being is not all body. There is a soul which resides in the body.[11] Its consciousness pervades over entire body.[12] If the consciousness, Svāminārāyaṇa would contend, is merely an outcome of the four elements, as maintained by Cārvāka materialists and behaviourists, then even the corpse can be conscious which, however, is against our experience. Consciousness in the body is always due to the contact of another substance whose essential quality is consciousness and this substance is jīva. Svāminārāyaṇa says that wrongly identifies its body with itself. Jīva is not body. It is different from body.[13]

Svāminārāyaṇa has gone to the extent of saying that so long as one identifies one's body, all one's knowledge becomes meaningless.[14] Dr. J.A. Yajnik has observed that "from the stand point of Svāminārāyaṇism is utterly wrong to regard the self as a by-product of material forces or a psychophysical series of saṅghāta or even a synthetic unity apperception".[15]

6. Self, Distinct from Body

According to Svāminārāyaṇa the self is distinct from the body.[1] Svāminārāyaṇa has again and again, emphatically said that the self is totally different from the body. He is never tired of pointing out that the self and the body are not one. According to Svāminārāyaṇa, the self and the body are not only not one, but are opposed to each other. The qualities of one are fundamentally different from the other. The self is conscious and the body is unconscious. The self is pure and the body is impure. The self is immortal and body is mortal. The self is blissful and the body is painful.[2] The body ages. The self does not age. The body is transitory and changes every moment. The self is permanent and changeless. It ever remains the same (ajara).[3]

According to Svāmināràyaṇa the body does not posses any attribute which is possessed by the self. There is not a single quality in the body which can be attributed to the self. Nor is there any quality in the self which can be attributed to the body.[4] Explaining the doctrine of fundamental difference between the self and the body, Svāmināràyaṇa has said that the self is different from gross, subtle and causal bodies[5] which are material (māyika) in nature.[6] According to him, the self is neither gross body, nor subtle body nor causal body. According to Svāmināràyaṇa self is different from three states of consciousness. The self is neither waking state nor dream state nor deep sleep state. So also self is neither cognitive senses nor conative senses nor internal senses (antaḥkaraṇa). Self is different from all these bodies, states and senses.[7] But due to ignorance the self identifies itself with these external and internal senses.[8] Svāmināràyaṇa says that if one realise one's self as different from the body, one will not have any attachment to the body. Nor will one have any attachment to any thing or person related to the body.[9] When one becomes free from the attachment to the body, one becomes free from the desire to enjoy sensuous objects.[10]

7. Dimension of the Self

The problem of the dimension of the self (jīva-parimāṇa) is not easy of solution. Since ancient times Indian mind has been thinking about it and yet the problem has remained as refractory as it was.

Indian philosophy gives four different answers to the question of the size of the soul. The first answer is that the dimension of the soul is atomic (aṇu-parimāṇa). The second answer is that it is of the size of the thumb (aṅguṣṭha parimāṇa). The third answer is that the soul is as big as the body (deha-parimāṇa). And the fourth answer is that it is neither atomic, nor of the size of the thumb, nor of the size of the body, but it is all pervasive (vibhu). The first view is adopted by the philosophers of different schools of Vaiṣṇavism. The second view is maintained by Śvetāśvatara Upaniṣad.[1] The third view is held by jaina philosophers. And the fourth view is advocated by Nyāya-Vaiśeṣika, Pūrva Mīmāsā, Sāṅkhya-Yoga and Advaita Vedānta. Svāminārāyaṇa holds the first view.[2] He says that the dimension of the soul is atomic. According to him, the soul is as subtle as the atom (aṇu-sūkṣma).[3]

This atomic view of Svāminārāyaṇa regarding the dimension of the soul is supported by Muṇḍakopaniṣad.[4] Rāmānujācārya[5] and Madhvācārya[6] also hold this view.

Strictly speaking in Advaita Vedānta there is no question of the dimension or the size of the soul. Soul is all-pervasive. It is identical with parabrahman, the one and the only reality. But according to Svāminārāyaṇa, the self is eternally different from parabrahman (God)[7] and, therefore, he does not accept this view. Now, of the remaining three views, one either accepts the atomic view (aṇuparimāṇavāda) or thumb-size view (aṅguṣ ṭha Parimāṇavāda) or body size view (deha parimāṇavāda). Svāminārāyaṇa believes that the self is formless (arūpa).[8] Size presupposes a form. And therefore Svāminārāyaṇa cannot accept body-size view. For the same reason he cannot accept thumb-size view. So far as body-size view is concerned there is another difficulty also. The difficulty is that this view makes the soul expanding and contracting. If the dimension of the self is identical with the body, the conclusion is inevitable that the soul is perishable like the body. Body size view purports to deprive the soul of its eternality and makes it non-eternal. Therefore, according to Svāminārāyaṇa, aṇuparimāṇavāda is the only acceptable view.

The Svāminārāyaṇa's view that the soul is atomic also deserves to be understood with some reservations or qualifications. It seems that the soul is said to be atomic in order to indicate its two characteristics : (1) eternality and (2) subtlety. This interpretation seems justified because Svāminārāyaṇa speaks of the soul also as formless (arūpa). The following section throws greater light on this point.

8. Self is Formless

According to Svāminārāyaṇa, every physical organism has a soul. In other words, all living bodies have souls.[1] According to Svāminārāyaṇa, the size of the soul is atomic.[2]

What do we mean by atomic? Atomic, obviously, means like an atom. What is the size of a material atom? It is smallest; so small that it cannot be perceived. It is a mere physical point with only position and no magnitude. It is imperceptible. It defies experience. Mathematics is the only instrument of dealing with it.[3]

According to Svāminārāyaṇa, soul is not a material entity. It is a spirit fundamentally different from matter.[4] Soul, according to Svāminārāyaṇism, is a spiritual "atom", so to say. Now if material atom cannot be perceived, how can a spiritual "atom" be perceived? This spiritual atom is a mere being (sattāmātra). It is a metaphysical point of mere existence. Now, such a metaphysical point can naturally have no shape. It cannot have any form. It must be shapeless and formless. Svāminārāyaṇa says that the soul is formless (nirākāra).[6] According to Svāminārāyaṇa, atomic soul is a mere being without any dimension and therefore it cannot have any shape or form. Soul is devoid of any shape or form.

Madhvācārya believes in the doctrine of soul as formal (Sākāratva).[7] The argument advanced by him for proving the form (ākāra) of soul is based on the analogy of the light of the lamp. According to Madhva, all illuminating substances always possess some form. Illuminating flame of the lamp possesses a form. Consciousness is of the nature of illumination. Soul is also of the nature of self-illumination (svaprakāśa). Therefore, soul should possess a form.[8] Svāminārāyaṇa would not accept this argument of Madhvācārya. Svāminārāyaṇa would argue against him and say that light had no form. If the consciousness is of the nature of illumination (prakāśa) and the soul is of the nature of consciousness, it cannot have any form. Svāminārāyaṇa would say that the argument of Madhvācārya was not well founded.

In fact Svāminārāyaṇa was required to face a situation as would arise from the doctrine of formal soul advocated by Madhvācārya. His own disciple, Brahmānanda, had argued that soul had a form. To the argument of Brahmānanda, Svāminārāyaṇa replies by a counterargument based on the authority of scriptures that if soul has a form, then it must also have hands, feet and other sense organs, But in the tenth part (daśama Skaṅdha) of Srīmad Bhāgvata it is mentioned that God creates sense-organs for the welfare of the soul. Now, if soul has a form, why should God take the trouble of creating sense-organs and other organs like mind and so on for the soul? If the soul, which is an eternally existing entity, has a form, it would not be necessary for God to create sense-organs for its welfare. Svāminārāyaṇa emphatically says that, on this evidence of scripture, the only conclusion possible is that the soul has only being (sattā) and no form.[9]

We shall now consider an interesting question in this context. According to Svāminārāyaṇa, God is never formless. God always has form and personality.[10] He is always in the two-handed human form.[11] Now, the question arises that if God is having a form (Sākāra), how can he indwell a formless (nirākāra) soul? Does God reside in the formless soul with personality (sākāra) or without personality (nirākāra)? In fact Nityānandasvāmi had raised this question before Svāminārāyaṇa[12]. Answering the question Svāminārāyaṇa says that God resides in the formless soul as its metaphysically sustaining principle. Thus according to Svāminārāyaṇa God resides in the soul as Antaryāmi[13] and not as transcendent divine personality which is always Dvibhuja (two-armed)[14].

9. Self Neither Male nor Female

There are males and females in the human, animal and plant world. According to Svāminārāyaṇa, all have souls (jīvas) distinct from their bodies.[1] A question would naturally arise : is the soul of a male of male gender and the soul of a female of female gender? The same question can be asked in other words like this: has the soul a gender? Svāminārāyaṇa has categorically answered the question. He says that the soul has no gender.[2] Svāminārāyaṇa makes it clear that the soul is neither male nor female. It is a genderless sentinent being. It is mere conscious existence.[3] Śaṅkarācārya also says the same thing. According to him, the soul has neither tongue, nor hands nor feet nor gential organs. According to him, soul is of the nature of consciousness and bliss[4].

Svāminārāyaṇa further clarifies that the soul is neither Brāhmin, nor Kṣatriya, nor Kanbi, nor son, nor father. It has neither nationality nor caste.[5] Śaṅkarācārya has also said that the soul is neither father, nor mother nor son. It has neither nationality nor caste.[6]

In Svāminārāyaṇa's view Varṇāśrama Dharma is far inferior to Bhāgavata Dharma[8] which is the same thing as Ekāntika Dharma.[9] This means that according to Svāminārāyaṇa what gives excellence to human life is neither Varṇa nor Āśrama but single-minded devotion to God. This being his view he has said in clear terms that a devotee of God, may be male or female or of any caste, after attaining release from the shackles of the body, would go to the Divine Abode (Akṣaradhāman) and assume a divine form to serve God.[10]

10. Location of Self

Where does the soul reside? Svāminārāyaṇa himself raises this question and answers it. He says that the soul resides in the heart and from there it carries on all its activities.[1] At several places in Vacanāmṛta Svāminārāyaṇa has made it clear that the subtle and atomic soul has its residence in the heart.[2]

This view of Svāminārāyaṇa is supported by Praṣṇopaniṣad which says that the soul has its seat in the heart.[3] Rāmānujācārya also holds the view that the soul has its seat in the heart (hṛtpadma).[4] Even Śaṅkarācārya says that the soul shines in the sky of heart (hṛdākāśa).[5]

According to Svāminārāyaṇa, in the heart, there is a disc (cakra) of flesh. It is the this disc of flesh that the soul resides.[6] How soul resides in this disc is explained by Svāminārāyaṇa with the example of a burning torch. He says that the torch, wrapped with rags wet with oil, holds fire. Here, according to Svāminārāyaṇa, the position is two-fold. The wet rays hold fire and the fire clings to wet rags. The same is the case with the soul vis a vis the disc of flesh. The disc holds the soul and the soul clings to the disc.[7]

Svāminārāyaṇa says that some one might raise an objection here. The objection might be to the effect that the soul is luminous and the disc of flesh is non-luminous: then how can luminous, soul cling to non-luminous disc?[8] In other words, how can two essentially opposite elements, namely the soul and the disc, meet each other? Soul is spiritual. The disc is material. How can spiritual cling to material? Svāminārāyaṇa answers this question and attempts to remove the doubt. He gives an illustration of earthen bowl with oil and a wick in it. He says that although the bowl, the oil and the wick are non-luminous, they can hold fire which is luminous. In other words, luminous fire can cling to non-luminous wick wet with oil. Again, fire does not remain suspended in the sky. It requires these non-luminous things to uphold itself. Similarly, the luminous soul requires non-luminous disc of flesh to uphold itself.[9] Just as bowl, oil and wick hold fire, the disc of flesh holds the soul. Although the soul and the disc of flesh are essentially different in nature, the soul clings to the latter. To bring home this point, Svāminārāyaṇa gives another illustration. He says that just as in a red-hot iron nail fire resides, in the same way the soul resides in the disc of flesh.[10] Thus we see that Svāminārāyaṇa has made a systematic attempt to show how the soul resides in the heart.

11. Classification of Selves

According to Svāminārāyaṇa, there are three kinds of souls. They are Anādi Mukta (eternally free), Mukta (liberated) and Baddha (bound). Anādi Muktas are eternally free souls like Nārada, Sanka, Śeṣa, Laxmi and others.[1] They have not been made free by any body. Nor have they become free by sermons of any saint.[2] They were never bound. They are ever free from forces of māyā.[3] The muktas are freed souls.[4] They were once bound, but they obtained liberation through devotion and by the grace of God.[5] The baddha are bound souls.[6] They are still in bondage. They are revolving in the circuit of birth and death on account of ignorance and bad actions. They can obtain liberation through knowledge and devotion by the grace of God.[7]

Svāminārāyaṇa classifies freed souls into two categories. They are Jñāni Muktas and Mahā Mukta. Jñani Muktas are those liberated souls who have determinate perception (savikalpa samādhi) and Mahā Muktas are those liberated souls who have indeterminate perception (nirvikalpa Samādhi).[8]

Bound souls are classified by Svāminārāyaṇa into two categories: Mumukṣu and Bubhukṣu. Mumukṣu souls are seekers of salvation[9], and Bubhukṣu souls are seekers of worldly enjoyment.[10]

Svāminārāyaṇa has also classified bound souls into another two categories which are somewhat similar to the two categories which we have just mentioned. They are Savāsanika and Nirvāsanika. Savāsanika soul is one which is full of wordly desires. Eventhough such a soul intensely worships God, it would not go to Divine Abode (akṣaradhāman) of God after leaving the body. It may go to any of the higher regions (loka), but not to Akṣaradhāman.[11] Nirvāsanika soul is one which has not desire for world by enjoyments. It loves God. It wants only God and nothing else. When such a soul leaves the body, it straight goes to Akṣaradhāman.[12]

Svāminārāyaṇa has also classified the bound souls into still another two categories: Daivi (of divine nature) and Āsuri (of demonic nature).[13] Daivi souls are those which are desireless (niṣkāma) for wordly enjoyments and which seek liberation through wisdom, virtue and devotion.[14] Āsuri souls are those which are highly desirous of wordly pleasure (sakāma) and which are involved in lust, anger, greed and vanity.[15] Svāminārāyaṇa says that Āsuri souls cannot become daivi souls because baser instincts are inherent in them since their birth.[16] But this does not mean that they can never attain divine nature (daivibhāva). If they again and again identify themselves with Brahman and live a virtuous life their demonic nature (asurabhāva) will vanish and divine nature will emerge.[17]

Madhvācārya makes a classification of the bound souls into three categories: Muktiyogya, Tamoyogya and Nityasamsāri.[18] The Muktiyogya bound souls are those which are eligible for release. If they love and worship God, they can attain liberation. Tamoyogya are those souls which are not eligible for release. They are condemned to eternal darkness (hell). Nityasansāri are those which are neither eligible for release nor condemned to eternal darkness. They are eternally bound to the wheel of birth and death. Svāminārāyaṇa does not accept this classification of Madhvācārya. According to Svāminārāyaṇa no soul is eternally damnable (tamoyogya). So also, no soul is eternally bound to the wheel of birth and death (nityasansāri). According to Svāminārāyaṇa every soul is eligible for final emancipation (ātyantika Kalyāṇa). The optimism and catholicity of Svāminārāyaṇa's outlook becomes most visible when he says that even a soul of an animal is eligible for attaining liberation. Then what wonder if man attains liberation?[19]

REFERENCES

1. Five Reals

1, V.G.L.S. 10; V.G.F.S. 7; V.G.M.S. 31.

2. No Distinction Between Jīva, Jīvātman and Ātman

1. V.G.F.S. 20; V.G.F.S. 44; V.G.F.S. 77; V.G.M.S. 3; V.G.M.S. 32; V.G.F.S. 38; V.G.F.S. 72; V.S.S. 6; V.G.M.S. 12.
2. V.G.F.S. 8; V.G.F.S. 37; V.G.F.S. 64; V.G.F.S. 25; V.G.F.S. 61; V.G.F.S. 73; V.S.S. 1; V.S.S. 3; V.S.S. 4; V.S.S. 12; V.L.S. 15; V.G.M.S. 35; V.G.M.S. 55; V.G.M.S. 57; V.G.M.S. 59; V.G.M.S. 69.

3. Svāminārāyaṇa Proves the Existence of Self

1. V.L.S. 7.

2. V.L.S. 7.
3. V.K.S. 1.
4. V.G.F.S. 38.
5. V.G.M.S. 62.
6. V.G.F.S. 72.
7. V.G.F.S. 72.
8. Radhakrishnan, An Idealist View of Life, (1947), p. 139.
9. Radhakrishnan, *Ibid.*, p. 140.
10. Dr. J.A. Yajnik, The Philosophy of Śri Svāminārāyaṇa (1972), p. 16.
11. Kant, Critique of Pure Reason, Translated by J.M.D. Meiklejohn (1978), p. 94.
12. Peter Koestebrown, "Religion in the Tradition of Phenomenology" in "Religion in Philosophical and Cultural Perspective" Edited by Clayton Fever and Others (1967), p. 186.
13. Dr. J.A. Yajnik, The Philosophy of Śri Svāminārāyaṇa (1972), p. 16.

4. What is Self?

1. Radhakrishnan, Indian Philosophy, Part I (1977) pp. 296, 298.
2. *Ibid.*, Part II, p. 188.
3. *Ibid.*, Part II, p. 189.
4. *Ibid.*, Part II, p. 417.
5. C.D. Sharma, Indian Philosophy (1952), p. 494.
6. Radhakrishnan, Indian Philosophy, Part I, pp. 390, 392, 393.
7. *Ibid.*, p. 667.
8. D.N. Shastri, Critique of Indian Realism (1976) p. 44.
9. Kant, Critique of Pure Reason, translated by J.M.D. Meiklejohn (1978), part II, chapter I.
10. Radhakrishnan, Indian Philosophy, Part II, p. 281, C.D. Sharma, *Ibid.*, p. 214.
11. Radhakrishnan, *Ibid.*, part II, p. 743.
    C.D. Sharma, Indian Philosophy (1952), p. 494.

5. Self is not By-product of Matter

1. Radhakrishnan, Indian Philosophy, Part I (1977), p. 279.
2. C.D. Sharma, Indian Philosophy, (1952), p. 46.
3. Radhakrishnan, Indian Philosophy, Part I (1977), p. 279.
4. C.D. Sharma, Indian Philosophy, (1952), p. 46.

5. C.D. Sharma, *Ibid.*, p. 46.
6. John Hospers, Introduction to Philosophical Analysis (1977), p. 39.
7. C.E.M. Joad, Guide to Modern Thought, (1948), p. 43.
8. John Hospers, Introduction to Philosophical Analysis (1977), p. 397.
9. V.G.M.S. 66 and V.G.M.S. 66.
10. Dehatrayavilakṣaṇam S.P. 116.
11. V.G.M.S. 2.
12. S.P. 105.
13. V.G.F.S. 44.
14. V.G.F.S. 44.
15. J.A. Yajnik, The Philosophy of Śri Svāminārāyaṇa (1972), p. 106.

6. Self Distinct from Body

1. V.G.E.S. 33; V.G.F.S. 25; V.G.L.S. 39; V.G.F.S. 61; V.S.S. 1.
2. V.S.S. 1.
3. V.S.S. 4.
4. V.S.S. 4.
5. V.G.M.S. 32.
6. V.S.S. 12.
7. V.P.S. 3.
8. V.G.M.S. 2; V.G.F.S. 44.
9. V.G.M.S. 35.
10. V.S.S. 1.

7. Dimension of Self

1. Śvetāśvatara Upaniṣad 3:13 and 5:18.
2. V.J.S. 2.
3. V.K.S. 8; S.P. 105.
4. Muṇḍakopaniṣad 3-1-9.
5. Radhakrishnan, Indian Philosophy, Part II, (1967), p. 691.
6. K. Narayana, An Outline of Madhva Philosophy (1962), p. 158.
7. V.G.F.S. 7.
8. V.P.S. 3.

8. Self is Formless

1. V.G.F.S. 72.
2. V.J.S. 2.

3. M.N. Roy, Science and Philosophy, (1947), p. 32.
4. V.G.F.S. 61.
5. V.G.M.S. 66.
   See also V.G.L.S. 33 and V.S.S. 12.
6. V.L.S. 15.
   See also V.P.S. 3.
7. K. Narayana, An Outline of Madhva Philosophy, (1962), p. 141.
8. K. Narayana, *Ibid.*, p. 141.
9. V.G.M.S. 66.
10. V.P.S. 7.
11. V.L.S. 4.
12. V.L.S. 4.
13. V.L.S. 15.
14. S.P. 107.
15. V.L.S. 18.

9. Self Neither Male nor Female

1. V.G.F.S. 61.
2. V.P.S. 3.
3. V.G.L.S. 22.
4. Nirvāṇaṣaṭkam–2.
5. V.G.L.S. 39.
6. Nirvāṇaṣaṭham–5.
7. V.G.F.S. 44.
8. V.G.L.S. 21.
9. V.G.L.S. 21.
10. V.G.L.S. 22.

10. Location of Self

1. V.J.S. 2.
2. V.K.S. 12; V.G.M.S. 34.
   See also S.P. 105.
3. Praśnopaniṣad 3.6
4. Radhakrishnan, Indian Philosophy II (1977), p. 691.
5. Śaṅkarācārya, Ātmabodha 67.
6. V.G.L.S. 4.
7. V.G.L.S. 4.
8. V.G.L.S. 4.

9. V.G.L.S. 4.
10. V.G.L.S. 4.

11. Classification of Selves

1. V.G.F.S. 32.
2. V.G.F.S. 18.
3. V.A.S. 2.
4. V.S.S. 5.
5. V.G.M.S. 69.
6. V.G.M.S. 31; V.G.M.S. 66; V.P.S. 3.
7. V.G.F.S. 21; V.G.M.S. 69.
8. V.G.F.S. 39 (99).
9. V.G.F.S. 21 (62).
10. V.G.F.S. 34.
11. V.S.S. 4.
12. V.G.F.S. 61
13. V.V.S. 7
14. Gītā, Chapter-16
15. *Ibid.*, Chapter-16
16. V.V.S. 7.
17. V.V.S. 7; V.V.S. 15.
18. B.N.K. Sharma, Philosophy of Madvācārya, (1962), p. 204.
19. V.G.F.S. 21.

CHAPTER 3

METAPHYSICS OF SELF

1. Plurality of Selves

A question was asked by Nityānanda Svāmi to Svāminārāyaṇa : does one soul reside in all the bodies or does each body have a separate soul?[1] The answer of Svāminārāyaṇa is that each living body has a separate soul. There are as many souls as there are living bodies.[2] It is not that only one soul resides in all the living bodies.[3]

Svāminārāyaṇa believes that the souls are innumerable (asaṅkhya).[4] He thus maintains the doctrine of the plurality of souls (Jīvasamūha).[5] According to him, souls are infinite in number.[6] Each soul is distinct from the rest.[7] God is the soul of all souls.[8] He comes down upon the earth for redemption of souls.[9] The plurality of souls is evident from the distribution of pleasures and pains.

The doctrine of the plurality of souls is almost a common feature of the Indian philosophy schools, and more particularly of Vaiṣḥṇavite schools. Even in Kaṭhopaniṣad we find a trace of this doctrine.[10] Rāmānuja,[11] Mādhva,[12] Sāṅkhya,[13] Yoga,[14] Nyāya,[15] Vaiśeṣika[16], Mīmāṁsā.[17] and Jainas[18] maintain this doctrine.

According to Svāminārāyaṇa, the plurality of souls remains in tact even in the state of emancipation (mokṣa) the emancipated souls (mukta jīvas) do not merge in God. They retain their individuality. Each liberated soul is distinct from the rest of the liberated souls. All the liberated souls are different from each other as regards their capacity of receiving knowledge and enjoyment of bliss of nearness of God.[19]

According to Svāminārāyaṇa infinite number of liberated souls reside in the divine abode (Akṣaradhāman) of God and are engaged in his service.[20]

2. Metaphysical Nature of Self

According to Svāminārāyaṇa, Jīvas are finite individual selves. They are basic spiritual units. They are many. Their number is infinite (asaṅkhya).[1] They are eternally different from God.[2] Each self is different and distinct from every other self.[3]

According to Svāminārāyaṇa, self is a spiritual substance (caitanya Vastu).[4] It is atomic (aṇumātra).[5] It is very subtle (sūkṣma) and imperceptible.[6] According to Śvetāśvatara Upaniṣad, the self is as subtle as one hundredth part of a one hundredth part of a hair point.[7]

According to Svāminārāyaṇa, self is eternal (nitya)[8] unique (vicitra)[9] and formless (arūpa).[10] It is whole, without parts (akhaṇḍa).[11] It is absolutely a pure (atiśuddha)[12] being (sattārūpa).[13] It is indivisible (akhaṇḍa)[14], imperishable (avināśi)[15], immortal (amara)[16], unchanging (nirvikāra)[17] and immutable (achyuta).[18] It cannot be pierced (abhedya). Weapons cannot cut it (acchedya).[19] Water cannot wet it (akledya)[20]. Wind cannot dry it (aśoṣya)[21]. Fire cannot burn it (adāhya).[22]

According to Svāminārāyaṇa, consciousness is the essential attribute of self (caitanyarūpa).[23] Knowledge is its inseparable quality (jñānarūpa).[24] It is different from three bodies (dehatraya Vilakṣaṇa),[25] namely, gross (sthūla), subtle (sūkṣma) and causal (Kāraṇa). Waking (jāgrata), dreaming (svapna) and sleeping (suṣupti) are three states (avasthā) of its consciousness. [26] By virtue of consciousness as its essence, it pervades all the three bodies[27] including manas (mind), buddhi (intellect), *cit* (awareness) and ahaṁkāra (ego).[28] It knows through antaḥkaraṇa (internal instruments of knowledge) which has four above said modes.[29] It is the real subject of knowledge (jñātā)[30], it is doer (kartā) and enjoyer (bhoktā) also. Nevertheless, by itself, it is not capable of knowing, doing or enjoying anything. All its power of knowing (jñānaśakti), willing (icchāśakti) and doing (kriyāśakti) comes from God who dwells in it.[31] For all purposes self is dependent on God (paratantra).[32]

According to Svāmināráyaṇa, self is existence (sat), knowledge (*cit*) and bliss (ānanda).[23] The self must exist. One can never talk about anything which does not exist. The self is aware of its own existence. Self is self-conscious (jñānarūpa).[34] In other words, the self is self-luminous.[35] Unless self is aware of itself there can be no knowledge at all. Self is bliss (sukharūpa).[36]

Svāmināráyaṇism is a system of Vedānta. Like other Vedānta systems, Svāmināráyaṇism recognises ānanda as an essential character of self. This character of self remains unmanifest due to ignorance (avidyā). So long as self remains associated with three bodies, it does not enjoy real bliss. When it is separated from them, it realises its true nature which is bliss.[37] By grace of God this character of self is revealed to it in the state of liberation.[38]

According to Svāmināráyaṇa, self is a real entity. It is knower. It has consciousness. It is not mere consciousness as Kevalādvaitins contend. Nor is it a mere appearance of Absolute as Bradley holds. Nor is it a "bundle of sensations" as Hume maintains. If we put the Svāmināráyaṇist stand point in Kantian way, we can say that self without consciousness is blind and consciousness without self is empty.

According to Svāmināráyaṇa, consciousness and bliss constitute the essential nature of self. This aspect of Svāmināráyana's philosophy might create some misunderstanding on account of its similarity with the philosophy of Śaṅkara. But it should be noted that the qualities of consciousness and bliss belong to self and they are not the same as the consciousness and bliss of parabrahman as in Śaṅkara Vedānta.

Thus, we notice four salient features about the concept of self as has been put forward by Svāmināráyaṇa namely, eternality of self, difference between self and God, difference between selves *inter se* and complete dependence of selves on God. Svāminārāyaṇa, like all orthodox systems of Indian philosophy, considers eternality as a necessary ingredient in the concept of self, without which no ethics would be possible. Unless self is believed to exist for ever, it would be impossible for it to experience good or bad consequences of its actions. The idea of permanence of self provides a rational basis for ethics.

3. Metaphysical Status of Self

There are four theories about the status of the soul vis a vis God. One, soul (jīva) is God (Brahman). This theory is advocated by Śaṅkarācārya and the followers of Advaita Vedānta.[1] Two, the soul is a portion (aṁśa) of God. This theory is held by Rāmānuja.[2] With slight difference from the theory of Rāmānujācārya, Madhvācārya also accepts the idea of parthood (aṁśatva) of soul. He explains the parthood of soul as reflection of God (Pratibimbāṁśaka).[3] Somewhat similar to this theory, the third theory propounds that God evolves souls out of his self. This theory is maintained by Judaism and Christianity.[4] And the fourth theory declares that God and the soul both are coeternal. According to this theory soul was never created. It always existed and will always exist. Soul is as eternal as God. Soul existed eternally with God and will exist eternally with God. Soul would neither have an end nor distinction.

Out of these four theories Svāminārāyaṇa adopts the fourth one. According to him, soul is never created. Soul is as eternal as God.[5] Soul is a subtle spiritual substance existing since eternity. Svāminārāyaṇa has very explicitly said that soul is not a part or portion (aṁśa) of God. It is an eternal entity.[6] The number of souls is infinite (asaṅkhya).[7] There can be no addition to the existing number of souls. New souls do not come into existence.[8] There can neither be addition to nor subtraction from this infinite number of souls. Infinity of souls remains constant. According to Svāminārāyaṇa, there is no question of increase in the number of souls.[8]

4. Doctrine of Intrinsic Difference

From the doctrine of plurality of selves the doctrine of intrinsic difference would logically follow. Of course, it is very difficult to define precisely what distinguishes one self from another. But the wide range of inequalities in the lives of living beings extending over human, animal, plant, aquatic and other spheres of life could not be satisfactorily explained except on the principle of intrinsic differences. The uniqueness of individual experience and inequalities of equipment point ultimately to the existence of inalienable essence of personality which underlies all states of experiences, and which is never seen to overlap in any two cases.[1] According to Svāminārāyana, the difference is not merely a component part of reality, but constitutes its very essence. So much so that to know a thing is to know it as distinct from all others.[2]

We have seen that God, matter (māyā) and selves (jīvas) are three major and distinct realities in Svāminārāyaṇa's metaphysical system.[3] God is distinct and independent of the other two realities which are dependent on God. Selves are unique and infinite in number.[4] Modifications of matter are innumerable.[5] Each order of reality is different from other.[6] Each self is different from the other. Each self is different from God.[7]

According to Svāminārāyaṇa, no self can become like God, even in the state of emancipation.[9] If the selves attain the position of absolute equality with God in the state of emancipation, it would be difficult to find a rational basis for difference, when they were in the state of bondage : because in bondage selves suffer miseries where as God is always untouched by miseries.[10]

If there is no intrinsic difference between the selves, the following questions would arise. How is it that some souls attains liberation ages before others? Why should others lag behind? The theory of Karma will not be able to answer these questions, because the difference in Karmas of different souls ultimately depends on their own intrinsic difference. Every individual experience is always unique. According to

Madhva the uniqueness of each individual experience is a sufficient reason for admitting the distinctiveness of each individual soul.[11] Svāminārāyaṇa finds the basis of the doctrine of plurality of selves in the intrinsic diversity of their essences.

Does one self become many? Śaṅkara would say "Yes", Svāminārāyaṇa would say "No". According to Svāminārāyaṇa one does not become many. Many are eternal and remain many eternally. If there is only one individual self, all selves would be automatically released, the moment a single self attains release. The very existence of both freed and bound selves at the same time is a proof of their distinction and plurality. The clarification of selves made by Svāminārāyaṇa is nothing but a comprehensive theory embodying the same idea of difference and distinction among selves.[12]

According to Svāminārāyaṇa, this distinction between selves persists even in the state of release. The released self knows God directly, but no two released selves have the same degree of knowledge of God.[13] Each self has a different degree of knowledge of God. In this context Svāminārāyaṇa gives two illustrations : One, of the ocean; the other, of the sky. He says that the ants, the beasts, the horses, the elephants, the crocodiles and the human beings take water from the ocean according to their capacities, but the water of ocean remains inexhaustible. Each realises the greatness of ocean according to its capacity.[14] Similarly, the mosquitoes, the sparrows, the hawks and the eagles all fly in the sky according to the strength and power of their wings and yet the sky remains boundless and unfathomable. Each realises its utter insignificance before the greatness of the sky.[15] In the same way, each self attains knowledge of God only proportionate to its receiving capacity.[16] Of course, Svāminārāyaṇa, has admitted growth in the capacity of self to know. The more the self attains the knowledge of greatness and glory of God, the more it realises the infinite character of the greatness and glory of God.[17] Greatness and glory of God being infinite and inexhaustible, the self would never have complete knowledge of God.[18] Each self realises the even increasing glory of God in accordance with the degree of its realisation.[19]

According to Rāmānuja, there are no qualitative distinctions among selves. The selves are many, but all of them are of the same quality. There is no difference between selves as regards jñāna and enjoyment of bliss.[20] This view of Rāmānuja is not acceptable to Madhva. According to him, plurality of selves without distinction is inconceivable. The selves, in his view, are qualitatively and quantitatively different from one another. For him, no two souls are alike. For explaining the qualitative pluralism of selves Madhva introduces two conceptions : One, svarūpabheda : the other, tāratamya. By conception of Svarūpabheda he shows that there are intrinsic distinctions in the nature of selves. By the conception of tāratamya he points out that there are gradations based on varying degree of knowledge and bliss, since beginningless time.[21] Each self has its own capacity to enjoy bliss. According to Madhva, if the selves are essentially the same, there would be no meaning in their qualitative plurality. A difference is no difference unless it makes a difference.[22] Madhva explains the conception of qualitative pluralism with the help of an illustration of sheep. To the ordinary passer by the sheep may all be just so may numerable units, but to the shephered who lives with them and has daily contact with them, they are real individuals each with very different features and characteristics. So with the divine shepherd each self is different from the other.[23] Svāminārāyaṇa agrees with Madhva in his conceptions of tāratamya.[24] He would also agree with Madhva in his conception of Svarūpabheda.

German philosopher Leibnitz also believes in the qualitative plurality of selves. He calls self 'Monad'. According to him, no two monads are exactly alike. Monads differ among themselves in the clearness of perceptions.[25] On these points Svāminārāyaṇa would agree with Leibnitz. But according to Leibnitz monads are windowless and there is no relation between them.[26] The 'Jīva' of Svāminārāyaṇa is not an exclusive windowless entity, but is related with so many selves in various ways. According to Svāminārāyaṇa, even in the state of liberation jīvas maintain social character in as much as they all aim at one and the same thing, namely, God. Thus, as they are all related to God, they can be said to be related to one another.[27]

5. Self Pervades the Entire Body

As we have seen above, the dimension of the soul is atomic. An objection can be raised that if the soul is atomic, it can only be in one place in the body and so it cannot perceive throughout the body. In other words, if the soul is aṇuparimāṇa, how can it be the knower of experiences all over the body? Svāminārāyaṇa attempts to meet the objection on the analogy of the lamp. He says that a lamp, placed at one spot in a room, extends from there light to the whole of the room. Similarly, the soul although residing in the disc of flesh in the heart extends its consciousness all over the body. Further, the flame of the lamp particularly pervades the wick and generally pervades the entire room. Similarly, the soul particularly pervades the disc of flesh and generally pervades the entire body.[1] Svāminārāyaṇa says that through its power of consciousness the soul pervades the entire body (akhilam tanum).[2]

A question can be asked : how is it that the consciousness of the soul is felt unevenly in different parts of the body? What is the reason of such uneven influence of soul on the body?[3] Answering the question Svāminārāyaṇa says that although the sun, through its rays, illumines all the objects, the intensity of the illumination depends on the purity of the object which it illumines. On the surface of the grass and on the surface of the pure water, the light of the sun would be experienced more than on the surface of the sand and on the surface of the dirty water. Although, the sun illumines all the objects equally, we will experience more light on pure objects and less light on the dirty or polluted objects. The reflection of the sun's rays varies in intensity according as the object is pure or polluted. Similarly, the pervasiveness of the soul is the same throughout the body, but it is felt more in the senses (indriyas) which are pure (svaccha). Our nose and years do not experience the same light as is experienced by our eyes. Again, the four internal psychological instruments (antaḥkaraṇa), namely manas, buddhi, cit and ahaṅkāra, experience the light of the soul more than the senses. Compared to the light experienced by four internal organs, the light experienced by senses is less.[4] So, the consciousness of the soul is experienced throughout the body, but it differs in intensity according to the purity of the experiencing organ.

Svāminārāyaṇa says that as the soul, through its power of consciousness, pervades the entire body, it experiences pleasure and pain that are caused to the body.[5] The pleasure and the pain of the body are the pleasure and pain of the soul. Thus, the soul is bhoktā and not away from the pleasure and pain of the body.[6]

6. Metaphysical Dependence of Selves on God

According to Svāminārāyaṇa there are two kinds of realities : One, independent (Svatantra), the other, dependent (Paratantra).[1] According to him, there are five realities; jīva, īśvara, māyā, brahman and parabrahman.[2] Out of these five realities, the last one, parabrahman (God) is the only independent reality. The rest of them are dependent realities.[3] Accordingly, individual selves are dependent realities.[4] They are dependent on God for their existence and activities.[5] Here it should be made clear that the term "independent" is not synonym for "eternal". The idea of Svāminārāyaṇa is not that only independent reality can be eternal. A reality, according to him, can be eternal and yet dependent.[6] A dependent reality also can be eternal. God is a reality. He is independent as well enternal. But the other four realities are eternal and yet dependent upon God for their existence.[7]

According to Svāminārāyaṇa, selves (jīvas) are eternally existing entities. Consciousness and bliss constitute their intransic nature. Even then, they are dependent upon God for their existence and activities. This dependence is not a passing phase in their lives. It is a permanent feature. It is the very condition of their being as finite entities. Even temporarily they cannot be independent of God. At all times, in bondage as well as liberation, they are dependent upon God. They have no power to experience fruits of their actions at their will. They can experience the fruits of their actions when God enables them to do so.[8] In fact, apart from God, they have no power of willing, feeling, thinking or doing. That power comes from God.[9] By themselves they can do nothing.[10] Their power of thinking, willing, feeling and doing is derived from the pervasion of God over selves. God pervades the selves and enables them to enter into various activities.[11] According to Svāminārāyaṇa, even in the state of liberation (mokṣa) they are dependent upon God for realisation of greater and greater bliss.[12] And after all what is liberation? According to Svāminārāyaṇa, it has two aspects : negative and positive. So far as negative aspect is concerned, it is nothing but release from the fetters which prevent the realisation of their true selves.[13] In its positive aspect liberation is the enjoyment of bliss in the eternal service of God.[13]

The dependence of selves arises from the limitations which they suffer. These limitations are partly extrinsic and partly intrinsic. The extrinsic limitations arise from the association of the self with the causal body, which evolves into subtle and gross bodies, since beginningless time.[15] The intrinsic limitations arise from their finite nature and inherent peculiarity. The finite nature warrants impossibility of the self to be like God. Svāminārāyaṇa has often said that no self can even attain the status, power, greatness and glory of God. Self can never become like God.[16] Inherent peculiarity entails uniqueness[17] which creates its own limitations. Of the two types of limitations, extrinsic limitations are removable by the process of sādhanā shown by Svāminārāyaṇa. The intrinsic ones remain for ever with the self. Thus, we see that dependence on God constitutes a distinctive mark of all finite selves at all times.

7. Self as Knower

According to Svāminārāyaṇa, the self, resides in the

body and God, in the form of Sākṣī (witness self) resides in the self.[1] Whether the self is bound (baddha) or free (mukta), Sākṣī dwells in it. Sākṣī is not affected by the bondage or freedom of the self,[2] because it is beyond (parā) of the self.[3]

According to Svāminārāyaṇa, there are three kinds of cognitive ways : indriyas (sense organs), antaḥkaraṇa (internal instruments) and Sākṣī (witness self). Mind (manas), buddhi (intellect) and citta (the faculty of reflection) are internal senses. External senses apprehend empirical objects. Mind and intellect interpret and decide. This is how perceptual knowledge originates. According to Svāminārāyaṇa, mana, buddhi and citta are products of matter (māyika) which is insentient (jaḍa)[4] and, therefore, these or any of them cannot be the subject of knowledge. According to Svāminārāyaṇa, the self is the real subject of knowledge (jñāta). He has said that "Buddhi is enabled to know because it is pervaded by the self and the self is enabled to know because it is pervaded by sākṣī.[5]

According to Svāminārāyaṇa, Sākṣī resides in the self, but it is not identical with the self. It is a mere witness of Jīva's activity. While Sākṣī is conscious of Jīva's activity, it is in no way moved by it. In Gītā this witness self (sākṣī) is described as Upadraṣṭā and the passer-self is described as Aṇumantā.[6]

According to Svāminārāyaṇa, the truth and knowledge of pleasure, pain, desire and such other thing cannot be cognised by ordinary instruments of knowledge. Inspired by Sākṣī the self has the direct knowledge of these things. Since knowledge of these things is direct, it is never subject to contradiction. It has to be accepted as certain, valid and infallible. When we have an experience of pain, say toothache, we never want its verification. We are certain about its truth. Svāminārāyaṇa says that one would not accept anything as true unless one has a personal experience of it.[7] This means that according to Svāminārāyaṇa, personal experience needs no verification.

8. Knowledge of Self

According to Svāminārāyaṇa, we cannot have knowledge of self by sense perception. Self is beyond the reach of senses. Sensuous knowledge of self is absolutely impossible.[1]

According to Svāminārāyaṇa, we can have knowledge of self by logical reasoning. Inference can give us knowledge of the self. Svāminārāyaṇa has, however, made it clear that the knowledge of self given by logical reasoning is mediate and not immediate (Sākṣātkāra).[2]

According to Svāminārāyaṇa there is a third kind of knowledge which is distinct from sensuous and logical knowledge. This is intuitive knowledge. Svāminārāyaṇa calls it non-sensuous and immediate knowledge. This intuitive knowledge arises from the direct and immediate experience of self.[3]

According to Svāminārāyaṇa, the knowledge of self derived from the logical reasoning and ordinary intuition is only about its existence and not about its metaphysical nature. By ordinary intuition self cannot know its own metaphysical nature. The self can know beauty, ugliness, childhood, youth, old age and a great number of things, but it cannot know anything about its own nature.[4]

According to Svāminārāyaṇa, metaphysical nature of self can never be known by ordinary means of knowledge. Some aspects of it can be immediately known through inference, Svāminārāyaṇa explains this position with the help of an illustration. He says that when one sees a large heavy sword weighing ten monads, one can infer that the person who wields this sword must be heaving a large and stout body. Similarly, from the fact that the self simultaneously pervades the entire body and illumines all the external and internal senses, we can infer that the self must be great and powerful.[5] Thus, the knowledge that self is great and powerful is inferential and not immediate. Immediate knowledge of the metaphysical nature is not attainable by ordinary means of knowledge, because, according to Svāminārāyaṇa, it belongs to a region where neither speech not mind can reach.[6] Thus, as Tillich has asserted, man must always remain a question mark to himself.[7] As Plato has pointed out, Socrates ever remained an unfathomable mystery to himself, although he devoted the whole of his life for understanding himself.[8]

According to Svāminārāyaṇa, intuition is of two kinds: One ordinary intuition (anubhava) and the other, mediative intuition (Samādhi). Meditative intuition can also be called yogic intuition. The ordinary intuition gives knowledge only of the existence of self. It does not give knowledge of the metaphysical nature of self. According to Svāminārāyaṇa, such knowledge of self can be derived from the state of samādhi.[9] It is only in the state of Samādhi that one goes beyond māya or Upādhi.[10] According to Svāminārāyana, when a person attains the state of samādhi, he experiences his true self and gains the knowledge of self.[11] For Bertrand Russel, "the question whether we are also acquainted with our bare selves as opposed to particular thoughts and feelings is a very difficult one".[12] Svāminārāyaṇa finds no such difficulty. According to him, we can be aquainted with our bare selves in state of Samādhi.

According to Svāminārāyaṇa, the attainment of self knowledge is not the goal. It is a preliminary towards a higher goal. It is a gateway leading into a new region wherein the realisation of God is made possible.[13] When the self enters into the supreme state of being in Samādhi, it becomes impossible for it to return to the ordinary existence.[14] This is comparable to Gītā's assertion that once the soul reaches the supreme abode of God, it never returns to earthly existence.[15]

It should however, be noted that Svāminārāyaṇa does not believe that the method of Aṣṭāṅga Yoga is the only method of attaining Samādhi.[16] According to him, Samādhi can also be attained by making our consciousness (citta vṛtti) undividedly and uninterruptedly absorbed in the form of God.[17] It is true that by control of breath, we can control the mind.[18] But it is also true that by control of mind, we can also control the breath.[19] According to Svāminārāyaṇa a devotee of God, whose consciousness has become completely united with the form of God, realises everything that can be realised by the practice of Aṣṭāṅga Yoga. Such a devotee, without practising Aṣṭāṅga Yoga, achieves all the benefits which can be achieved by its practice.[20]

REFERENCES

1. Plurality of Selves

1. V.G.F.S. 13.
2. V.G.F.S. 13.
3. V.G.F.S. 13.
4. V.A.S. 5.
5. V.G.L.S. 37.
6. V.A.S. 5.
7. V.S.S. 17.
8. V.G.L.S. 37.
9. V.A.S. 5.
10. Kaṭhopaniṣad 2.5.13.
11. Radhakrishnan, Indian Philosophy, Part II, p. 691.
12. *Ibid.*, p. 743.
13. Sāṅkhya Kārikā 18.
    See also Ibid., p. 282.
14. *Ibid.*, p. 342.
15. *Ibid.*, p. 148.
16. *Ibid.*, p. 190.
17. *Ibid.*, p. 409.
18. *Ibid.*, p. 320.
19. V.S.S. 17.
20. V.G.F.S. 21.

2. Metaphysical Nature of Self

1. V.A.S. 5.; V.A.S.7.; V.G.L.S. 39.
2. V.G.F.S. 7.
3. V.G.F.S. 41.
4. V.G.M.S. 66; V.J.S. 2.
5. V.J.S. 2.; S.P. 105.
6. V.K.S. 8.

7. Śvetāśvatara Upaniṣad, 5-9
8. Gītā 2-4.
9. V.V.S. 6.
10. V.P.S. 3.
11. V.G.F.S. 13.
12. V.P.S. 3.
13. V.G.L.S. 33; V.S.S. 12.
14. V.F.F.S. 13.
15. V.J.S. 2; V.S.S. 1; V.L.S. 10.
16. V.S.S. 4; V.S.S. 12.
17. V.L.S. 10.
18. V.G.F.S. 13.
19. V.J.S. 2; V.G.F.S. 8; V.G.F.S. 25; V.S.S. 12
20. S.P. 105; Gītā 2. 24.
21. S.P. 105; Gītā 2-24.
22. S.P. 105; Gītā 2-24.
23. V.J.S. 2; V.P.S. 3.
24. V.S.S. 12.
25. S.P. 116.
26. V.G.F.S. 23.
27. S.P. 105; V.G.L.S. 4
28. V.K.S. 4.
29. V.G.M.S. 63.
30. V.G.L.S. 39; V.G.F.S. 38.
31. V.G.L.S. 4.
32. V.G.F.S. 68.
33. V.G.F.S. 8.
34. V.S.S. 12.
35. V.G.L.S. 39; V.G.M.S. 35; V.G.L.S. 33; V.K.S. 8.
36. V.S.S. 12.
37. V.G.M.S. 66.
38. V.S.S. 11.
39. V.G.F.S. 38.

3. Metaphysical Status of the Self

1. Śaṅkarācārya, Brahmajñānāvalīmālā, 20.
2. Radhakrishnan, Indian Philosophy, Part II (1977), p. 693.
3. K. Narayana, An Outline of Madhva Philosophy, (1962), p. 143.

4. Genesis 1.27.
5. V.G.F.S. 7; V.G.M.S. 31.
6. V.G.L.S. 10.
7. V.A.S. 5.
8. V.G.L.S. 10.

4. Doctrine of Intrinsic Difference

1. V.G.M.S. 67.
2. V.S.S. 17.
3. V.G.F.S. 7; V.G.M.S. 31.
4. V.A.S. 5; V.A.S. 7; V.G.L.S. 37.
5. V.G.F.S. 12.
6. V.G.F.S. 7.
7. V.G.F.S. 41.
8. V.G.L.S. 39.
9. V.S.S. 17.
10. J.A. Yajnik, the philosophy of Śrī Svāminārāyaṇa, p. 63.
11. B.N.K. Sharma, Madhva's Teachings (1979), p. 91.
12. *See,* Note on Classification above.
13. V.S.S. 17.
14. V.S.S. 17.
15. V.S.S. 17.
16. V.G.F.S. 24.
17. V.S.S. 17; V.S.S. 17.
18. V.G.L.S. 37.
19. V.S.S. 17.
20. B.N.K. Sharma, Philosophy of Shri Madhvāchārya (1962), p. 199.
    See also A.K. Lad, The concept of Liberation in Indian Philosophy (1967), p. 143.
21. B.N.K. Sharms, *Ibid.,* p. 199.
22. B.N.K. Sharma, *Ibid.,* p. 200.
23. B.N.K. Sharma, *Ibid.,* p. 200.
24. V.G.F.S. 41.
25. Leibnitz, Monadology, 9.
26. Leibenitz, Monadology, 7.
27. Dr. K.J.A. Yajnik, The Philosophy of Śrī Svāminārāyaṇa, p. 109.

5. Self Pervades the Entire Body

1. V.G.L.S. 4.
2. S.P. 105.
3. V.L.S. 15.
4. V.L.S. 15.
5. V.G.L.S. 4.
6. V.G.L.S. 4.

6. Metaphysical Dependence of Selves on God

1. V.G.F.S. 64; V.G.M.S. 21
2. V.G.F.S. 7
3. V.G.F.S. 68; V.G.F.S. 64.
4. V.G.F.S. 64; V.G.F.S. 52.
5. V.G.F.S. 52.
6. See Dr. Yajnik J.A. The Philosophy of śrī Svāminārāyaṇa, p. 52
7. V.G.M.S. 21; V.G.F.S. 64
8. V.G.F.S. 65; V.G.F.S. 65.
9. V.G.F.S. 52
10. V.G.F.S. 52
11. V.G.F.S. 65.
12. V.G.F.S. 71
13. V.G.M.S. 66.
14. V.S.S. 17.
15. V.K.S. 12.
16. V.K.S. 8; V.K.S. 13; V.G.L.S. 39.
17. V.S.S. 17.

7. Self as Knower

1. V.G.L.S. 4.
2. V.S.S. 5.
3. V.L.S. 10; V.V.S. 4
4. V.G.F.S. 12; V.G.M.S. 34
5. V.G.M.S. 63; V.K.S. 4.
6. Gītā 13.23.
7. V.G.L.S. 35.

8. Knowledge of Self

1. V.G.L.S. 3.
2. V.K.S. 1.

3. V.G.F.S. 20.
4. V.G.F.S. 20.
5. V.G.F.S. 20.
6. V.G.L.S. 3.
7. J.A. Yajnik, The Philosophy of Śrī Svāminārāyaṇa, p. 108.
8. Plato, Pheadrus, 229 A.
9. V.A.S.1; V.G.M.S. 27.
10. V.G.M.S. 20.
11. V.G.M.S. 20.
12. Bertrand Russel, The Problems of Philosophy (1943), p. 78.
13. V.G.F.S. 24.
14. V.G.F.S. 73.
15. Gītā 15.6.
16. V.A.S.
17. V.G.M.S. 14.
18. V.G.F.S. 25.
19. V.G.F.S. 25.
20. V.G.F.S. 25; V.G.F.S. 25.

CHAPTER 4

SELF AND GOD

1. Various Names of God

Svāminārāyaṇa makes reference to God by various names. He refers to God as Bhagavān, Puruṣottama,[1] Parameśvara,[2] Nārāyaṇa,[3] Naranārāyaṇa,[4] Laxmīnārāyaṇa,[5] Puruṣottamanārāyaṇa,[6] Śrī Kṛṣna,[7] Vāsudeva,[8] Parabrahman,[9] Rājādhirāja[10] and Saccidānanda.[11] But largely he uses the word "Bhagavān" for God.

2. Svāminārāyaṇa Proves the Existence of God

Saint Acquinas advances five arguments for proving the existence of God : argument from (1) Motion, (2) Cause, (3) Necessity (4) Gradation and (5) Design.[1] There are and can be many more arguments for proving the existence of God. But generally the arguments for proving the existence of God can be classified into five types : Ontological, Cosmological, Teleological, Moral and Religious. Out of these five, Svāminārāyaṇa advances three types of arguments for proving the existence of God : the teleological argument, Moral argument and the argument from religious experience.

First, we shall take up the teleological argument. What is a teleological argument? This is a very popular argument, both in the West as well as in the East, for proving the existence of God. The argument points out that everywhere in the world there are clear signs of order in accordance with a purpose. This purposive order cannot be due to the blind working of the mechanical laws. This order, so runs the argument, cannot be explained by anything in the things themselves. The order has to be conceived as imposed on things by some intelligent agency outside them. Saint Thomas Acquinas has very sharply formulated this argument. He argues that we see that things which lack knowledge such as natural bodies, act for an end, and this is evident from their acting always in the same way so as to attain the best result. Hence it is plain that they achieve their end, not fortuitously, designedly. Now, whatever lacks knowledge cannot move towards an end, unless it is directed by some being endowed with knowledge and intelligence, as the arrow is directed by the archer. Therefore, some intelligent being exists by whom all natural things are directed to an end; and this being we call God.[2] Svāminārāyaṇa presents a similar argument. He says, Look at the universe. We find everything orderly. Everything behaves in an orderly way. None deviates from the order.[3] And order is the result of design. God is the Master Director. He directs everything and every activity. He designs everything.[4] There is nothing in the universe which is outside his design.[5] Unless directed, not even a blade of grass can move.[6] This is how Svāminārāyaṇa has formulated his teleological argument.

Another argument, for the existence of God, that can be traced in the Vacanāmṛta is the moral argument of which Immanuel Kant is the Chief Exponent. The moral argument runs as follows : We see uniformity in the natural order. According to Kant, natural order is also a moral order.[7] From the moral order we can rationally think that world is controlled by a morally perfect Being. Reason tells us that there ought to be a being who controls everything and apportions happiness according to desert. In order to do this, such a being must be all-wise, all-good and all-powerful. The inviolability and certainty of moral law inevitably leads to the concept of a morally perfect being having adequate power and wisdom to adjust world to the supreme teleological end. Without such an enforcing power, moral values would, be meaningless, and such a being is God.[8]

Svāminārāyaṇa would completely subscribe to Kant's formulation of the moral argument. According to Svāminārāyaṇa, we see uniformity in the natural order.[9] This presupposes one supreme being who controls everything.[10] According to Svāminārāyaṇa, God is the controller (niyantā) of everything.[11] All the actions and their consequences are within his control. The inviolability of moral law is due to over-all control of God. God is the Supreme controller.[12] He apportions happiness according to deeds.[13] He is the cause of all causes.[14] Moral law implies supreme good.[15] God is the supreme good (ātyantika Kalyāṇa).[16] On realizing which nothing remains to be realised.

The third argument that we can trace in Vacanāmṛta for proving the existence of God is the argument from religious experience. According to this argument the occurrence of religious experience proves the existence of God.

According to F.R. Tennant the religious experience is enjoyed at the highest stage of raptness which can be attained through mystical contemplation. The experiences induced by raptness are not of the ineffable kind, but admit in some measure or even full measure, of translation into terms of ordinary imagery and knowledge. Mystics are able to visualise otherwise than by eye and to understand otherwise than understanding the mystery of God.[16] Svāminārāyaṇa would fully endorse this view of Tennant and add that because the mystical or religious experience is most objective and translatable into ordinary language through the use of symbols and analogies from ordinary experience of the natural world, it is possible to prove the existence of God on its basis.

For Svāminārāyaṇa the religious experience constitute is the most important argument for establishing the existence of God. In Vacanāmṛta he repeatedly talks about his personal experience of God. He claims to be in constant touch with God.[17] Svāminārāyaṇa enjoys the religious experience in mystical raptness, and translates it in terms of ordinary imagery. He emphatically says to his disciples, "Do believe me. I see God even right now."[18] He further reiterates, "I talk about God from my highly personal experience of God." He swears in the name of Paramahaṅsas and says that he describes God from his knowledge of having personally seen (join) Him.[19] Thus, his religious argument is based on his direct personal experience of God. It should be made clear that, although in Vacanāmṛta we can trace the aforesaid arguments for proving the existencc of God, neither God nor proofs for the existence of God, as Dr. J.A. Yajnik has rightly pointed out presented any problem to Svāminārāyaṇa. He was constantly feeling his presence.[20]

3. Form and Personality of God

Parabrahma or Puruṣottama is God of Svāminārāyaṇa. Puruṣottama is the supreme personality. The concept of Puruṣottama is highest one in Svāminārāyaṇism. The personality of Puruṣottama occupies the central position not only in Akṣ aradhāman[1] but also in the totality of existence.[2]

In Vacanāmṛta Svāminārāyaṇa shows great concern about the form and personality of God. He regards them as important aspects of God's being. Svāminārāyaṇa seeks to establish beyond doubt the form and personality of God, and refutes the doctrine which denies them. In very unambigous terms Svāminārāyaṇa says that the form and personality of God are like those of a human being.[3] God has two arms and two legs.[4] Personality of God is very beautiful.[5] But the body of God is not material (māyika). It is divine (divya).[6]

According to Svāminārāyaṇa, God is never formless (nirākāra). It is always with form and personality (sākāra).[7] In his view, formless God can do nothing without form and personality activities of God are inconceivable.[8] Those who quote Śruti to establish formlessness and impersonality of God are mistaken. They do not understand its real import.[9] What Śruti negates is the material form and not the divine form of God. Śruti never negates the divine form of God.[10] On the contrary Śruti speaks of it.[11] Svāminārāyaṇa says that, in Śruti it is mentioned that God looks at māyā.[12] If God has no eyes, how can He look at māyā? Now, if He has eyes, He must also have ears, hands and legs.[30] In the same way He also must have all the fourteen sense organs. God possesses all the faculties of cognition and connotion. But

His sense organs are not material. They are divine.[14] When Śruti declares God to be formless, it only means that God has no material form. Śruti negates only the materiality of divine form.[15] According to Svāminārāyaṇa, if God is not personal, how can He be the object of man's love, devotion and worship?[16] The desire to behold and know the form of God is the highest desire of mumukṣu.[17]

The supreme puruṣottama, of Svāminārāyaṇa is thus person. He has a character of His own. God of Svāminārāyaṇa is not a mere abstraction. He is not only an ultimate ground of the universe but also an object of love, devotion and worship of devotees. It is a personality that can be behold and experienced. Svāminārāyaṇa has no regard for the Absolute Brahman of Śaṅkara.[18] Radhakrishnan says "the absolute of Śaṅkara rigid, motionless and totally lacking in initiative, cannot call forth our worship."[19] Svāminārāyaṇa would completely agree with this observation of Radhakrishnan. According to Svāminārāyaṇa, to conceive God as formless and impersonal is the greatest crime against Him.[20] No one should listen to the person who says that God is formless and impersonal.[21]

4. Man in the Image of God

The Jewish doctrine of creation is found in the account given in chapters 1 and 2 of the Book of Genesis in the old Testament. The description of the creation of the world by God is given in vivid pictorial language. God created firmament, waters, earth, beasts and so on. Then God said, "let us make man in our image, after our likeness.[1] God willed to create man and created him in his own image. And thus God created man in his own image, in his own likeness.[2] This view of creation of man would not be completely acceptable to Svāminārāyaṇa. However, we find Svāminārāyaṇa in full agreement with the view in so far as the complete similarity of the images of man and God is concerned. Here also a difference in the two views is worth noting. It is this : unlike old Testment Svāminārāyaṇa does not say that man is like God, he rather says that God is like man. Thus the Svāminārāyaṇist belief is that the visible form of a human being is the true form of God.[3] Just as a human being has a two armed and two-legged figure, God has also a two-armed and two legged figure, God also has two-armed and two-legged form.[4] Svāminārāyaṇa very clearly says that the form of God is like that of man.[5]

It may be argued that, according to Svāminārāyaṇa, God has created man[6] and, therefore, God is prior to the creation of man. Now, when form of God resembles that of man and God is prior to the creation of man, it becomes pretty obvious that, God created man in His own image, in his likeness. This argument will not hold good because according to Svāminārāyaṇism there is no beginning of creation. It is beginningless (anādi). Hence, the point of God being "prior" is not at all relevant. This means that the Christian and Svāminārāyaṇist positions are comparable but not identical.

According to Svāminārāyaṇa, when Jiva after leaving the physical body, goes to Akṣaradhāman, the divine body given to it is also the likeness of divine form of God. It is very interesting to note in this connection that Svāminārāyaṇa doctrine in this respect goes farther than Biblical one. Whereas the Biblical doctrine of similarity between man's image and God's image is limited to Jiva's physical body in this world only, Svāminārāyaṇa doctrine goes beyond physical plane and postulates similarity between divine body of jiva and divine body of God in Akṣaradhāman also.

5. The Doctrine of Double Soul

Svāminārāyaṇa has expounded the doctrine of double soul. According to him, every living creature has a double soul. By doctrine of double soul, it is not meant that every living creature has two souls. The doctrine does not mean that. In its true connotation it is a doctrine of soul within soul.

According to Svāminārāyaṇa, there is a soul in every living body. And the soul also has a soul within it. Svāminārāyaṇa says that just as jīva resides in the heart, God resides in jīva by his antaryāmī śakti.[1] So the soul which indwells the soul of every living creature, according to Svāminārāyaṇa, is none else than God himself.[2] This view has found expression in number of religious leaders and traditions. For example, śrī Aurobindo says that the indwelling God is the inner light and the inner voice of the mystic.[3] He calls the indwelling God, The Hidden Guide.[4] Saint Augustine says, "thou art more inward to me than my most inward part."[5] Thomas Acquinas says, "the Holy Ghost inhabits the mind by his substance."[6] In Kaṭhopaniṣad we find the doctrine of double soul. According to Kaṭhopaniṣad, the wise men, who perceive God as dwelling in their own selves, attain eternal peace and none else.[17] In Gītā also we find this doctrine. According to Gītā, God resides in the heart of man.[8] This means Jīva resides in the heart and God resides in Jīva is a widely acceptable doctrine.

Svāminārāyaṇa has repeatedly said that God resides in the soul of every living creature. The peculiarity of Svāminārāyaṇa's assertions consists in the fact that he repeatedly authenticates the truth of this doctrine by his own personal experience. He says that he sees the person of God in the illumination which exists in his heart.[9]

A question may arise, How can God, who is eternally and intrinsically different from jīva reside in jīva? To this question Svāminārāyaṇa gives a very clear answer. He says just the fire exists in the wood, although its nature is intrinsically different from that of wood, God resides in each and every soul, although His nature is different from jīva.[10]

According to Svāminārāyaṇa without God residing in it, Jīva cannot do anything.[11] It even cannot enjoy the fruits of its own actions. It can only do what it is enabled by God to do.[12] God is independent, Jīva is not. Jīva is dependent upon God for its existence and activities.[13] Just as a human body without a soul is unable to do anything, Jīva without Purusottama would not be able to do anything. God is the soul of soul, the self of self and the life of life.[14]

The doctrine of double soul does not imply that God is present in everything with the same fullness. According to Svāminārāyaṇa he is more fully present in Akṣarabrahman than in Puruṣa–Prakṛti.[15] In the same way, He is more fully present in man than in birds and beasts.[16] The doctrine of degrees of fulness with which God is present in different things is explained by Svāminārāyaṇa with the Leaf of illustration. He says that in a sense, it can be said that a long fire is present in a long log of wood and a curved fire in a curved log of wood.[17] It is in this sense that Svāminārāyaṇa speaks of greater or lesser fullness of presence (Nyūnādhikabhāva) of God in different degrees of realities.[18] God is more present in higher reality than in a lower reality. His manifestation depends upon the kind of reality in which He is immanent.[19] Thus, as Dr. Yajnik has pointed out, "God is immanent in each and every being, not partially, but wholly and indivisibly."[20]

With reference to the presence of God in jīva, it should be noted that God as God in jīva and God as witness self (Sākṣī) in jīva refer to two different things. The former has an ontological implication and the latter has an epistemological context. From the stand point of ontology God resides in jīva as ultimate reality and supports very existence. From the standpoint of epistemology God resides in jīva as sākṣī and enables it to know all that it can know.

6. Relation Between Self and God

As we have seen according to Svāminārāyaṇa there are five enternal reals.[1] He conceives two types of reals : One, independent (Svatantra) and this other dependent (Paratantra).[2] He has drawn a bold line of demarcation between these two types of ultimate reals.

According to Svāminārāyaṇa, God, as the only independent real is the highest ontological principle. Nārāyaṇa, whom he also calls Bhagavāna and Puruṣottama, is the only independent reality.[3] All other realities are viewed as dependent on Him.[4] Under the dependent type of realities are covered

Akṣarabrahman, Māyā, Īśvara and Jīvā. It should be noted that all eternals, whether independent or dependent, are equally real, and so are the differences between them.

Although jīva are eternal realities, eternally different and distinct from God, they depend upon Him for their existence and activities. They exist in and through God. Their existence cannot be conceived except through God. God constantly sustains them. He is eternally independent of them. God is sovereign. His will is final. He is the only ultimate reality to which all other existences stand in relation of constant and complete dependence. All other reals are subject to His will and power. They are metaphysically dependent upon God for their being and becoming.[5]

This relation of metaphysical dependence of Jīva has been explained by Svāminārāyaṇa in terms of Śarīraśarīrī relation. God is the self of all the lesser realities which constitute His body.[6] God is the soul of soul, self of self and life of life.[7] Svāminārāyaṇa has explained Akṣarabrahman, Māyā, Īśvara and Jīva to be God's body in the sense that they are pervaded by Him, just as physical body is pervaded by jīva, jīva is pervaded by God. Just as physical body without soul is incapable of doing anything, in the same way jīva without God indwelling it is incapable of doing anything.[8]

According to Svāminārāyaṇa, this relation of metaphysical dependence continues between jīva and Puruṣottama even at the transcendent level. In the state of liberation there is complete realisation of metaphysical dependence of jīva upon Puruṣottama. In a sense it can be said that liberation is jīva's realization of its enternal metaphysical dependence on Puruṣottama at transcendent level, which results in eternal Svāmī Sevaka relation.[9]

Here it is necessary to point out, as it has been stated by Dr. J.A. Yajnik, that "Dependence is a kind of relation and there is nothing in the concept of this relation which makes it impossible to apply this relation to eternal substances. Similarly, the notion of eternity is not necessarily connected with the notion of independence."[10] This means that one need not suppose that what is eternal cannot be dependent on another eternal. Simply, an eternal entity is determined by another eternal entity, it does not mean that the determined eternal entity loses its eternal character. An eternally dependent entity by its being eternally dependent on another eternal entity does not cease to be eternal. Even in dependence it remains eternal. Similarly, the depended eternal entity by its caprice cannot render depending eternal entity non-eternal. It is well known that the eternal atoms of Nyāya-Vaiśeṣika Philosophy are not exempt from the sway of God. Eventhough atoms are moved by God, they remain eternal. What is eternal is eternal. Eternal can never become non-eternal. There is no logical difficulty in holding that eternal realities can be eternally dependent on God.

It should also be pointed out that notion of "eternality" is not necessarily associated with the notion of independence. What is meant by an eternal entity is only this that it was never created by anyone at any time nor will it be destroyed at any time.

7. Jīva, Law of Karma and God

According to Svāminārāyaṇa, God is Karmaphalapradātā.[1] Although jīva is bound by Law of Karma and has to suffer or enjoy according to its dessert, it cannot enjoy the fruits of its own action at its will and by its own effort.[2] It is only when God enables jīva to enjoy the fruits of its action, it can do so. Not otherwise.[3] No one can go, against the will of God. He controls everything and every activity in the universe. No one can do anything nor enjoy anything otherwise than in accordance with the will of God.[4] Only God is rewarder of all actions.[5] It is God who creates objects of ordinary sense experience as well as dream objects.[6] Jīva does not create dream objects. He simply cannot create them.[7] Even in dream it cannot enjoy the objects of its choice. Dream objects are given by God. Not only this. Even states (avasthā) of jīva are determined by Him, jīva by itself cannot go from one state to another. It is He who takes jīva from the state of waking (jāgrata) to the state of dream (svapna) or from the states of dream to the state of deep sleep (suṣupti).[8] Other aspects of this point are discussed in the Chapter on Law of Karma.

8. God as the Goal

What is the ultimate goal of human existence? In very clear terms Svāminārāyaṇa has said that realisation of God is the supreme goal (paramapada) of human life.[1] There is no other goal higher than God. God is not only the metaphysical ground and the moral governor of the universe, but He is the Supreme Value (paramsāra) also.[2]

According to Hoffding, every religious standpoint gathers up into its conception of God the highest known values.[3] There are three ultimate values commonly recognised in the East as well as in the West. They are truth (satyam), goodness (śivam) and beauty (sundaram). Svāminārāyaṇa recognises these three values.[4] Svāminārāyaṇa also recognises eternal bliss as a value.[5]

These values are indefinable. But they are not unintelligible. It is a matter of common experience that truth satisfies the intellect, good satisfies the will and beauty satisfies the feeling. These supreme values are not mere social conventions. The religious consciousness regards them as possessing objective validity. These values are ideals realised in God. God is the eternal embodiment of truth, beauty, goodness, bliss, perfection and righteousness. According to Svāminārāyaṇism, these values constitute important aspects of the supreme personality of God.[6] Svāminārāyaṇa's view of God establishes relation between values and spiritual reality. Individual selves achieve approximations to the supreme personality of God and share in God's highest values.[7] When jīva attains Sādharmya with God,[8] on liberation, it attains not only in form, but in the embodiment of values also.[9]

According to Svāminārāyaṇa, God is not only the most beautiful and the most perfect Being,[10] but supreme bliss also.[11] No bliss is Superior to the bliss of God.[12] According to Saint Augustine, God is the Chief good. Nothing is better than God.[13] Svāminārāyaṇa completely agrees with Saint Augustine and says that God is the chief good (Paramasāra).[14]

According to Svāminārāyaṇa, the greatest good of man lies in the realisation of God, and no where else.[15] There is no gain greater than that of God.[16] Having gained God nothing remains to be gained.[17] God is the highest goal. He has the greatest value of human life.[18] We thus see that "the philosophy of Svāminārāyaṇa starts with the conception of Parabrahman as the ground of finite existence, and ends with the emphasis that realisation of Parabrahman, who is immanent in man, is the highest goal of human existence."[19]

9. Self's Knowledge of God

According to Svāminārāyaṇa, God can be known. Let us see by what method and how much of God can be known.

As it has been worked out by Dr. J.A. Yajnik, "sense reason and intuition are the three ways accepted by Svāminārāyaṇa as valid method of knowing reality.[1] Generally it is true that the use of all the three is necessary if reality is to be fully grasped.[2] Now, the sense experience is not always beyond doubt. Knowledge given by sense is not always certain. This is the limitation of sense experience. Logical reasoning is also not without its limitation. Logical knowledge has certainty, but it lacks in immediacy. Logical knowledge is mediate knowledge. This is the limit of Logical knowledge. And, therefore, very obviously God cannot be known through sense experience or logical reasoning.[3] Svāminārāyaṇa has said that God is beyond the reach of sense and reason.[4]

The intuitive knowledge is free from these limitations. It is certain as well as immediate. The intuition is rooted in the very being of the self and functions completely independent of the psycho-physical organism. This being so, knowledge given by intuition is immediate, certain and beyond all doubt. According to Svāminārāyaṇa, intuition (anubhava) is the only way of knowing God.[6]

According to Svāminārāyaṇa, God can be known, but can never be completely known. Svāminārāyaṇa has emphatically pointed out the inexhaustible character of God. God's glory, greatness and power are inexhaustible and can never be fully known by any one.[7] The liberated soul residing in Akṣaradhāman, directly knows God. But it does not know Him completely. It knows only within its capacity to know. Its knowledge of God is proportionate to its receiving capacity.[8] Of course, Svāminārāyaṇa has accepted the possibility of growth in this capacity. According to Svāminārāyaṇa, the capacity to receive knowledge of God admits of continuous growth. More jīva knows God, more develops its capacity to know Him.[9] This capacity will continuously go on developing further and further, but infinite nature of God can never be completely known.

Thus we see that Svāminārāyaṇa denies absolute unknowability of God. But at the same time, he also denies the absolute knowability of God. According to Him, God is never fully known, never fully unknown. For him God is known as well as unknown. "It is interesting to note" to quote Dr. J.A. Yajnik, "that the Svāminārāyaṇist view regarding the knowability of God is strikingly similar to one maintained by Pringle Pallison in his "Idea of God." Both conceive God as the Known-Unknown.[10]

10. Jīva's Sādharmya with God

Referring to the Śruti text Nirañjanam Paramam Sāmyamupaiti,[1] Svāminārāyaṇa says that jīva attains similarity with God.[2] According to Svāminārāyaṇa, when the self attains liberation, it goes to Akṣaradhāman, where it acquires a divine body (Bhāgavati tanu) which is similar to the divine body of God.[3] In Akṣaradhāman there are infinite number of liberated souls (muktas) who have attained similarity with God.[4]

The doctrine of attaining similarity (sādharmya) with God is explained by Svāminārāyaṇa with the help of the illustration of bee. Svāminārāyaṇa says that a bee catches hold of a worm (iyala) and gives it a sting and then hovers over the insect making a buzzing sound. Because of the processes that take place in the worm due to sting and the buzzing sound, it gets transformed into a bee. It ceases to be a worm and becomes a bee like a real bee.[5] In the same way, according to Svāminārāyaṇa, when temporal processes of Sādhanā are undergone, Jīva gets transformed into a divine form like that of God.[6] Svāminārāyaṇa says that by these processes of Sādhanā the devotee of God gets transformed into divinity, even though embodied.[7]

The liberation, ultimately, is a self-discovery. And when the self is discovered, jīva finds that it has similarity with God both in form as well as in the enjoyment of divine bliss. The devotee of God, who acquires knowledge of greatness and glory of God, when it leaves the body and goes to Akṣ aradhāman, it attains the glory greatness, bliss and charm similar to those of God.[8] The devotee of God who attains self-realisation and God-realisation also attains sādharmya with God.[9]

This point is further discussed in the section on liberation.

11. Can Jīva become God?

According to Svāminārāyaṇa, this question is out of place. Such a question is not warranted in Svāminārāyaṇīya theism. In Svāminārāyaṇism such a question is irrelevant and inconceivable.

According to Svāminārāyaṇa, there are five enternal realities. God is the supreme reality. These five realities are eternally different from one another, One cannot become the other. At least, none can become God, one can at the most attains Sādharmya with God. But one cannot become God nor absolutely like God.[1]

In advaita Vedānta of Śaṅkara, Jīva, can realise itself as Brahman. According to Śaṅkara jīva and Brahman are identical. In Svāminārāyaṇism jīva can realise itself as essentially of the nature of Akṣarabrahman. But jīva can never become Akṣarabrahman, or Puruṣottama. Jīva eternally remains jīva. According to Svāminārāyaṇa, Puruṣottama is absolutely unfathomable and can never be fully known by any one.[2] And, therefore, there is no question of any one ever becoming Puruṣottama.

Svāmināārāyaṇa argues that if jīva can become Puruṣottama, then there would be many Gods. Each God would decide on a different course of action with the result that there would be no order and uniformity in the functioning of the universe.[3] But, because no one can become Puruṣottama and there is only one Puruṣottama, the order and uniformity in the universe are maintained.

REFERENCES

1. Various Names of God

1. V.G.F.S. 44.
2. V.K.S. 12.
3. V.L.S. 13.
4. V.J.S. 5.
5. V.G.F.S. 4.
6. V.G.M.S. 3.
7. V.G.F.S. 5.
8. V.G.M.S. 31.
9. V.G.M.S. 3.
10. V.L.S. 18.
11. V.L.S. 18.

2. Svāmināārāyaṇa Proves the Existence of God

1. Saint Thomas Acquinas, Summa Theologica, in Introduction to Philosophy, (Readings) Edited by Arthur Smulyan and others (1967), p. 333-336.
2. Saint Thomas Acquinas, *Ibid.*, p. 336.
3. V.G.L.S. 39.
4. V.G.L.S. 39.
5. V.G.F.S. 18.
6. V.G.F.S. 18; V.G.F.S. 37.
7. Frank Thilly, A History of Philosophy (1949), p. 382.
8. *Ibid.*, p. 386.
9. *See above* V.G.L.S. 39.
10. V.G.L.S. 39.

11. V.G.F.S. 64.
12. V.G.L.S. 39.
13. V.G.F.S. 65.
14. V.G.L.S. 38.
15. V.G.M.S. 61;
    See also V.K.S. 7.
16. F.R. Rennant, The Nature of Belief, From Introduction to Philosophy (Readings) Edited by Arthur Smulyan and others, p. 379.
17. V.G.M.S. 13.
18. V.G.M.S. 13.
19. V.G.M.S. 13.
20. Yajnik J.A. The Philosophy of Śrī Svāminārāyaṇa, p. 46.

3. Form and Personality of God

1. V.G.M.S. 42.
2. V.G.M.S. 42.
3. V.G.M.S. 13.
4. V.G.M.S. 13.
5. V.L.S. 18.
6. V.G.F.S. 45.
7. V.G.F.S. 45; V.P.S. 7; V.P.S. 1; V.G.L.S. 35; V.V.S. 13.
8. V.P.S. 1.
9. V.G.F.S. 66.
10. V.G.F.S. 45.
11. V.G.F.S. 45.
12. V.G.F.S. 45.
13. V.G.F.S. 45; V.G.F.S. 8.
14. V.G.F.S. 8.
15. V.G.F.S. 8; V.G.F.S. 8.
16. V.G.L.S. 37; V.G.F.S. 40.
17. V.P.S. 1; V.S.S. 1.
18. V.L.S. 14.
19. Radhakrishnan, Indian Philosophy, Part-II (1977), p. 659.
20. V.G.M.S. 39; V.G.F.S. 71.
21. V.G.M.S. 34.

4. Man in the Image of God

1. Genesis 1.26.

2. Genesis 1.27.
3. V.K.S. 8.
4. V.G.M.S. 13.
5. V.G.M.S. 13.
6. V.G.F.S. 41.

5. The Doctrine of Double Soul

1. S.P. 107
2. V.G.F.S. 13; V.G.L.S. 4; V.G.L.S. 37.
3. Aurobindo, Life Divine, (1965), p. 207.
4. Aurobindo, *Ibid.*, p. 207.
5. Saint Augustine, Confessions, 3-11.
6. C. Gent, Thomas Acquinas IV, 18.
7. Kaṭhopaniṣad 2.5.13.
8. Gītā 18-61.
9. V.G.M.S. 13.
10. V.G.L.S. 371.
11. V.G.F.S. 52.
12. V.G.L.S. 37.
13. V.G.F.S. 64.
14. V.G.L.S. 37.
15. V.G.F.S. 41.
16. V.G.F.S. 41.
17. V.G.F.S. 41.
18. V.G.F.S. 41.
19. V.G.F.S. 41.
20. Dr. J.A. Yajnik, The Philosophy of Śrī Svāminārāyaṇa, p. 54.

6. Relation between Self and God

1. V.G.F.S. 7.
2. V.G.F.S. 64.
3. V.G.F.S. 64.
4. V.G.F.S. 64.
5. V.G.F.S. 52.
6. V.G.F.S. 64; V.G.F.S. 72; V.G.S. 10.
7. V.G.L.S. 37.
8. V.G.F.S. 64.
9. V.G.M.S. 67.

10. Dr. J.A. Yajnik, The Philosophy of Śrī Svāminārāyaṇa, p. 52.

7. Jīva, Law of Karma and God

1. S.P. 107.
2. V.G.F.S. 65.
3. V.G.F.S. 65.
4. V.G.P.S. 78.
5. *See above* S.P. 107.
   See below V.G.M.S. 11.
6. V.G.M.S. 21.
7. V.G.M.S. 21.
8. V.G.F.S. 66.

8. God as the Goal

1. V.G.M.S. 8.
2. V.G.M.S. 56.
3. Hoffding, Philosophy of Religion (1906), p. 61.
4. V.L.S. 18.
5. V.G.M.S. 10.
6. V.G.M.S. 56.
7. V.K.S. 1.
8. V.K.S. 1; V.L.S. 13
9. V.K.S. 1.
10. V.P.S. 4; V.L.S. 18.
11. V.G.M.S. 10.
12. V.P.S. 1.
13. Saint Augustine, On the Morals of the Catholic Church, in Readings edited by Arthur Smullyan (1967), p. 241-242.
14. V.G.M.S. 56.
15. V.G.M.S. 57; V.P.S. 1.
16. V.P.S. 1.
17. V.G.F.S. 63; V.G.M.S. 56.
18. V.G.L.S. 37; S.P. 108.
19. Dr. J.A. Yajnik, The Philosophy of Śrī Svāminārāyaṇa, p. 82.

9. Self is Knowledge of God

1. Dr. J.A. Yajnik, The Philosophy of Śrī Svāminārāyaṇa, p. 18.
2. V.L.S. 7.
3. V.P.S. 4.

4. V.L.S. 7.
5. V.L.S. 7, V.P.S. 4.
6. V.L.S. 7.
7. V.G.L.S. 37.
8. V.G.F.S. 66.
9. V.S.S. 17.
10. Dr. J.A. Yajnik, The Philosophy of Śrī Svāminārāyaṇa, p. 82.

10. Jīva's Sādharmya with God

1. Muṇḍaka Upaniṣad, 3-1-3.
   V.K.S. 1; V.L.S. 13.
2. V.L.S. 13.
3. V.S.S. 14; V.K.S. 1.
4. V.G.M.S. 67.
5. V.K.S. 1.
6. V.K.S.1.
7. V.K.S. 1; V.K.S. 1.
8. V.G.M.S. 67.
9. V.G.M.S. 62; V.K.S. 1.

11. Can Jīva become God?

1. V.G.M.S. 67; V.G.M.S. 67; V.K.S. 10; V.L.S. 4; V.L.S. 13; V.P.S. 2; V.G.L.S. 39; V.G.L.S. 37.
2. V.G.L.S. 37; V.L.S. 4.
3. V.G.L.S. 39; V.G.L.S. 39;
   Because no body can become second God
   V.G.L.S. 39.

CHAPTER 5

JĪVA AND AKṢARABRAHMAN

1. Introductory Remark

According to Svāminārāyaṇa, as we have seen, there are five eternal realities which are intrinsically different and distinct from one another. Akṣarabrahman is one of them. The other four are : God, Māyā, Īśvara and Jīva.[1]

Akṣarabrahman occupies second rank in the metaphysical order of the ultimate realities in Svāminārāyaṇism.[2] Its position in hierarchy of real is very unique and important. And yet, it is not self-existent. Only God is self-existent. Akṣrabrahman exists only in and through God, it is metaphysically dependent on God for its existence and activities.[3] Its uniqueness and importance is due to God.[4] Akṣarabrahman is not.[5] It is eternally different from God. Akṣarabrahman cannot become God. No one can become God.[6]

2. Second in Rank

As already seen, according to Svāminārāyaṇa, there are five eternal realities. They are : parabrahman (Puruṣottama), Akṣarabrahman, Māyā, Īśvara and Jīva. Parabrahman (God) is the highest reality both in the order and the value.[1] Parabrahman is the supreme ontological entity. Akṣarabrahman is immediately next to Parabrahman in the order and is subordinate to Him. Except Parabrahman it is subordinate to none. Svāminārāyaṇa always mentions Akṣarabrahman as the second in the order of eternal realities. Whenever he mentions Akṣarabrahman along with other four realities, he never changes the order. If he places Parabrahman first in the order, then Akṣarabrahman is placed second. If he places

Parabrahman as the fifth, then Akṣarabrahman is placed fourth.[2]

Akṣarabrahman is higher than Māyā, Īśvara and Jīva, God is described as Akṣarātīta which means God is higher than Akṣarabrahman.[3] The term "Akṣarātīta", which is used to describe Parabrahman as higher than Akṣarabrahman and there being none higher than God, Akṣarabrahman naturally falls in the second rank.

Akṣarabrahman is a dependent reality.[4] It occupies a very important position in the metaphysical hierarchy of ultimate realities in Svāminārāyaṇism. Akṣarabrahman is a very important ontological category in Svāminārāyaṇa metaphysics. Except God it is second to none. It is second only to God.

3. Personal Aspect of Akṣarabrahman

This Akṣarabrahman has two aspects : formal (sākāra) and formless (nirākāra). In other words, Akṣarabrahman has personal as well as impersonal aspects.[1] We shall first deal with the personal aspect.

In its personal aspect Akṣarabrahman has a form and personality, which resembles God.[2] God is eternally in the form of a human being.[3] Akṣarabrahman, in its personal aspect, is always in the human form with two hands and two feet. But its form and personality are not material (māyika). They are divine (amāyika). Akṣarabrahman is beyond three guṇas of prakṛti and hence it is called triguṇātīta.[4]

Akṣarabrahman is eternally liberated.[5] There is a distinction between liberated (mukta) and eternally liberated (nitya mukta). Liberated soul was in bondage prior to its liberation. It attained liberation through the temporal process of sādhanā. Eternally liberated souls were never in bondage, and their state of liberation is not due to any process of sādhanā. They are free and liberated since eternity.[6] Akṣarabrahman is liberated since eternity (anādimukta). It was never in bondage. Akṣarabrahman is nitya mukta.

Akṣarabrahma is a devout servant of God. It is the nearest and dearest devotee eternally in the service of God.[7] Akṣarabrahman always enjoys communion with God and eternally worships God in love. Akṣarabrahman is the first devotee of God. If the expression be permitted, Akṣarabrahman is the personal attendant of God. It serves God always and everywhere. It serves God not only in His divine abode, but also in all places where He incarnates. It is impossible to think of Akṣarabrahman away from God in SvāmināRāyaṇiya theology. Wherever Akṣarabrahman is, God is present.

Akṣarabrahman in its personal aspect is supreme knowledge and service in love personified. Akṣarabrahman is the supreme ideal of love, service and devotion to God. It is the best example of the highest state of liberation eternally realised. In its personal aspect. Akṣarabrahman is an eternally existing ideal for spiritual aspirants. It provides eternal inspiration for finite selves, either in bondage or in liberation, to endeavour to attain a position similar to Akṣarabrahman.[8] Its eternal service to God is proverbial : serve God like Akṣarabrahman.

4. Impersonal Aspect of Akṣarabrahman

Simultaneously with the personal aspect Akṣarabrahman expresses itself in another aspect as an impersonal entity. According to Svāminārāyaṇa, Akṣarabrahman, in its impersonal aspect is formless, homogeneous, undifferentiated consciousness pervading everywhere.[1] It consists of an infinite mass of effulgence overflowing endlessly in all directions.[2] It is extremely luminous and radiates infinite flood of light.[3] It is eternal, non-empirical, infinite and partless whole. It is existence (sat), consciousness (cit) and bliss (ānanda). It is beyond the ambit of māyā (aprākṛta).[4] It never contracts or expands. It is unchanging and always remains in the same state. It is same for ever.[5] It is variously described in Vacanāmṛta as Akṣara, Brahman, Akṣarabrahman, Ātma, Akṣaradhāman, Cidākāśa, Brahmamehola,[7] Brahmapura,[8] Brahmadhāma,[9] Brahmajyoti[10] and Saccidānanda.[11]

In its impersonal aspect also Akṣarabrahman serves God by being His divine abode. God eternally resides in it[12]. It also serves the liberated souls as the transcendent supreme abode for their eternal habitation.[13] It is a most desired place for all mumukṣus who aspire to be in communion with God.[14]

This cidākāśa is not a created entity. It is eternally there. It is not destructible. It has eternal existence.[15] It serves as the substratum and support of all elements.[16]

5. Jīva's Sādharmya with Akṣarabrahman

Svāminārāyaṇa has expounded the doctrine of jīva sādharmya with Akṣarabrahman. According to Svāminārāyaṇa the single minded devotee (Ekāntika Bhakta) of God, after leaving the body, goes to Akṣarabrahman and attains similarity (sādharmya) with Akṣarabrahman. On reaching Akṣaradhāman, the disembodied self gets a divine body (Brahmamaya śarīra) similar to that of Akṣarabrahman.[1] Now, Svāminārāyaṇa also says that jīva, on reaching Akṣaradhāman, attains similarity with Puruṣottama. This tends to create a confusion in the mind of one who seriously tries to understand the position. A question would naturally arise in one's mind, How can jīva attain similarities both with Akṣarabrahman as well as God?

Svāminārāyaṇa himself answers the question and clears up the confusion. He says the Akṣarabrahman has sādharmya with Puruṣottama.[3] Now, as jīva has sādharmya with Akṣarabrahman and Akṣarabrahman has sādharmya with God, Jīva has also sādharmya with God. The position is just similar to a mathematical formula like this. A is equal to B and B is equal to C. Therefore, A is equal to C. This position can also expressed in the form of Hypothetical Syllogism (H S) which is one of the Rules of Inference in the Propositional calculus in Symbolic Logic. Stated symbolically, the formula can be expressed as under :

A B
B C
A C

But it is not necessary to resort to the above mentioned Rule of inference to prove that Jīva has sādharmya with Puruṣottama. As seen above, Svāminārāyaṇa himself has said that on reaching Akṣaradhāman jīva attains sādharmya with God. Thus, we can see that jiva has sādharmya both with Akṣarabrahman as well as Puruṣottama. To say that jīva has sādharmya with Akṣarabrahman is the same thing as to say that jīva haṣ sādharmya with God. Thus Svāminārāyaṇa expounds the doctrine of Double Sādharmya. It means that in Akṣaradhāman, God, Akṣarabrahman and all liberated jīva posses similar forms and similar nature.

6. "Going to" and "Residing in" Akṣaradhāman

What is the meaning of "Going to" and "residing in" Akṣaradhāman? This question came up for consideration before Dr. J.A. Yajnik. According to him, "going to" Akṣaradhāman does not mean travelling in space and reaching at some place. So also, according to him, "residing in" does not mean residing in some locality. According to him, Akṣ aradhāman is not a place and there is neither "going to" or "residing in" Akṣaradhāman. In his view, "one who goes beyond māyā and attains the state of saccidānanda can be said to have reached or gone to Akṣaradhāman.[1]

Now, the question is whether this interpretation given by Dr. J.A. Yajnik is borne out by the internal evidence available in Vacanāmṛtà. Let us see, Firstly, Svāminārāyaṇa always refers to Akṣaradhāman as if it is a vast place in which society of the liberated souls is located. From the said references made by Svāminārāyaṇa to Akṣaradhāman, one gets an impression that Akṣaradhāman is a residential locality, of course infinitely vast. Secondly Svāminārāyaṇa has described Akṣaradhāman in detail. He inter alia describes the patterns of building and types objects and articles available in Akṣaradhāman.[3] From this description of Akṣaradhāman one definitely feels the Akṣaradhāman is a City of God. Svāminārāyaṇa himself calls Akṣaradhāman a city of Brahman (Brahmapur).[4] The use of the word "Brahmapur" for Akṣaradhāman shows that Svāminārāyaṇa regards it as a divine place for eternal habitation of liberated souls. Dr. Yajnik has observed that "Svāminārāyaṇa has never described Akṣ aradhāman in the way in which the paradise of popular imagination is described." It appears to me that this observation of Dr. Yajnik is against the evidence contained in Vacanāmṛta, Thirdly, Svāminārāyaṇa refers to the passage by which Jīva travels and reaches Akṣaradhāman. He calls it the way of Light (arcimārga).[5] Fourthly, he mentions the vehicles by which souls travel to reach Akṣaradhāman.[6]

So, we can see that the interpretation given by Dr. Yajnik is not borne out by the internal evidence of Vacanāmṛta. Dr. Yajnik himself refers to the "Social Character" of the liberated souls. According to him, the liberated souls are related to one another in the way in which the bound souls are related, because they all aim at one and the same thing, God. In his view, the liberated souls are related to one another in the sense that they are all related to God.[7] Now, "Social Character" of liberated souls connotes a "Society" of liberated souls. And "Society" presupposes a place where it is located. So, willynilly Dr. Yajnik has to concede, if not directly, then indirectly, to the position that Akṣaradhāman is a place in Svāminārāyaṇiya theology.

Again the interpretation given by Dr. J.A. Yajnik to the expressions "going to" and "residing in" has not Svāminārāyaṇiya, but Śaṅkarite Flavour. The interpretation appears to be in the vein of Śaṅkara's Brahmavāda which is against the tenor of Svāminārāyaṇa's theistic philosophy. However, the standpoint of Dr. Yajnik is that Svāminārāyaṇa accepts Śaṅkara's position up to a point and then goes beyond it.[8]

7. Akṣaradhāman as the Goal

According to Svāminārāyaṇism, Akṣaradhāman is the highest goal for the devotee of God. In Akṣaradhāman is located the society of liberated souls. It is a perfect society. It is full of joy and beauty. Every devotee of God, in Svāminārāyaṇism, desires to go to Akṣaradhāman and eternally reside there. The devotee very keenly aspires to enjoy communion with God in Akṣaradhāman. Akṣaradhāman is the most cherished goal of all aspirants (mumukṣus) in Svāminārāyaṇism.[1]

But, it is to be noted that Akṣaradhāman is not the ultimate goal. The ultimate goal is God. It is through realizing the goal of Akṣaradhāman that the devotee can realise the ultimate goal of having communion with personal God. Thus, God is the goal of goal. Akṣaradhāman is the goal to be realised in the first instance with a view to realise the ultimate goal which is God. Thus we see that Svāminārāyaṇism has accepted the theory of two goals. But as Dr. Yajnik has pointed out, "though Akṣarabrahman is a goal, it is not to be preferred to the goal of the realization of the personal God."[2]

Gītā also accepts the theory of two goals. According to Gītā, Akṣara is Brahman.[3] There are two puruṣas : Kṣara (jīva) and Akṣara (Brahman).[4] God is greater than both.[5] Akṣara is the divine abode of God.[6] It is a place of supreme illumination.[7] A devotee having gone there never returns.[8] God is superior to Akṣara.[9] Gītā speaks of the worship of Akṣara. According to Gītā, the goal of Akṣara is to be attained for realising the higher goal of being near God and serving Him in great love and devotion.[10]

According to Svāminārāyaṇa the goal of eternally enjoying the commune with God cannot be achieved by those who meditate upon the formless effulgent consciousness (nirākāra caitanya teja) of Akṣarabrahman. So also those who believe God to be impersonal and formless cannot achieve the goal. Such devotees cannot realise God. They lose their consciousness of individuality and are merged in the formless effulgence of Akṣarabrahman from which they never come out.[11] Only those who meditate upon the personal form of God achieve the goal.[12]

8. Akṣarabrahman of Svāminārāyaṇa and Brahman of Śaṅkara

From what has been said before it will be clear that Akṣarabrahman of Svāminārāyaṇa is in many respects similar to Brahman of Śaṅkara's philosophy. Like Brahman of Śaṅkara, Akṣarabrahman of Svāmīnārāyaṇa has saguṇa and nirguṇa aspects.[1] But there are vital differences between the Brahman of Śaṅkara and Akṣarabrahman of Svāmīnārāyaṇa. In Śaṅkara's philosophy, Brahman is the highest reality, whereas in Svāmīnārāyaṇa's philosophy Brahman is not the highest reality. Brahman is subordinate to Puruṣottama. Puruṣottama is the highest reality. There is another difference also. In Śaṅkara's philosophy jīva is Brahman. In Svāmīnārāyaṇism jīva is not Brahman. So also jīva is not puruṣ ottama. All the three are eternally different.[2] In Śaṅkara's philosophy jīva is identical with Brahman, the highest reality. In Svāmīnārāyaṇism, jīva is identical neither with Brahman nor with Puruṣottama.

REFERENCES

1. Introductory Remark

1. V.G.F.S. 7.
2. V.G.F.S. 7.
3. V.G.F.S. 64.
4. V.L.S. 13.
5. V.L.S. 13; V.G.F.S. 64.
6. V.L.S. 13.

2. Second in Rank

1. V.G.F.S. 37.
2. V.G.L.S. 7; V.G.L.S. 10; V,S.S. 6; *See also* V.S.S. 5
3. V.S.S. 4, *See also* V.G.M.S. 13; V.L.S. 18, *See* V.G.M.S. 13.
4. *See above* V.G.F.S. 64.

3. Personal Aspect of Akṣarabrahman

1. V.G.F.S. 21; V.G.F.S. 21; V.G.F.S. 71; V.G.F.S. 31.
2. V.L.S. 13
3. V.K.S. 8; V.L.S. 4; V.L.S. 18; V.G.M.S. 13; V.V.S. 18.
4. V.G.M.S. 10; V.G.M.S. 42.
5. V.G.F.S. 21.
6. V.G.F.S. 32.
7. V.G.F.S. 21.

8. V.G.F.S. 21.

4. Impersonal Aspect of Akṣarabrahman

1. V.G.F.S. 21.
2. V.L.S. 14.
3. V.L.S. 14; V.G.M.S. 13.
4. V.G.F.S. 12.
5. V.G.F.S. 63.
6. V.G.M.S. 13.
7. V.G.F.S. 21; *See also* V.G.F.S. 46.
8. V.G.F.S. 71; V.L.S. 11; V.V.S. 1.
9. V.A.S. 6.
10. V.G.L.S. 36.
11. *See above* V.G.F.S. 12.
12. V.A.S. 6; V.G.F.S. 63; V.P.S. 1; V.G.F.S. 21; V.G.M.S. 64; V.G.M.S. 64.
13. V.G.F.S. 121; V.G.F.S. 12.
14. V.G.F.S. 12.
15. V.G.F.S. 46.
16. V.G.F.S. 46.

5. Jīva's Sādharmya with Akṣarabrahman

1. V.G.F.S. 21; V.G.F.S. 21; V.G.F.S. 40; Also see of Akṣara's sādharmya with Puruṣottama; V.L.S. 13.
2. V.G.M.S. 67; V.G.L.S. 39; V.K.S. 1.
3. Akṣara's sādharmya with Puruṣottama; V.L.S. 13.

6. "Going to" and "Residing in" Akṣaradhāman

1. Dr. J.A. Yajnik, The Philosophy of Śrī Svāminārāyaṇa, p. 101.
2. V.P.S. 1; V.L.S. 13; V.L.S. 14.
3. V.A.S. 6.
4. V.A.S. 6.
5. V.G.F.S. 21.
6. V.G.F.S. 1.
7. Dr. J.A. Yajnik, The Philosophy of Śrī Svāminārāyaṇa, p. 109.
8. Dr. J.A. Yajnik, *Ibid.*, p. 102 and 103.

7. Akṣaradhāman as The Goal

1. V.G.M.S. 22; V.G.F.S. 21.
2. Dr. J.A. Yajnik, The Philosopy of Śrī Svāminārāyaṇa, p. 101.

3. Gītā 8.3.
4. Gītā 15.16.
5. Gītā 15.17.
6. Gītā 8.21.
7. A place of high illumination, Gītā 15.6.
8. Gītā 15.6, *See also* Gītā 8.21 above.
9. Gītā 15.18.
10. Gītā 18.54.
11. V.G.F.S. 64.
12. V.G.L.S. 30; V.G.M.S. 9.

8. Akṣarabrahman of Svāminārāyaṇa and Brahman of Śaṅkara

1. V.G.M.S. 42.
2. V.G.F.S. 7.

PART THREE

EMPIRICAL NATURE OF SELF

CHAPTER 6

DEHATRAYA

1. Introductory Remark

According to Svāmināràyaṇa, the self (jīva) in its wider sense is two fold : higher and lower. The real, pure self is higher self and the self as associated with body, senses and antaḥkaraṇa is the lower self.[1] Referring to the higher aspect of the self Svāmināràyaṇa says that the self in its true being (vyatireka) is different from three bodies, four antaḥkaraṇās and ten senses.[2] With reference to the lower aspect of the self he says that, till liberation, it remains inseparably associated with the causal body.[3]

According to him, causal body evolves into subtle and gross bodies.[4] The subtle and gross bodies, with which the lower self is associated, are all material in nature (māyika).[5] Through ignorance the self wrongly identifies itself with them.[6] The pleasures and the pains of the body are regarded by self to be its own.[7] From this identification arises the empirical nature of the self.[8] Thus, there are two aspects of the nature of the self : One, metaphysical (vyatireka); the other empirical (anvaya).[9] We have dealt with the metaphysical aspect. Now, we shall proceed to deal with empirical aspect.

2. Doctrine of Dehatraya

According to Svāmināràyaṇa the self experiences the objects of the world through the body.[1] Svāmināràyaṇa has used the terminology of Gītā,[2] and has described the body as the field and the self as the knower of the field (Kṣetrajña).[3]

According to Svāmināràyaṇa, there are three bodies (dehatraya); gross (sthūla), subtle (sūkṣma) and causal (karaṇa).[4] We shall, now, proceed to see what Svāminārāyaṇa has to say about these bodies.

3. Sthūla Śarīra

Svāminārāyaṇa himself raised three questions. One, of how many elements is the gross body constituted? Two, of how many elements the subtle body is constituted? Three, are these elements equal in both the bodies or are they more or less?[1] And he himself answered these questions. He has said that the gross body is constituted of five gross elements (pañca mahābhūtās) namely, earth, water, fire, air and space.[2]

4. Sūkṣma Śarīra

The subtle body is constituted of nineteen elements, namely, five congnitive organs, five conative organs, five kinds of vital air (pañca prāṇās) and four internal instruments (antaḥkaraṇās).[1]

5. Relation between Sthūla and Sūkṣma Śarīra

According to Svāminārāyaṇa, when the five elements of the gross body and the nineteen elements of the subtle body remain concomitantly associated, then and then only the body would function. Not otherwise.[1] Svāminārāyaṇa says that the joint functioning of the subtle and the gross bodies is inevitably necessary for experiencing the objects of the world. By mere cavities of sense organs (golakas) the experience of objects is not possible. These cavities of sense organs have got to be associated with the elements of subtle body for experiencing the objects.[2] Without their association with the elements of the subtle body the cavities by themselves cannot function. Therefore, the gross body is said to be constituted of twenty four elements.[3] Similarly when the nineteen elements of the subtle body function with the five elements of the gross body, then only the subtle body can have experience of the subtle objects.[4] And, therefore, the subtle body is also said to be constituted of twenty four elements.[5] Svāminārāyaṇa has said that the subtle body remains in complete concomitance with the gross body which becomes evident when sexual intercourse in dream results in the discharge of semen through physical body.[6] From this, according to Svāmināрāyaṇa, it follows that the gross body functions in absolute harmony with the waking and dream states of the subtle body.[7]

If this is the position, then the subtle body is almost on par with the gross one. Now, the actions performed by the gross body have an effect on the self as per the law of Karma. Then the question would arise whether the action performed by the subtle body would have a similar effect on the self? In fact such a question was raised before Svāmi-nārāyaṇa.[8] In reply to this question Svāmināрāyaṇa has said that if the self identifies with the causal body as it mostly does in case of gross body, then the actions performed by the subtle body would have the same impact on the self as the actions performed by the gross body.[9] But he who has no such ego sense for the subtle and the gross bodies is not bound by the actions of any of the two bodies, for he remains only as self.[10] Thus according to Svāmināрāyaṇa, the knower of the self (ātmajñānī), one who has self-realisation, is not bound by the action of his gross as well as subtle bodies.[11]

The twenty four elements, which constitute the gross and subtle bodies are triguṇātmika,[12] because they are evolved from māyā (prakṛti) which is of the nature of three guṇās.[13] These twenty four elements are material and nonliving (jaḍacidātmaka)[14]. But they appear to be living and sentient because of their association with the self.[15] From this it becomes clear that it is the self and not the body which experiences the pleasure and pain. It is the self which is the enjoyer (bhoktṛ) of the sense-objects. And thus the self is not away from the pleasures and the pains of the body.[16] In other words the self is one with the pleasures and the pains of the body. However, it should be noted that the jīva enjoys the sense-objects through sense-organs. It cannot enjoy these objects independently of sense organs.[17]

6. Karaṇa Śarīra

According to Svāminārāyaṇa, gross and subtle bodies are beginninglessly associated with the causal body just as the seed is associated with the tree.[1] This causal body is material (māyika)[2] and therefore, ignorant in nature (avidyātmaka).[3] It retains the accumulated impressions of the actions (Karmas) of the past births. The causal body of every jīva is constituted of sañcitakarmas which are the results of the beginningless ignorance of the self.[4] Svāminārāyaṇa maintains that just as a seed has a beginningless association with its husk or the earth has a beginningless association with the small, the jīva has a beginningless association with the causal body.[5]

The jīva by nature is pure conscious being (caitanyavastu),[6] but it is enwrapped by avidyā, that is, the causal body. It is because of this that the causal body is described as the māyā of jīva.[7] This causal body evolves into subtle and gross bodies and, therefore, all the three bodies are called māyā of the jīva.[8] According to Svāminārāyaṇa it is with these causal bodies that the jīvas rest in the womb or māyā in the state of final dissolution (ātyantikapralaya).[9]

Svāminārāyaṇa says that just as the seed is the cause of the growth of the tree, the causal body is the cause of further births of the bound jīva. And therefore, it is called causal body.[10] The māya attached to jīva in the form of the causal body is inseparable from it.[11] But if one meditates upon the divine form of God, it will be separated from jīva, as the skin of the tamarind seed is separated when backed.[12]

A question was raised before Svāminārāyaṇa : In what sense is the jīva said to be immanent in its respective bodies and in what sense is it said to be transcendent? In reply to the question Svāminārāyaṇa says when the jīva is in a completely identified state with its bodies and in such a state suffers the agonies of births and deaths, it is said to be immanent in its bodies. But the jīva in its pure being (sattāmātra), which is eternal and indestructible is always separate from and transcends these three bodies.[13]

7. Creation and Destruction of Soul

Because of his belief in the metaphysical dependence of all finite realities upon God for their existences and activities, Svāminārāyaṇa holds that all finite entities are in some way created, sustained and destroyed or otherwise determined in numerous ways by God.

Svāminārāyaṇa has said that God is the creator, sustainer and destroyer of this universe.[1] He has further said that God is the creater and destroyer (Kartā-hartā) of the finite universes.[2] Now, the universe is composed of matter (māyā) and spirits (jīvas). Svāminārāyaṇa says that God, out of Himself, creates all the spiritual entities, right from Brahma to Stamba and others.[3] He creates human beings and all the movable and immovable selves (sthāvara jaṅgama jīvas).[4] Again, when God is the destroyer of the universe, He is also the destroyer of selves. To put it plainly, God is the creater and the destroyer of selves.

Now, on one hand, Svāminārāyaṇa says that God is the creater and the destroyer of the selves, and on the other hand, he says that selves are eternal entities.[5] No new selves come into being. Their number is constant and invariable. No new self is ever born.[6] He further says that self is immortal (amara)[7] and indestructible (avināśī).[8] These apparently opposite assertions of Svāminārāyaṇa may create confusion in his philosophical position. To clear up this confusion, it is necessary to examine the theory of creation in Svāminārāyaṇa's philosophy. Let us try to examine it.

As already seen, God (Bhagvān), selves (jīvas) and matter (māyā) are eternal realities. Jīvas and maya are not the creations of God. They are co-eternal with God. They are there since all eternity along with God. They all possess equal eternality. No one, including God is Before or After.

As seen above, the universe is composed of matter and spirits which are co-eternal with God. God does not create jīva and matter. Then, what does God create when He creates the universe? What does Svāminārāyaṇa mean when he says that God creates souls?

According to Svāminārāyaṇa, universe is not a modification of or emanation from God. For Svāminārāyaṇa universe is merely an actualisation of what is already in the womb of māyā (matter) by the action of God. At the time of Pralaya (dissolution) the selves are lying in the womb of maya. God, at His will, gives them intellect (buddhi), senses (indriyas), mind (manas) and actualises them.[9] A.N. Whitehead says that "God does not create eternal objects."[10] God "is not Before creation, but With Creation."[11] These observations of Whitehead would be applicable to God of Svāminārāyaṇa without any reservation. Unlike God of Mosaic theism,[12] God of Svāminārāyaṇa theism does not create Ex Nihilo (from nothing) or De Novo (anew). Like Demiurge (God) of Plato's Timacus,[13] God of Svāminārāyaṇa is shaping already existing raw materials into various forms. In other words, God, when He creates, gives shapes and forms to existing eternal realities. According to Svāminārāyaṇism, creation is nothing more than giving forms to existing eternal realities. Then, a question would arise, in what sense eternal self is created by God?

Self, in Svāminārāyaṇism, is eternal. It is not created by God. When Svāminārāyaṇa talks of creation of self, at first thought, it appears incompatible with his idea of eternality of self. But Svāminārāyaṇa explains the idea of creation of self by its association with qualifications (Upādhis). According to him, these Upādhis give a qualified appearance to the eternal and beginningless self which is pure as it transcends these Upādhis.[14]

For Svāminārāyaṇa creation of self signifies association of qualifications (Upādhis). According to Svāminārāyaṇa, creation of self means emergence of its qualified appearance caused by its association with Upādhis. These Upādhis consist of three bodies, causal, subtle and gross, which are material in nature.[15] When Svāminārāyaṇa speaks of creation of self, all that is meant by him is the association of the self with the Psycho-physical organism. There is no birth of self as spirit. Passing from one state of dependence to another is itself a new birth in respect of self. This is creation in the sense of change in state that depends on the will of another, that is God. This philosophical position is called Parādhīnaviśeṣāpti by Madhvācārya.[16] Although Svāminārāyaṇa does not expressly refer to the doctrine of Parādhīnaviśeṣāpti, he means to convey the idea contained in it. Such a view of Svāminārāyaṇa in respect of creation of eternal objects is similar to the view held by Thomas Acquinas. The view of Thomas Acquinas as shown by B.N.K. Sharma is known as the doctrine of Eternal Creation which posits eternal and incessant dependence of all finite realities in their each and every state of being and becoming.[17] This is how Svāminārāyaṇa shows that even eternal things can, in a sense, be said to be created. It is in this sense that Creation of eternal entities is to be understood.

We have seen that God is all-powerful. He can do and undo[18]. He can create as well as destroy the universe[19]. When He composes the universe with eternal things and gives them shapes and forms, it is creation. When He decomposes and reduces them to their pre-creation state it is destruction.[20]

Self is eternal. Eternal means everlasting. Everlasting means never coming to an end. In other words, the existence of eternal self can never come to an end. Self can never be destroyed. But Svāminārāyaṇa talks of destruction of eternal self.[21] The question arises, in what sense can eternal self be said to be destroyed?[22]

According to Svāminārāyaṇa, the purpose of creation is to enable the self to experience the sense objects properly and endeavour to attain liberation (mokṣa).[23] In Svāminārāyaṇism attainment of liberation is the ultimate goal of life. Now, self in human body, with senses and four antaḥkaraṇas, would be in a better position to make endeavours for attainment of liberation. Svāminārāyaṇa says that if, due to its Karmas, the self happens to find itself in an immovable and insentient body of mountain or some such body, it will not be in a position to make endeavours for the attainment of liberation for a very very long time. In the body of a mountain the self is unable to do anything for attainment of liberation. It becomes impossible for the self to make any endeavour for it. In such cases, according to Svāminārāyaṇa, the self can be said to have been destroyed.[24] Svāminārāyaṇa explains the position with the help of an illustration of eunuch. According to him, eunuch cannot be called either male or female. An eunuch is useless for the purpose of procreation. Eunuch is unable to procreate. Similarly, when the self becomes unable to make any endeavours for the attainment of liberation, it can be said to have been destroyed.[25] It is in this sense that the Destruction of eternal self is to be understood.

8. Jīva in Pralaya

According to Svāminārāyaṇa, there are innumerable universes (anantakoṭi brahmāṇḍa).[1] A universe is a cosmos. Each universe has a cosmic God (brahmāṇḍābhimānī īśvara)[2] in other words, each universe has a separate cosmic God (īśvara) incharge of it. Svāminārāyaṇa has admitted plurality of Īśvaras. According to him, there are infinite number of Īśvaras (Anantakoṭi Virāṭ Puruṣa).[3]

Each universe is created by God. According to Svāminārāyaṇa God creates the universe for the redemptive purpose of the jīvas.[4] God not only creates the universe, but maintains and dissolves it also. He maintains and dissolves it for the emancipatory benefit of jīvas.[5] For providing rest to the jīvas incessantly moving in the cycle of births and deaths, God, out of compassion for them, enters into the activity of dissolution (pralaya).[6]

According to Svāminārāyaṇa, the dissolution of the universe is of four kinds : Nityapralaya (daily dissolution) Nimittapralaya (Cosmic dissolution) Prākṛtikapralaya (material dissolution) and Ātyantikapralaya (final dissolution).[7]

Svāminārāyaṇa has explained these four kinds of dissolution. According to him, the state of suṣupti (dreamless deep sleep) of jīva is called Nityapralaya.[8] Jīva's external adjunct (Upādhi) is merged in the daily dissolution.[9] Svāminārāyaṇa says that bodies of human and other beings are getting destroyed every moment. According to him, this is also Nityapralaya.[10]

The state of suṣupti of the cosmic God (īśvara) is called Nimittapralaya (cosmic dissolution).[11] The body of Īśvara is called Virāṭ (cosmos). This age of the body of Īśvara is dviparārdha,[12] that is, 200,000,000,0000,000,000 human years. One day of Īśvara is equal to fourteen Manus, that is, fourteen manvantaras.[13] His night is equal to his day.[14] During his day the life of cosmos (triloki) is sustained.[15] When his night falls, Īśvara rests and goes in suṣupti. During the suṣ upti of Īśvara cosmos is dissolved. This is called Nimitta-pralaya (cosmic dissolution).[16] The external adjuncts (Upādhi) of Īśvara are merged in the cosmos dissolution.[17] The daily dissolution of Īśvara is the cosmos dissolution of jīva. When Īśvara is in the state of suṣupti, the jīva residing in his cosmos will also be in the state of suṣupti.

When the evolutes of māyā (cosmic matter) merge in māyā, it is called Prākṛtikapralaya.[18] In the state of Prākṛtika-pralaya all the external adjuncts (Upādhi) of Puruṣa are dissolved.[19] According to Svāminārāyaṇism this Prākṛtika-pralaya would be suṣupti of Puruṣa. In the state of suṣupti of Puruṣa (higher cosmic God) the jīva and the Īśvaras functioning under the dominion of Puruṣa would also be in the state of suṣupti.

The distinction between Puruṣa and Īśvara requires to be noted. According to Svāminārāyaṇa, the entire creation is by God.[20] At the time of creation God casts a glance at Akṣarabrahman and a Puruṣa comes out of it.[21] This is Akṣarapuruṣa. Now, God as Akṣarapuruṣa, enters into the womb of Māyā and innumerable pairs of Pradhānas and Purūṣas are created.[22] There are innumerable universes.[23] Each pair of Pradhāna-Puruṣa is the cause of a universe.[24] God, then, as Puruṣa enters into the womb of Pradhāna and Mahattatva is created.[25] From Mahattatva three kinds of Ahaṅkāra are created. From Ahaṅkāra mind, Intellect, Prāṇas, Pañca Mahābhūtas, Pañca Tanmātras and senses are created.

Out of these elements Īśvaras emerge.[26] Īśvaras (Virāṭa Puruṣas) are infinities in number.[27] According to Svāminārāyaṇism, Īśvara is in charge of a universe. Thus, Puruṣa is the cause of the universe and Īśvara is the manager of the universe.

In the state of Ātyantikapralaya (final dissolution) everything including Prakṛti, also called Māyā,[28] merges in the divine light of Akṣarabrahman just as night merges in the day.[29] Ātyantikapralaya is also called Mahāpralaya (great dissolution). In the state of Mahāpralaya all the creation of Prakṛti and Puruṣa (Akṣara Puruṣa) gets totally dissolved.[30] In Mahāpralaya all the universes are dissolved.[31]

What happens to the jīvas when all the universes are dissolved in Mahāpralaya; the devotees of God go to the divine abode (Akṣaradhāman) of God, while the jīvas, who are in bondage and moving in the cycle of births and deaths in various universes, have rest (viśrāma) in the womb of māyā.[32]

According to Svāminārāyaṇa there are three bodies : gross (sthūla), subtle (sukṣma) and causal (karaṇa).[33] The gross and the subtle bodies are associated with the causal body in the same way in which the seed is associated with the tree.[34] This causal body evolves into gross and subtle bodies.[35] Causal body causes subtle and gross bodies. Just as the seed is the cause of the growth of the tree, the causal body is the cause of further births. And, therefore it is called causal body.[36]

This causal body is material (māyika)[37] and, therefore, ignorant in nature,[38] and yet it retains the impressions of the actions (Karmas) performed in the past births. In other words causal body is constituted of accumulated impressions of actions (Sañcitakarmas). Svāminārāyaṇa says that just as a seed has a beginningless association with its husk or as the earth has a beginningless association with the smell, in the same way the jīva has a beginningless association with the causal body.[39] The causal body is, therefore, described as the māyā or ignorance of the jīva.[40]

It is with these causal bodies that the jīva rest in the womb of māyā during the final dissolution. In the words of

Dr. Radhakrishanan,[41] they lie in deep slumber, as it were. But as the consequences of their deeds are not yet exhausted, they have again to enter into an embodied existence as soon as God wills to create a new material world.

Dr. J.A. Yajnik has pointed out that God in Svāminārāyaṇism is not conceived as the material cause of the world. God is only the instrumental cause of the world.[42] Svāminārāyaṇa has explained the point of creation of the new world by an analogy of the earth, the seed and the rain.[43] He says that are innumerable seeds lying in the earth. They lie in deep slumber, as it were. But as soon as they come in contact with the rain-water, they sprout up and grow abundantly. In the same way the jīvas resting in māyā evolve in the state of creation and assume forms, in accordance with their past karmas, by the will of God who is the giver of the fruits of deeds (Karma phalapradātā).[44] Thus the work of God in respect of jīvas lying in māyā is like that of rain which enables the seed to grow and to fulfill its end.[45]

We must conclude this point with a note that, according to Svāminārāyaṇa, even during the state of final dissolution (ātyantikapralya), God and His devotees, with their divine forms, enjoy divine bliss in Akṣaradhāman.[46]

9. Disembodied State of Jīva

As we have seen the soul in its mundane existence, has three bodies : gross, subtle and causal. According to Svāminārāyaṇa, a bound (baddha) soul is never without a body. At the time of death, when the soul leaves the gross physical body, it retains the subtle and causal bodies. In the state of final dissolution (ātyantika Pralaya) also, when, according to Svāminārāyaṇa all the universes are dissolved, the soul, resting in māyā, retains the causal body[1] which is material in nature.[2] Even in the state of final release (ātyantika Kalyāṇa) the soul residing in the divine abode of God (Akṣaradhāman) possesses a divine body.[3] In any condition, whether in bondage or in release, in the mundane world or in Akṣaradhāman, the soul is never without a body : the body may be one or two or three; may be material (māyika) or divine (bhagavati).

An interesting question arises in this context. Is there any time when the soul is without a body? Is there any time when the soul has disembodied existence? According to Svāminārāyaṇism, there is a time when the soul has a disembodied existence; there is a time when the soul is without a body. When is that time? Let us see.

According to Svāminārāyaṇa, the soul in its true nature is formless.[4] When it is in the state of bondage it is inseparably attached to the causal body.[5] Since beginningless time the causal body is associated with the soul.[6] The causal body evolves into the subtle and gross bodies.[7] The causal body remains attached to the soul till liberation (mokṣa) is attained. When, on death, the liberated soul leaves the physical body, the causal body attached to it falls off and along with it subtle body also falls off. And the soul emerges in its true formless being.[8] At this moment the soul becomes disembodied; at this moment the soul is without any king of body. We can say that the soul at this moment is in the "naked" condition. This disembodied state of the soul continues till it reaches the Akṣaradhāman where God gives it a divine body (bhagavti tanu)[9]

Thus, we see that, according to Svāminārāyaṇism, the soul is never in disembodied condition except between the time, when after liberation, it leaves the gross body and enters the Akṣaradhāman.

REFERENCES

1. Introductory Remark

1. V.G.F.S. 7.
2. V.P.S. 3.
3. V.V.S. 6.
4. V.K.S. 12.
5. V.G.M.S. 66.
6. V.G.F.S. 44; V.G.M.S. 2.
7. V.G.F.S. 78.
8. Dr. J.A. Yajnik, The Philosophy of Śrī Svāminārāyaṇa, p. 137.
9. See above, V.G.F.S. 7.

2. Doctrine of Dehatraya

1. V.G.F.S. 7; V.G.F.S. 78; V.S.S. 5.
2. Gita 13.2.
3. V.G.M.S. 17; V.K.S. 12; V.G.M.S. 1.
4. V.V.S. 6; V.S.P. 116.

3. Sthūla Śarīra

1. V.S.S. 14.
2. V.S.S. 14.

4. Sūkṣma Śarīra

1. V.S.S. 14.

5. Relation between Sthūla and Sūkṣma Śarīra

1. V.S.S. 14.
2. V.S.S. 14.
3. V.S.S. 14.
4. V.S.S. 14.
5. V.S.S. 14.
6. V.S.S. 14.
7. V.S.S. 14.
8. V.S.S. 14.
9. V.S.S. 14.
10. V.S.S. 14.
11. V.S.S. 14.
12. V.G.F.S. 12; S.P. 106.
13. V.V.S. 5.
14. V.G.M.S. 34; V.G.F.S. 12.
15. V.G.M.S. 34.
16. V.G.L.S. 4.
17. V.L.S. 15.

6. Kāraṇa Śarīra

1. V.V.S. 6.
2. V.K.S. 12.
3. V.V.S. 6.
4. V.V.S. 6.
5. V.V.S. 6.
6. V.G.M.S. 66.
7. V.K.S. 12.

8. V.K.S. 12.
9. V.V.S. 6.
10. V.K.S. 12.
11. V.K.S. 12.
12. V.K.S. 12.
13. V.S.S. 5; V.G.F.S. 7.

7. Creation and Distruction of Soul

1. V.P.S. 1; V.G.M.S. 31.
2. V.L.S. 1.
3. V.G.F.S. 13.
4. V.G.L.S. 13.
5. V.G.L.S. 10.
6. V.G.L.S. 10.
7. V.S.S. 12.
8. V.G.L.S. 4; *See also* V.L.S. 10 and V.J.S. 2.
9. V.P.S. 1.
10. A.N. Whitehead, Process and Reality (1929), p. 363.
11. A.N. Whitehead, *Ibid.*, p. 486.
12. A Dictionary of Philosophy (1979) Edited by Antony Flew and others, p. 76.
13. *Ibid.,* p. 76.
14. V.S.S. 9.
15. V.K.S. 12.
16. B.N.K. Sharma, Madhva's Teachings (1979), p. 126.
17. B.N.K. Sharma, Philosophy of Shri Madhvāchārya, (1962), p. 55.
18. V.L.S. 13.
19. L.L.S. 1.
20. L.L.S. 2.
21. V.V.S. 11; V.G.L.S. 12
22. V.G.L.S. 12.
23. V.P.S. 1.
24. V.V.S. 11.
25. V.G.L.S. 12.

8. Jīva in Pralaya

1. V.L.S. 4; *See also* V.A.S. 5; V.A.S. 7; V.G.L.S. 39.
2. V.L.S. 15.

3. V.G.F.S. 63.
4. V.K.S. 1.
5. V.K.S. 1.
6. V.K.S. 1.
7. V.L.S. 9.
8. V.A.S. 3.
9. V.A.S. 3.
10. V.G.F.S. 12.
11. V.A.S. 3; V.G.F.S. 12.
12. V.G.F.S. 12; *See also* V.G.M.S. 31.
13. V.G.F.S. 12.
14. V.G.F.S. 12.
15. V.G.F.S. 12.
16. V.G.F.S. 12.
17. V.S.S. 3.
18. V.A.S. 3.
20. See above V.P.S. 1.
21. V.G.F.S. 41.
22. V.G.F.S. 12; V.G.F.S. 41.
23. V.L.S. 1; V.L.S. 2.
24. V.G.F.S. 12.
25. V.G.F.S. 12.
26. V.G.F.S. 41; V.G.F.S. 12.
27. V.G.F.S. 63.
28. V.G.F.S. 12; *See also* V.G.F.S. 13.
29. V.A.S. 3; V.G.F.S. 12.
30. V.G.L.S. 10.
31. V.G.F.S. 12.
32. V.G.F.S. 12.
33. V.V.S. 6.
34. V.V.S. 6.
35. V.K.S. 12.
36. V.V.S. 6.
37. V.V.S. 12.
38. V.V.S. 6.
39. V.V.S. 6.
40. V.K.S. 12.

41. Radhakrishnan, Indian Philosophy Part II, (1977), p. 551.
42. J.A. Yajnik, The Philosophy of Śrī Svāmīnārāyaṇa, p. 52, 53.
43. V.G.L.S. 10.
44. V.V.S. 6; V.G.L.S. 10.
45. J.A. Yajnik, The Philosophy of Śrī Svāmiārāyaṇa, p. 52.
46. V.P.S. 7.

9. Disembodied state of Jīva

1. V.V.S. 6.
2. V.K.S. 12.
3. V.S.S. 14.
4. V.P.S. 3.
5. V.V.S. 6.
6. V.V.S. 6.
7. V.K.S. 12.
8. V.G.M.S. 66.
9. V.S.S. 14.

CHAPTER 7

ANTAḤKARAṆA

1. Nature of Antaḥkarṇa

What is Antaḥkaraṇa? According to Svāminārāyaṇa, it is internal organ of knowledge. The self directly does not know any object. It knows through antaḥkaraṇa. The cause of cognition is not the consciousness of the self alone, but this consciousness as qualified by the internal organ.[1] This internal organ differs with each individual and, therefore cognition by one does not mean cognition by all.

According to Svāminārāyaṇa, there are four antaḥkaraṇās. They are : manas (mind), buddhi (intellect), Citta (facility of reflection) and ahaṅkāra (ego).[2] The stuff of antaḥkaraṇa, according to Svāminārāyaṇa is subtle matter.[3]

2. Manas

Mind is the central internal organ. According to Svāminārāyaṇa, the mind is the region where wordly desires originate.[1] In its nature mind is always unsteady. It cannot remain without thought. Mind is engaged in the play of opposites (saṅkalpa—vikalpa). Opposite thoughts pertaining to different desires (vāsanā) serve as food for the mind.[2]

According to Maitreyī Upaniṣad, mind is the cause of bondage as well as release. Bondage, if it is attached to objects; release if detached from them.[3] This idea of Upaniṣad is acceptable to Svāminārāyaṇa. He says that one, who has conquered the mind, has conquered the world.[4] According to Svāminārāyaṇa, mind governs the sense organs. All the ten sense organs work under the control of mind. The sense organs are dependent upon mind for their functioning.[5] It is only when the mind is in conjunction with the sense organs that it is possible to have any perceptual knowledge.[6]

3. Buddhi

Out of four internal organs (antaḥkaraṇas), Buddhi (intellect) is regarded by Svāminārāyaṇa as the most important internal organ. He regards buddhi higher than mind.[1] The reason for his so regarding is that it has a cognitive function. It pervades not only each of the ten sense organs, but, manas, citta and ahaṅkāra also.[2] In other words, buddhi pervades the body from toe to the top of head.[3] Because of such pervasion, buddhi knows simultaneously the functioning of all organs of the body[4], and hence, according to Svāminārāyaṇa, every experience involves a judgement. Svāminārāyaṇa says doubting, deciding, remembering and forgetting are due to buddhi.[5] A question may be asked. How can buddhi, which is material (māyika) and insentient (jada), know? Svāminārāyaṇa answers the question by saying that jīva pervades buddhi and inspires it to know and, therefore, it is the jīva who knows. Svāminārāyaṇa further clarifies that God as Sākṣin (witness self) resides in the jīva and hence it is ultimately Sākṣin who knows and through Sākṣin jīva knows.[6]

4. Citta

Mahattattva (the great element) is the cosmic intelligence. According to Svāminārāyaṇa, it is the first product of evolution of prakṛti (māyā). It is the cause of the universe.[1] What Sāṅkhya calls "Mahat" Yoga calls "Citta".[2] According to Svāminārāyaṇa Citta and Mahattattva are the same.[3]

According to Svāminārāyaṇa, citta is pure, luminous changeless and quiet.[4] The function of citta is to reveal the nature of objects of knowledge.[5] Svāminārāyaṇa says that citta is like a big mirror. The mirror, without discrimination, reflects the images of dogs, donkeys and saints who appear before it.[6] Similarly, the attention of citta is drawn to any thing which may be heard, seen or remembered, irrespective of its being good or bad.[7] Even trifles attract its attention.[8]

5. Ahaṅkāra

Ahaṅkāra is self–sense. It is the principle of individuation. It forms the basis of egoity or I–hood.

According to Svāminārāyaṇa, Ahaṅkāra in its cosmic aspect consists of three guṇās, namely, sattva, rajas and tamas. It is the cause of the generation of five elements (pancabhūtās), sense organs, antaḥkaraṇa and prāṇa (vital air). By nature ahaṅkāra is quiet, grave and obscure (vimūdha).[1] In the context of ahaṅkāra, Dr. G.N. Joshi has noted that "It makes possible the appropriation of things in the form of "my" and "mine". The function of ahaṅkāra is abhimāna or self–love. Ahaṅkāra is the sense of subjectivity of an individual in virtue of which one mentally separates one's self from others.[2] Svāminārāyaṇa would endorse this view of ahaṅkāra with respect to its individual aspect.

6. Process of Decision–Making

According to Svāminārāyaṇa, when the sattva guṇa predominates, the antaḥkaraṇa (conscience) remains pure. When the rajoguṇa predominates, it is disturbed and overflows with thoughts. When the tamas predominates, it becomes void (sūnya).[1] According to Svāminārāyaṇa, internally the senses and antaḥkaraṇās are attached to the self and externally they are attached to empirical objects.[2] Describing the process of decision-making, Svāminārāyaṇa has said that at first decision is made by the senses; and then it is made by the ego (ahaṅkāra), then by the faculty of reflection (citta), then by mind (manas), then by intellect (buddhi) and ultimately by the self.[3] However, Svāminārāyaṇa makes it clear that the self accepts the decision of the intellect and, therefore, decision of the intellect can be said to be the decision of the self.[4]

According to Svāminārāyaṇa, the antaḥkaraṇa has greater consciousness then senses and the self has greater consciousness than antaḥkaraṇa.[5] Gītā also speaks in the same tone. It says that the mind is superior to senses; the intellect is superior to mind; and the self is superior to intellect.[6] It should be noted that Svāminārāyaṇa also regards the intellect (buddhi) as superior to mind.[7]

According to Svāminārāyaṇa, when senses come in contact with empirical objects, the desire to experience them is generated, first through outside contact. The outside object, then travels inside and enters into the antaḥkaraṇa as the object of its desire and through antaḥkaraṇa it enters into the self.[8]

7. Four Modes of Antaḥkaraṇa

According to Svāminārāyaṇa, the self knows through the antaḥkaraṇa.[1] The activities of antaḥkaraṇa are the activities of self.[2] According to him, antaḥkaraṇa is one, but it functions in four modes (chāra vibhāga).[3] When it has mode of indetermination (saṅkalpa–vikalpa or manana), it is called mind. When it has the mode of determination (niścaya), it is called intellect (buddhi). When it has the mode of attention (cintavana), it is called citta.[4] And when it has the mode of self–sense, it is called ego (ahaṅkāra).

8. Relation between the Mind and the Self

The nature of the mind and its constituents have been agitating the minds of people for a long time. In the West there are philosophers who equate mind with the self. For them there is no distinction between the mind and the self. Indian philosophers, from the very beginning, have recognised mind (manas) as something distinct from the self (jīva).

According to Svāminārāyaṇa, mind is not self. The self is different from mind.[1] The mind, as contrasted with the self, belongs to lower prakṛti.[2] It consists of subtle matter as opposed to gross matter of which the body is formed.[3] It functions as one of the four internal instruments (antaḥkaraṇa) of the self.[4] According to Svāminārāyaṇa, the self, which is non–material and which has consciousness as its essential attribute[5], is capable of associating, in an almost inseparable manner, with matter in the form of mind.[6] The fact of such association is accepted by almost all the systems of Indian Philosophy. Svāminārāyaṇism also accepts it.

According to Svāminārāyaṇa, the mind, which is evidenced by its thoughts, is able to think because it is pervaded by the self.[7] Self pervades the mind in the same manner in which the fire pervades the iron rod.[8] And this solves the problem as to how there can be association between non-material (caitanya) self and the material (māyika) mind. Svāminārāyaṇa would agree with Saraswatī Chennakeshavan when she observes that "mind which is of a such a fine matter that it can absorb consciousness which in its turn is capable of being reflected in mind. Both are always seen, known and experienced together."[9]

Apart from Svāminārāyaṇa saying that there is a soul and that it is different from mind, it is not impossible to have a direct knowledge of the soul. We can conceive soul. But such a conception of soul is empirically not important, because, as Svāminārāyaṇa says, we cannot directly experience self. We have knowledge of it only through inference.[10] But so far as mind is concerned, we have direct experience of it. According to Svāminārāyaṇa, as the mind is associated with the self in an inseparable manner, it is possible to have the experience of the self combined with the mind. According to Svāminārāyaṇa, we always have experience of self–mind combination. And when we have the experience of this combination, we feel that mind is not different from self.[11] In such a state of experience, mind and self are experienced as one and not two. According to Svāminārāyaṇa, mind is nothing but the reflection (Kiraṇa) of the self.[12] So from the standpoint of psychology, the self is nothing more than its empirical nature, which is reflected in the overflowing and ever rushing desires of the mind.[13] It is only owing to these desires that the empirical life of the self is made possible. Svāminārāyaṇa says that the self always seeks to have experience of empirical objects (pañca viṣayās). Either the self experiences these objects through external senses or it experiences them internally through mind. But it cannot, even for a moment, remain without having experience of them.[14]

In respect of the nature of mind, Svāminārāyaṇa gives an analogy of heat and cold. Just as a man becomes miserable on account of the extreme heat in the summer, in the same way, the self, associated with the mind, becomes unhappy and miserable when desired objects are not experienced. Just as a man becomes inactive on account of the extreme cold in the winter, in the same way, when the desires are fulfilled, the self becomes happy and due to happiness it becomes inactive for attainment of liberation (Kalyāṇa).[15] So also, when a desire is fulfilled, the empirical self seeks to have the same delight again. But the struggle to regain the same delight results in pain and suffering. The very desire for repetition of pleasure brings about pain and suffering. Again, the fulfilment of a desire gives rise to so many desires rooted in lust, anger, greed, infatuation, arrogance and jealousy.[16] According to Svāminārāyaṇa, the empirical self is perpetually engaged in seeking fulfilment of unfulfilled desires. But all the desires can never be fulfilled. And, therefore, seekers of the worldly happiness are day and night burning by the fire of unfulfilled desires.[17]

According to Svāminārāyaṇa, mind directs the senses and itself is directed by the self.[18] Svāminārāyaṇa maintains that what is necessary for perceptual knowledge is neither mere sense or its proper functioning in conjunction with mind, but the self which perceives through these.[19] The same idea is allegorically expressed in Kaṭhopaniṣad which says that the mind is the internal sense organ directed by self and itself directing other sense organs.[20] According to Svāminārāyaṇa, the self is responsible for the activities of mind. Mind plays only a secondary role in the formation of knowledge. It is not mind which is of primary interest to Svāminārāyaṇa, but the self, the Knower, which causes the mind to function. It is that which is of primary interest to Svāminārāyaṇa.

REFERENCES

1. Nature of Antaḥkaraṇa

1. V.G.M.S. 63; V.K.S. 1; *See also* V.J.S. 2.

2. V.G.M.S. 12; *See also* V.V.S. 4, V.J.S. 2, V.G.F.S. 18; V.G.M.S. 12, and V.G.M.S. 63.
3. V.G.F.S. 12; V.G.M.S. 34.

2. Manas

1. V.G.F.S. 38; *See also* V.G.F.S. 12.
2. V.G.M.S. 8; *See also* V.G.F.S. 12.
3. Maitreyī Upaniṣad, 4.11.4.
4. V.G.F.S. 2.
5. V.G.F.S. 12.
6. V.G.M.S. 63.

3. Buddhi

1. V.K.S. 1; V.P.S. 1.
2. V.K.S. 1.
3. V.K.S. 4.
4. V.K.S. 4.
5. V.G.F.S. 12.
6. V.K.S. 4; V.K.S. 1.

4. Citta

1. V.G.F.S. 12.
2. Radhakrishnan, Indian Philosophy, Part II, (1977), p. 345.
3. V.G.F.S. 12.
4. V.G.F.S. 12; V.G.M.S. 6.
5. V.G.M.S. 6.
6. V.G.M.S. 6.
7. V.G.M.S. 6; V.G.M.S. 6; V.G.M.S. 6.
8. V.G.M.S. 6.

5. Ahaṅkāra

1. V.G.F.S. 12.
2. Dr. G.N. Joshi, Ātman and Mokṣa, (1965), p. 346.

6. Process of Decision–making

1. V.G.F.S. 32.
2. V.G.M.S. 2.
3. V.K.S. 1.
4. V.K.S. 1.
5. V.G.M.S. 2.
6. Gītā 3-42, *See also* Kaṭhopaniṣad 1.3.10.

7. *See above* V.K.S. 1 and V.P.S. 1.
8. V.G.M.S. 2.

7. Four Modes of Antaḥkaraṇa

1. V.G.M.S. 63; V.K.S. 1; V.J.S. 2.
2. V.G.M.S. 2.
3. V.G.M.S. 63.
4. V.J.S. 2.

8. Relation between the Mind and the Self

1. V.P.S 3.
2. V.G.F.S. 12.
3. V.G.F.S. 12.
4. V.G.M.S. 63.
5. V.V.S. 1.
6. V.G.M.S. 2.
7. V.K.S. 1; V.K.S. 4.
8. V.G.L.S. 4.
9. Saraswati Chennakeshavan, The Concept of Mind in Indian Philosophy (1980), p. 157.
10. V.K.S. 1.
11. V.G.M.S. 23.
12. .G.M.S. 23.
13. Dr. J.A. Yajnik, The Philosophy of Śrī Svāminārāyaṇa, p. 140; V.V.S. 4.
14. V.A.S. 3.
15. V.G.M.S. 23; V.G.M.S. 23.
16. V.G.F.S. 24.
17. V.G.F.S. 24.
18. V.K.S. 4.
19. V.K.S. 4.
20. Kaṭhopaniṣad 1.3.3.

CHAPTER 8

DOCTRINE OF AVASTHĀTRAYA

1. Introductory Remark

Svāminārāyaṇa has expounded the doctrine of avasthātraya. According to Svāminārāyaṇa, the experience of empirical objects is possible only when the jīva enters into a particular state (avasthā) of the body. The state of body in which the jīva is enabled to experience the empirical objects is called avasthā.[1] Thus, an avasthā is a state of empirical consciousness during its association with the body. There are three such states : waking (jāgrata), dream (svapna) and dreamless deep sleep (suṣupti)[2].

The scientists of the materialist world have taken up for themselves the world of objects as their field of inquiry, while religious and philosophies have taken up the world of subject for their inquiry. During their inquiries in the inner world, as a logical consequence, they identified the three facts of the empirical consciousness as the waking, the dream and the deep sleep. In these three planes of consciousness, we find that in each one of them, we act differently as though we in ourselves are three different entities. The "Waker" in us is different from the "dreamer" and both are different from the "sleeper".[3]

2. Jāgrata Avasthā

The first state of the empirical consciousness, according to Svāminārāyaṇa, is jāgrata avasthā (waking state). It has its root in the state of sustenance (sthiti avasthā) of cosmic god (īśvara).[1] It has its location in the eyes.[2] The attributes of sattvaguṇa are predominant in it. The sattvaguṇa connotes the quality of "Knowledge". Owing to the preponderence of the sattva guṇa, the experience in the waking is clear, distinct and objectively true.[3]

The jīva in this state has consciousness of the body (piṇḍa) which is a miniature form of cosmos (brahmāṇḍa or Viśva)[4]. According to Svāminārāyaṇa, the jīva in this state identifies itself with the gross body and is known as Viśvābhimāni. The individual waking self is called Viśva and Cosmic Waking Self is called Virāṭa. The jīva, as Viśva, is conscious of the external world. It experiences the empirical objects through the media of ten external senses (indriyas) and four internal senses (antaḥkaraṇas). The only experience known to it is in the field of sense objects (pañca viṣayas), namely, the sound (śabda), the touch (sparśa), the form (rūpa), the taste (rasa) and the smell (gandha).[5] According to Māṇḍūkya Upaniṣad, the characteristic of this state is attainment (āpti).[6] It is during this state that man works for various attainments. In this state man makes his choices and decisions. It is a state of outward moving consciousness (bahih prājña).[7] Svāminārāyaṇa would fully agree with this idea of Māṇḍūkya Upaniṣad.

The objects of the world experienced in the waking state are not regarded by Svāminārāyaṇa as illusory as Śankara did nor as "bundle of sensations" as Hume did, Svāminārāyaṇa does not believe that there are no other things the thinking beings and that we perceive our own ideas as the subjective idealists hold. Nor does Svāminārāyaṇa believe that the knower gives form to the world of phenomena as Kant maintains. According to Svāminārāyaṇa, the external object that the mind perceives exists irrespective of its being perceived. Svāminārāyaṇa has taken a strictly realistic position. He, therefore, holds that the world of external objects is common to all perceiving mind.

3. Svapna Avasthā

The second state of empirical consciousness, according to Svāminārāyaṇa, is the Svapna Avasthā (dream state). It has its root in the state of creation (Utpatti avasthā)[1] of cosmic God (hiraṇyagarbha).[1] It has its location in the region of throat.[2] The attributes of rajoguṇa are predominant in it.[3] Rajoguṇa connotes the quality of "action".

In the waking states the physical body is active and moving. In the state of dream as well as the dreamless sleep it lies inactive like a machine at rest. In the state of dreamless sleep a little of rajoguṇa still persists through which digestion of food, blood circulation and other internal functions continue. But when rajas increases and predominates during dreamless sleep dreams start appearing. Owing to the preponderance of rajoguṇa the jīva experiences empirical objects in the dream state.[4] The experience of objects in the dream state is dim, unstable and objectively false. The reason for its being so, according to Svāminārāyaṇa, lies in the peculiarity of the region of throat wherein infinite varieties of dream objects originate.[5] Just as in a temple, the walls of which are decorated with mirrors, a lamp, placed in the centre, appears in many images, in the same way the thought of a desire (saṅkalpa) assumes infinite forms in the region of throat.[6]

According to Svāminārāyaṇa, the jīva in this state identifies itself with the subtle body and is known as Taijasābhimānī. The individual dreaming self is called Taijas (bright) and the Cosmic Dreaming Self is called Hiraṇyagarbha. Dream is inward moving consciousness. In this state the jīva as Taijas is conscious only of the internal world, and experiences subtle objects (vāsanāmaya bhoga) through the media of subtle indriyas and antaḥkaraṇa.[7] According to Māṇḍūkya Upaniṣad the characteristic of this state is "Upsurge" (utkarṣa)[8]. The "Upsurge" indicates something that takes one beyond one's range. Upsurge results in superiority. One experiencing Upsurge has a superior Knowledge. Svāminārāyaṇa would completely endorse the above view of Māṇḍūkya Upaniṣad.

According to Svāminārāyaṇa, dream objects represent unfulfilled desires of jīva in the waking state. The nature of jīva does not change in the dream state from what it was in the waking state. The desires which arise in the waking state spring up in the dream state.[9] Svāminārāyaṇa would agree with Freud when he says that "the dream in its innermost essence, is the fulfilment of a wish."[10] As Dr. J.A. Yagnik has pointed out, Svāminārāyaṇa would agree with the psycho-analyst that the experience of the dream state need to be interpreted, and such an interpretation, if it is true, throws a good deal of light upon the character of the person whose dreams are interpreted.[11]

A question was raised before Svāminārāyaṇa by Svāmi Nirlobhānanda : Many a time it happens that the objects never seen or heard in the waking life spring up in the dream state. What is the reason of it?[12] In answer to this question Svāminārāyaṇa has said that the unfulfilled desires of the past birth crop up in the form of objects.[13] This means that according to Svāminārāyaṇa objects of dream experiences are ultimately objects created on the basis of the memory or sanskāras of the experience of the objects of waking state. This is the reason why Svāminārāyaṇa would not agree with John Hospers when he says that "It seems impossible to distinguish dreams from waking–life experiences on the basis of any qualitative dissimilarity between dream experiences and waking life experiences."[14] Moreover, according to Svāminārāyaṇa, dream state is completely different from the waking state, and therefore, the nature of experiences in both these states are bound to be different. Thus the view of John Hospers is not in consonance with the view of Svāminārāyaṇa about dream and waking–life experiences.

Emphasising the spiritual quality of the self, Svāminārāyaṇa has said that the consciousness of the person, if coupled with spiritual vigour, becomes so purified that bad dreams do not appear to him.[15] According to Svāminārāyaṇa the jīvas cannot assume the dream state nor can they create the dream state at their choice. It is God, who, as the giver of fruits of action (Karmaphalapradātā), presents the dream objects to the individual selves in accordance with their dessert.[16] Dr. J.A. Yajnik has noted that "Svāminārāyaṇa would not agree with psycho–analyst in regarding experiences of dream as purely subjective and fantastic fabrications woven with the images of memory."[17]

4. Suṣupti Avasthā

The third state of empirical consciousness, according to Svāminārāyaṇa, is suṣupti avasthā (dreamless sleep or deep sleep, state). When we have transcended both the states of waking and dreaming, we shall be in this state.

The difficulty in describing the deep sleep is that during the time of sleeping we experience none of the worlds of our usual instruments of cognition as they are not at work then. Deep sleep is a state in which gross body becomes inert and the internal instruments (antaḥkaraṇas) retire. It is a state of living in which all the instruments of knowledge are closed down.

Svāminārāyaṇa has given a good description of the state of deep sleep. According to him, the root of this state is in the state of dissolution of the cosmic god (īśvara).[1] It has its location in the heart.[2] The attributes of tamoguṇa are predominant in it.[3] The tamoguṇa connotes the quality of inertia. Actions performed under the predominant influence of Tamas induce the self into the state of deep sleep.[4]

In the state of deep sleep the jīva experiences a mere all round ignorance, a complete negativity. There are no objects to experience, either gross or subtle, and hence there is no experiencer. The sleeper does not desire any object nor does he see any dream. Owing to the preponderance of tamoguṇa, the self becomes oblivious of the desire to experience empirical objects, of knowledge (jñātāpaṇuṅ) of such desires and the ego of doership (Kartāpaṇuṅ), all of which merge in the causal body.[5] The self does not have any kind of contact with the empirical objects. The self becomes just like a stone, that is, the jīva becomes almost unconscious in this state. It does not have any kind of knowledge.[6] The only thing the self experiences is a state which has neither form, nor sound, nor taste, nor touch.

According to Svāminārāyaṇa, in this state the self identifies itself with the causal body and is known as prājña (the wise). The self, in this state, remains fully absorbed in the bliss of Pradhāna Puruṣa who is known as Saguṇa Brahman in Svāminārāyaṇism.[7] Thus, the self gets a temporary relief from the sufferings and agonies of empirical life. But this does not mean that the self derives real bliss. In this state the self gets only the shadow of the supreme bliss. It is called shadow because the self does not experience positive bliss. Māyā (avidyā) with its three guṇas persists in this state. According to Svāminārāyaṇa, the deep sleep is not a state of real bliss. The real bliss can be experienced only when the self goes beyond three guṇas of māyā and is established in its true being (ātma Sattā).[8]

According to Māṇḍūkya Upaniṣad, the characteristic of this state is Apiti (final end).[9] As Rohit Mehta has pointed out, the literal meaning of the word Apiti is "Approaching" or "Entering In To." The state of deep sleep is a state where man is approaching the Portal of Truth. It is a condition where man is entering into a new realm.[10] Svāminārāyaṇa would be in complete agreement with this view of Māṇḍūkya Upaniṣad.

5. Intermingling of the Three States

In Yogavāsiṣṭha the doctrine of composite state is propounded. According to this doctrine, anyone of the three states may include in itself the remaining one or other states.[1] Svāminārāyaṇa has admitted this doctrine. According to him, the three states are not exclusive of each other. Any one of them may involve the other two.[2] A man may be waking in a state and yet be in the dream state totally unaware of the surroundings. At Dr. J.A. Yajnik has put it, "This happens so because the differentia of any of the three states of consciousness is in preponderance of any one of the three guṇas; and the guṇas are, by their very nature, capable of mixing with one another in any proportion. Thus, it is quite possible that in any one of the three states of consciousness, the experiences peculiar to the remaining state of states of consciousness may also arise."[3]

According to Svāminārāyaṇa, the experience in the waking state is distinct and objective (Yathārtha). But, what would be the state (avasthā) in which man experiences rope as snake? Svāminārāyaṇa would reply the question like this. He ways that if the jīva, in the waking state, is overtaken, by a sense of promiscuity (bhrānti), it will experience the empirical object as what it is not (ayathārthapaṇe). According to Svāminārāyaṇa, this is a case in which the waking state is coloured or dominated by the dream state.[4] This can be said to be a composite state in which the elements of both the waking state and the dream state are present. In such a composite state, the man sees rope as snake, even though apparently he seems to be in the waking state.

Svāminārāyaṇa, also, mentions an instance of the composite state wherein the elements of both the waking state as well as the deep sleep state are present. He says that if the jīva, in the waking state, becomes oblivious of the outer environment due to the influence of fatigue and compunction, it will not be able to experience empirical objects discriminately. Under such a condition it will experience them indiscriminately (viveka rahita). In such a case the waking state is coloured or dominated by the deep-sleep state.[5]

According to Svāminārāyaṇa, when in the dream state the jīva experiences the empirical objects of its desire (vāsanāmaya bhoga) knowing them with discrimination as it does in the waking state, then it is called waking state in the dream state.[6] Similarly, when it experiences such objects in the dream state without discriminatory knowledge of them on account of inertness, it is called deepsleep state in the dream state.[7]

According to Svāminārāyaṇa, if, during the state of deep-sleep, the sense of doership (Kartṛ Vṛtti) arises due to previous deeds (Karmas), such a state is called dream state in the deep-sleep state.[8] Sufferings and agonies experienced in waking and dream states are dissolved in the blissful states of deep sleep. Now, if the self experiences bliss with the knowledge of bliss as opposite of suffering, then such a state, according to Svāminārāyaṇa, is called waking state within the deep-sleep state.[9]

6. The Individual and the Cosmic Aspects of the Three States

In the foregoing pages, in this chapter, we have pointed out, along with other aspects, the individual and the cosmic aspects of the three states of consciousness. But, it would be worth-while to bring these aspects out of their general setting and place them here so that we may have a clear and concise picture of the individual and cosmic aspects of these three states of waking, dream and deep-sleep.

As seen, according to Svāminārāyaṇa, self in the waking state indentifies itself with the gross body and is known as Viśvābhimānī. The individual waking self is called Viśva and the cosmic waking self is called Virāṭa. The self, as viśva, is conscious of the external world.

According to Svāminārāyaṇa, as seen, the self in the dream state identifies itself with the subtle body and is known as Taijasābhimānī. The individual dreaming self is called Taijas and the Cosmic Dreaming Self is called Hiraṇyagarbha. The self, as Taijas, is conscious only of internal world.

According to Svāminārāyaṇa, as seen the self, in the deep-sleep state, identifies itself with the causal body and is known a prājña. The self, in this state, remains fully absorbed in the bliss of Pradhāna Puruṣa who is known as Saguṇa Brahman in Svāminārāyaṇism.

From the above-mentioned aspects of the three states of consciousness, it becomes clear that Svāminārāyaṇa has adopted a thoroughly realistic position. Svāminārāyaṇa, does not believe in dṛṣṭisṛṣṭivāda. According to him, although the self is metaphysically dependent on God and experiences empirical objects in and through God, nevertheless the objects of the world are real and not the constructions of mind.

Herein lies an important difference between Śankara and Kant on one side and Svāminārāyaṇa on the other. Śaṅkara regards objects of the world as unreal, as being creations of avidyā. Kant regards them as mental constructs. Svāminārāyaṇa regards them as objectively real. What is attempted above is nothing more than a simple comparison between the world of self and the world of Īśvara (cosmic God). The comparison indicates the fundamental unity of spiritual character of the world without taking away the least of its objective reality.

7. The Fourth State

Thus we see that Svāminārāyaṇa has given us a analysis of empirical consciousness. As we have seen, in waking state both senses and mind are not at work. In dream state the senses are at rest and only mind is at work. In deep-sleep state both senses and mind are at rest. The waking state is a state of outward movement. Dream state is a state of inward movement. And deep-sleep state is a state of no movement.

According to Svāminārāyaṇa, the self cannot choose to be in a particular state it likes. The self which experiences the fruits of deeds (Karmas) in its waking, dreaming and sleeping states cannot independently do so. God, who is the giver of fruits of actions (Karmaphalapradātā) enables it to go through these states according to its Karmas.[1] For example, a self, when it is in the state of waking, cannot go to the state of dreaming, even if it desires to do so, because God controls its movements (Vṛttis). Again, if it desires to go from the dream state to the waking state, it cannot do it, nor can it go into the state of deep-sleep. It is only when God helps it to go through these states according to its Karmas, that it can experience the fruits of its actions in these three states.[2]

Thus, we have seen the characteristics of three states of consciousness as has been explained by Svāminārāyaṇa. But according to Svāminārāyaṇa, these three states are not all. There is a fourth one which comprehends all the three states. Svāminārāyaṇa calls it Turīyapada. He also calls it Antaryāmi,

Draṣṭā, Brahman and Parabrahman. According to Svāminārāyaṇa, it is by this Turīyapada that the self is enabled to distinguish between these three states.[3] All the three states are included in the fourth one. Turīya is the consciousness of unity. According to Māṇḍūkya Upaniṣad, the characteristic of this state is Amātra (Partless).[4] In this state the self is in the state of pure consciousness. According to Svāminārāyaṇa, the highest is not the deep-sleep state, but the fourth state.[5] This fourth states brings out positive aspect of the negative emphasised in the state of deep-sleep. However, as Radhakrishnan has pointed out, Turīya, like suṣupti, is not a normal occurrence of man's life.[6]

This point should be concluded with a note that the Buddhist discrimination of four states of Kāma, Rūpa, Arūpa and Lokottara answer to the four states of consciousness mentioned above.[7]

REFERENCE

1. Introductory Remark

1. V.S.S. 6.
2. V.S.S. 6; V.G.L.S. 78.
3. Swāmī Chinmayānand, Māṇḍūkya Upniṣad (1953), p. 33.

2. Jāgrata Avasthā

1. V.S.S. 6; V.S.S. 6; V.G.F.S. 65.
2. V.S.S. 6.
3. V.K.S. 12.
4. V.G.F.S. 65.
5. V.S.S. 6.
6. Māṇḍūkya Upniṣad-9.
7. Māṇḍūkya Upniṣad-3.

3. Svapna Avasthā

1. V.S.S. 6.
2. V.S.S. 6.
3. V.S.S. 6.
4. V.G.F.S. 15.
5. V.G.M.S. 21.

6. V.G.M.S. 21.
7. V.S.S. 6.
8. Māṇḍūkya Upaniṣad 10.
9. V.G.L.S. 18.
10. Freud, The Dream As Wish-Fulfilment, in The Philosophers of Modern Science, Modern Pocket Library (1954), p. 332.
11. J.A. Yajnik, The Philosophy of Śrī Svāminārāyaṇa, p. 139.
12. V.G.L.S. 18.
13. V.G.L.S. 18.
14. John Hospers, Introduction to Philosophical Analysis (1977), p. 514.
15. V.G.F.S. 63.
16. V.G.M.S. 21.
17. J.A. Yajnik, The Philosophy of Śrī Svāminārāyaṇa, p. 139.

4. Suṣupti Avasthā

1. V.S.S. 6.
2. V.S.S. 6.
3. V.S.S. 6.
4. V.G.F.S. 65.
5. V.S.S. 6.
6. V.G.F.S. 65.
7. V.S.S. 6.
8. V.G.M.S. 51.
9. Māṇḍūkya Upniṣad 11.
10. Rohit-Mehta, The Call of Upaniṣad (1970), p. 166.

5. Intermingling of the Three States

1. Yogavāsiṣṭha, Sthitiprakaraṇa, Sarga 19, Verses 9 and 10.
2. V.S.S. 6.
3. Dr. J.A. Yajnik, The Philosophy of Śrī Svāminārāyaṇa, p. 140.
4. V.S.S. 6.
5. V.S.S. 6.
6. V.S.S. 6.
7. V.S.S. 6.
8. V.S.S. 6
9. V.S.S. 6.

7. The Fourth State

1. V.G.F.S. 65.

2. V.G.F.S. 65.
3. V.S.S. 6.
4. Māṇḍūkya Upaniṣad 12.
5. V.S.S. 6.
6. Radhakrishnan, Indian Philosophy, Part-I (1977), p. 162.
7. Radhakrishnan, *Ibid.,* p. 161.

CHAPTER 9

JĪVA AND ĪŚVARA

1. Plurality of Īśvaras

Īśvara is the cosmic self. He is one of the five eternal realities admitted by Svāminārāyaṇa. He was never created. He is an eternally existing metaphysical entity.[1]

Like jīvas, Īśvaras are infinite in number,[2] Svāminārāyaṇa has accepted the doctrine of plurality of Īśvaras. Svāminārāyaṇa has specifically said that no new jīva (self) comes into existence. In respect of Īśvara Svāminārāyaṇa has not expressly said so. But since Īśvara is an eternally existing ontological category, his creation cannot be logically conceived. Thus, according to Svāminārāyaṇa, no new Īśvara comes into existence.

According to Svāminārāyaṇa, there are infinite number of universes.[3] Each universe is headed by an Īśvara. Īśvara who is the head of a universe, is called Brahmāṇḍābhimāni.[4] Each universe (Brahmāṇḍa) has usually more than one Īśvara. Every Īśvara has been assigned the duty and responsibility of governing and taking care of universe of a department of it. According to Svāminārāyaṇa, Brahmā and such others are Īśvaras.[5] According to this view of Svāminārāyaṇa, Brahmā, Viṣṇu, Rudra, Mahāviṣṇu, Pradhāna Puruṣa, Hiraṇyagarbha, Bhūmapuruṣa and even Mahattattva are Īśvaras. They handle some or the other department of their universe. Thus, from Brahma to Virāṭ Puruṣa, all are included in the category of Īśvaras.

2. Metaphysical Nature of Īśvara

Īśvara is essentially different from his three bodies.[1] His real metaphysical nature is Saccidānanda.[2] The real nature of God is also Saccidānanda.[3] But that does not mean that God has transformed himself as Īśvara.[4] God is eternally different from Īśvara. There is eternal difference between God and Īśvara.[5]

Īśvara is knower, doer and enjoyer.[6] In the context of the universe with which he is attached, he is omniscient. He is omniscient in the sense that he knows everything pertaining to universe with which he is connected.

Īśvara is not an independent reality. Like Jīva, Īśvara is dependent reality. Howsoever large his grossbody (virāṭ) may be, and compared to jīva, howsoever great his powers of action may be, still Īśvara is a finite entity and depends on God for his existence and activities.[7] He simply exists in and through God. He is not only dependent on God in the state of bondage, but also in the state of liberation. His metaphysical limitations are not merely external. They are intrinsic also. The external limitations can be eradicated by the Upāsanā of God. But the intrinsic limitations remain for ever.[8]

3. Three Bodies of Īśvara

Like jīva, Īśvara is bound by the law of Karma till he attains liberation, he remains in bondage.[1] He is bound by māyā in the form of three bodies. He three bodies are : Virāṭ (gross body), Sūtrātma (subtle body) and Avyākṛta (causal body).[2] All the three bodies are constituted of twenty elements.[3]

Virāṭ is his outer body. The shape of this gross body of Īśvara is like that of a human body. Īśvara has a two-armed and two-legged personality.[4] He possesses a macro- cosmic (virāṭ) body. His body is so large that one cannot have any view of it.[5] He acts and performs his duties through this body.

Sūtrātma is the subtle body of Īśvara. It is evolved from māyā which is of the nature of three guṇas.[6] The twenty four elements of which the subtle body is formed are non-living (jadacidātmaka).[7]

According to Svāmināryaṇa, Avyākṛta is the causal body of Īśvara. This causal body is very much similar to the causal body of Jīva.[8] This causal body is material.[9] It possesses the accumulated Karma of the past births of Īśvara.[10] This causal body evolves into subtle and gross bodies[11] and, therefore, all the three bodies are called maya of Īśvara.[12] It is with this causal body that Īśvara rests in the womb of māyā during the state of final dissolution (ātyantika Pralaya)[13] This māyā attached to Īśvara is inseparable from him. But if he meditates upon the divine form of God, it will be separated from Īśvara.[14]

4. Three States of Īśvara

Like Jīva, Īśvara has also three states. These three states are : Utpatti (creation), Sthiti (sustenance) and Pralaya (destruction).[1]

The waking state of "Īśvara" is the state of creation (utpatti).[2] In this state "Īśvara" crates the cosmos. The dream state of "Īśvara" is the state of sustenance (sthiti).[3] In this states "Īśvara" sustains what he has created. Just as Jīva enjoys empirical objects in the state of dream (Svapna), so also "Īśvara" enjoys the objects which are created for him by God according to his dessert.[4] The deep sleep state of "Īśvara" is the state of dissolution (Pralaya). In this state "Īśvara" goes in the deep sleep. And when "Īśvara" goes in the deep sleep the whole cosmos is dissolved.[5]

5. Four Forms of Speech of Īśvara

According to Svāmināryaṇa, four forms of speech function both in the body of jiva as well as in the body of Īśvara.[1] Svāmināryaṇa has explained in details the nature of these four forms of speech.

According to Svāmināryaṇa, there is a thousand petalled lotus in the head of Īśvara. At the time of creation of cosmos, God enters into this thousand-petalled lotus. The entry of God gives rise to a divine sound (Akṣarabrahmātmaka Nāda) in the lotus.[2] The divine sound so created in the lotus travels downwards through Suṣumnā and reaches the navel region (Nābhikaṇḍa) of Īśvara and there makes a great reverberation. The Nāda which makes this reverberation is called Parā Vānī (Supreme Word).[3] This Parā Vānī then proceeds upwards and enters into the heart region (Hṛdayākāśa) of Īśvara where it spreads its resonance. The Nāda resounding in the heart region is called Paṣyantī Vāṇi (Perceiving Word).[4] From there it further proceeds Upwards and enters the throad region of Īśvara. The Nāda vibrating in the throat region of Īśvara is called Madhyamā Vāṇi (Intermediate Word).[5] From the throat region the Nāda surges out through the mouth of Īśvara. As it comes out of the month, it gets converted into fifty two letters and results in four Vedas. The Nāda which jushes out from the mouth of Īśvara is called Vaikharī Vāṇi (Expressed Word).[6] This is how, according to Svāminārāyaṇa, the four forms of speech function in the body of Īśvara.[7]

According to Svāminārāyaṇa, similar four forms of speech function in the body of jīva.[8] God resides in jīva as antaryami (indweller). God is connected with all the three states of jīva.

According to Svāminārāyaṇa, the speech which can describe the divine form of God and which can distinguish Ātma from Anātma and which can clearly point out the eternal difference between Jīva, Īśvara, Māyā, Akṣara and Puruṣottama, is called Parā Vāṇi.[9] The speech which can clearly represent the empirical object as they are and can distinguish them through spoken word is called Vaikharī Vāṇi.[10] The speech which does not clearly represent the empirical objects but creates an ambiguity about them is called Madhyama Vāṇi.[11] And the speech which creates absolute confusion in representing the objects is called Paśyantī Vāṇi.[12]

These four forms of speech are connected with the working state (Jāgrata Avasthā) of the Jīva.[13] But the four forms of speech which are connected to the dream and deep sleep states of jīva can be known only by one who attained the state of Samādhi. They cannot be known by persons of common accomplishment.[14]

6. Parabrahman in Īśvara

As we have seen, Īśvara is one of the five reals admitted by Svāminārāyaṇa. Although, Īśvara is eternally different from Puruṣottama, Īśvara is not independent of Puruṣottama, Īśvara is metaphysically dependent on Puruṣottama, without Puruṣottama, Īśvara can do nothing.[1] Just as Puruṣottama resides in jīva, he also resides in Īśvara, he could not do anything with that body. He even could not get up. It is only when Puruṣottama entered into him that he got up[2] and started his activities of creation, maintenance and destruction.[3] By His antaryāmi Śakti Puruṣottama resides in Īśvara. It is God who, through the instrumentality of Īśvara creates infinite universes, sustains and destroys them.[4]

7. Birth, Death and Re-birth of Īśvara

According to Svāminārāyaṇa, all creation comes to an end in the state of final dissolution (ātyantika Pralaya). At the will of God the cosmic evolution starts again. According to Svāminārāyaṇa, when God wills to create, He simply looks at Akṣara and a Puruṣa emerges out of it.[1] This is the Primordial Puruṣa. From the union of this Primordial Puruṣa and the Primordial Prakṛti, Pradhāna Puruṣa is born.[2] From Pradhāna Puruṣa evolves Mahattattva.[3] From Mahattattva evolves three kinds of ego : Sātvika, Rājasika and Tāmasika. From ego evolve five gross elements (Pañcamahābhūtas), five subtle elements (Pañcatanmātra), five senses of cognition, five senses of connation and four internal senses (antaḥkaraṇas).[4] All these twenty four elements combine and give birth to Īśvara.[5] This is, in short, the story of the birth of cosmic self.

The age of the body of Īśvara is dviparārdha years.[6] During his age, he carries on activities of creation, sustenance and destruction of comos. His nights and days are equal. During his day cosmos comes into existence. At the fall of his night it gets destroyed. This daily destruction is called Nimitta Pralaya.[7] This goes on till the expiry of his age. At the end of his age his body is dissolved and the twenty four elements constituting his body get merged in Mahāmāyā. The death of his body results in Prakṛta Pralaya.[8]

When the states of final dissolution ends, the same old wheel of births and deaths gets moving once again.[9]

8. Liberation of Īśvara

During his life time, Īśvara worships Sankarṣaṇa, Aniruddha and Pradyumna[1] which are the saguṇa forms of God.[2] The worship of these saguṇa forms gives him strength and power to carry on activities of creation, sustenance and destruction.[3] So long as he worships these forms, he is unable to free himself from the entanglements of māyā.[4] So long as he worships these forms cycle of his births and deaths keeps on moving. But when he worships God, he realises his brahmahood and becomes free from the bondage of maya. It is only when he worships and meditates upon Parabrahman, the supreme reality, that he realises his true nature and attains his liberation. The Upāsanā of Parabrahman enables Īśvara to attain release from the fetters of māyā and to enjoy eternally the bliss of self-realisation and God-realisation.[5]

According to Svāminārāyaṇa, the process of attaining liberation and the state of liberation in Akṣaradhāman are the same as those of Jīva. In these things Īśvara is very much similar to jīva.[6] So far as state of liberation in concerned, Svāminārāyaṇa has not admitted any distinction between Īśvara and Jīva.

9. Similarities between Jīva and Īśvara

According to Svāminārāyaṇa, the nature of Īśvara is very much similar to that of Jīva.[1] From the foregoing discussion we find that there are striking similarities between Jīva and Īśvara. The nature of Īśvara as revealed by Svāminārāyaṇa in Vacanāmṛta discloses that Īśvara is a sort of higher soul. And therefore, certain similarities are bound to be there.

One thing comes out very conspicuously that Īśvara is not essentially different from Jīva. Although Īśvara as an ultimate metaphysical reality, is eternally different from Jīva, there is no intrinsic difference between the two. The essential nature of both of them is the same.

Now, let us bring out prominent similarities between Jīva and Īśvara. It would be worthwhile to count them one by one.

1. Both Jīva and Īśvara are finite selves. Jīva is individual self. Īśvara cosmic self.
2. Both are eternally existing realities.
3. Both are infinite in number.
4. No new Jīva comes into existence. Similarly, no new Īśvara comes into existence.
5. Both have limited embodied existence. Embodied life of jīva is hundred years.[2] Embodied life of Īśvara is dviparārdha years. Their bodies die on the completion of their ages.
6. Both are in bondage. They are bound by māyā as well as by Law of Karma.[3]
7. Both have three bodies. Jīva's bodies are sthūla, Sūkṣma and Karaṇa. Īśvara's bodies are Virāṭa, Sūtrātma and Avyākṛta.[4] The Sthūla, Sūkṣma and Karaṇa are the māyā of Jīva and Virāṭ, Sūtrātma and Avyākṛta are the māyā of Īśvara. The association with prior three bodies constitute māyā of jīva and with latter three bodies constitute the māyā of Īśvara.[5]
8. The bodies of both Jīva and Īśvara are constituted of 24 elements.
9. When embodied, both have similar type of outer bodies. Both have two-armed and two-footed bodies.
10. Both have three states of Consciousness. Jīva's states are jāgrata, Svapna and Suṣupti. Īśvara' states are Utpatti, Sthiti and Pralaya.[6]
11. For both of them God creates dream objects and enables them to experience those objects according to their desert.[7]
12. Both are dependent realities. Both are subordinate to God. Both of them depend upon God for their existence

and activites. Both exist in and through God. Both have type of metaphysical dependence upon God in bondage as well as in liberation.

13. Both are knower, doer and enjoyer.
14. Both of them are incapable of doing, knowing or enjoying anything without God.[8]
15. Both have to worship Parabrahman to realise their true nature and to attain liberation. Upāsanā of Parabrahman enables both of them to get release from māyā and attain eternal bliss of self-realisation.
16. Both go to Akṣaradhāman on attaining liberation and enjoy the bliss of vision and nearness of God.
17. Puruṣottama resides in both of them.
18. Both have four forms of speech.

10. Difference between Jīva and Īśvara

Svāminārāyaṇa has said that jīva is essentially of the nature of Akṣarabrahman.[1] He has also said that Jīva is similar to Īśvara. It is, therefore, clear that Īśvara is essentially of the nature of Akṣarabrahman. According to Svāminārāyaṇa, as already seen, the bodies of both jīva and Īśvara are constituted of twenty four elements. From these and other aforementioned similarities, one is likely to believe that both Jīva and Īśvara are similar in essence and substance, and that there is no difference between them.[3] But Svāminārāyaṇa has ruled out the possibility of such a belief. He has clearly said that one should not believe that jīva and Īśvara are the same or similar.[4] Inspite of their glaring similarities, both are fundamentally different.[5] Both are eternally different from one another.[6] Emphasizing the difference between Jīva and Īśvara, Svāminārāyaṇa has said that one should evolve a proper logical understanding by which one can appreciate the difference between the two.[7]

A very great difference between Jīva and Īśvara is that jīva is an entity of limited knowledge (alpajña) whereas Īśvara is an omniscient entity (sarvajña).[8] But here it should be clarified that by "omniscient" is not meant that Īśvara has knowledge of the infinite universes. It is only meant that he knows everything of the universe with which he is attached. In other words, in the context of the universe with which he is associated, he is omniscient.

Another important difference between Jīva and Īśvara which has been pointed out by Svāminārāyaṇa is that the elements of which the body of jīva is constituted are of inferior competence (alpa), whereas those constituting the body of Īśvara are of superior competence (samartha).[9] The elements forming the body of Īśvara function as substratum of bodies of other living beings. Those forming the body of jīva cannot function as substratum of other bodies.[9]

A difference which deserves mention is that the entire universe constitutes the body of Īśvara, whereas body of jīva is of a very limited measure. The effect of this difference is that Īśvara can experience the entire universe, whereas the experience of Jīva is limited only to its body. To use Dr. J.A. Yajnik's words, "The experiences of Īśvara are co-extensive with the whole universe."

The waking, dreaming and deep sleep of the body constitutes three states of Jīva's consciousness. The states of Jīva's consciousness are connected with a particular body. The three states of Īśvara's consciousness are entirely different from those of Jīva's consciousness. Creation, sustenance and destruction of the universe constitute the three states of īśvara's consciousness. This brings out an important difference between Jīva and Īśvara that Īśvara creates the universe; Jīva does not; cannot. One important difference between Jīva and Īśvara in regard to their relationship with Māyā should be noted. According to Svāminārāyaṇa, the Māyā of Jīva is inseparable from it. Māyā is inseparably associated with Jīva since beginningless time. Even at the time of dissolution Jīva is unable to break with it. In the state of dissolution Jīva lies in the womb of Māyā. This is not the case with the Māyā of Īśvara. Īśvara's association with Māyā is not inseparable. At the time of dissolution Īśvara can easily sever his connection with it. But Jīva, even at the time of dissolution cannot separate itself from Māyā.[11]

Svāminārāyaṇa has warned his disciples that they should not equate Jīva with Īśvara. Svāminārāyaṇa has said that Īśvara can come down on earth. He can take an incarnation (avatāra).[12] Of course, it is only when God "enters" Īśvara that he can take an avatāra. This means that God at times incarnates through Īśvara.[13] No such thing is possible for Jīva till it is in bondage. A liberated soul can, at its will, take birth on earth without getting itself entangled in the forces of Māyā. When born, it remains completely beyond the forces of Māyā.[14] Such a birth of a liberated soul is similar to the descent of an avatāra. But it is not an avatāra.

11. Relation between Jīva and Īśvara

Jīva and Īśvara are eternally different from each other. The question is, Is there any relation between Jīva and Īśvara? Can there be any relation between two eternally different ontological entities? Let us try to find the answer.

We have seen that there are three states of the consciousness (avasthā) of Jīva, Jāgrata, Svapna (dream) and Suṣupti (deep sleep). Like Jīva, Īśvara also has three states of consciousness. They are Uptatti (creation), Sthiti (maintenance) and Pralaya (dissolution). Svāminārāyaṇa has said that the three states of Jīva's consciousness have their roots in the three states of Īśvara's consciousness. According to Svāminārāyaṇa, jīva's Jāgrata state has its root in the Utpatti State of Īśvara.[1] Jīva's Svapna state has its root in the Sthiti state of Īśvara.[2] And Jīva's Suṣupti state has its root in the Pralaya state of Īśvara.[3] Thus, Jīva and Īśvara are related through their states of consciousness. That is, the states of Jīva's consciousness are ultimately created by Īśvara.

But a very important aspect of Jīva's relation with Īśvara is this : the twenty four elements which constitute the body of Īśvara function as substratum of bodies of all jīvas. So far as bodies of jīvas are concerned, they are materially connected with Īśvara's body.

Moreover, jīva exists in the universe which is headed by īśvara. In the area of the universe īśvara is the highest power, subordinate only to the supreme authority of God. In a particular universe, īśvara, under the paramountcy of God, is sovereign and jīvas are, as it were, his subjects. So far as the universe is concerned relationship between īśvara and jīva is that of the ruler and the ruled. Jīva's cannot interfere with the execution of the decree of īśvara for either creation or maintenance or destruction. Jīvas have no alternative but to abide by that decree.

We have seen that for attaining release from the forces of māyā, jīva has to worship and meditate upon God. Īśvara has also to worship and meditate upon God for attaining release from the forces of māyā. God is their common object of worship and meditation. Their meditational relation with God constitute relation between them also. Jīva and Īśvara are related through God with whom both are devotionally related. Both have common goal : liberation and God.

As we have seen, the essential nature of Jīva is also the essential nature of īśvara. Both are Brahmarūpa. On liberation, both realise their essential nature. On reaching Akṣaradhāman both get divine bodies (Bhagavati tanu) and both become the citizens of the city of God (Akṣaradhāman). Both find their place and position in the divine society of liberated souls (muktas). In Akṣaradhāman they have a social character about them because they aim at one and the same thing, God. And thus īśvara and jīva can be said to be related to one another in the sense that both are related to God. So far as the state of liberation is concerned, Svāminārāyaṇa does not make any distinction between jīva and īśvara.

As we have seen, for attaining liberation, the temporal process of Upāsanā, both for jīva as well as īśvara is the same. And so through Upāsanā a comradeship is created between them.

We have seen that Puruṣottama resides in Jīva. Svāminārāyaṇa has said that Puruṣottama pervades jīva and enables it to undertake the activities of feeling, willing and thinking.

Similarity, Puruṣottama resides in Īśvara. Puruṣottama pervades Īśvara and enables him to enter into activities of feeling, willing and thinking. Thus God resides in both jīva and Īśvara. God is common self (jīvana) between them. Thus, we see that jīva is related to Īśvara through Puruṣottama, both internally as well as externally. Internally Puruṣottama is the indweller (antaryāmi) of both and externally He is the object of worship (Upāsya) of both.

In no way Īśvara helps jīva in its redemptive endeavour. Svāminārāyaṇa has said that as Īśvara is bound like jīva, he is not in a position to help jīva for attaining liberation.[4] Of course, in a sense, Īśvara inspires jīva to worship God and attains liberation. When jīva realises that even a cosmic God like Īśvara has to worship God for attaining liberation, it is inspired to worship Him for attaining the same.

12. Can Jīva become Īśvara?

As seen, when Jīva is released from the forces of māyā, it realises that the essential nature of Akṣarabrahman is also its own essential nature. And when, on leaving the physical body, it goes to Akṣaradhāman, it acquires a divine body and attains sādharmya both with Akṣarabrahman and Puruṣ ottama. This is the highest position to which Jāva can rise, of course, on attaining release from bondage.

The question is, when in bondage, how high can jīva rise above the lower plane of spiritual existence? The answer of Svāminārāyaṇa is that, while remaining in the state of bondage, jīva can raise itself to the position of Īśvara.[1] This does not mean that jīva becomes Īśvara. Jīva is eternally different from Īśvara. However, high jīva may rise in its spiritual states, it cannot become Īśvara. But it can raise itself to a higher plane of spiritual existence similar to that of Īśvara. So, jīva can become like Īśvara, but it cannot become Īśvara. If jīva was ever to become Īśvara, Svāminārāyaṇa would not be justified in saying that jīva, Īśvara, māyā, Akṣarabrahman and Parabrahman are five distinct realities. Thus the Svāminārāyaṇa position here in quite consistent with his central doctrine of "Five Reals."

13. Īśvara becomes Jīva in Akṣaradhāman

As already seen, the nature of Īśvara is very much similar to that of jīva. Īśvara is as bound (baddha) as jīva. Like jīva, īśvara has to worship God for attaining liberation. On attaining liberation, like jīva, īśvara gets a divine body and acquires similarity (sādharmya) both with Akṣara and Puruṣottama. Thus, jīva and īśvara both attain similarity with Akṣarabrahman and Puruṣottama, and thus they attain similarity with each other. Both become like each other. Svāminārāyaṇa has not admitted any distinction between jīva and īśvara in the state of release. It means that in the state of release, jīva and īśvara enjoy a similar spiritual existence. Now, Svāminārāyaṇa has not admitted any separate category of liberated īśvaras in Akṣaradhāman. In Akṣaradhāman, there is only one category and that is the category of liberated jīvas. So it comes to this that in the state of release īśvara loses his īśvaraness and becomes as good as jīva. In other words, in the state of release, īśvara becomes jīva. It is very interesting to note that in the state of bondage jīva cannot become īśvara, but in the state of release īśvara becomes jīva.

It must, however, be noted that Svāminārāyaṇa has neither categorically admitted nor categorically denied the distinction between jīva and īśvara. I have worked out the above implication because I found it very interesting. The implication, though based only on partial evidence, is certainly not baseless. It deserves consideration.

14. Īśvara of Svāminārāyaṇa and the Overmind of Aurobindo

Just as there are four spiritual categories in the philosophy of Svāminārāyaṇa, in the same way, there are four spiritual categories in the philosophy of Aurobindo. In the philosophy of Svāminārāyaṇa, we have Puruṣottama, Akṣarabrahman, Īśvara and Jīva. In the philosophy of Aurobindo, we have Puruṣottama (Saccidānanda), Supermind, Overmind and Mind.

Some similarities, may therefore, be attempted to be drawn. Puruṣottama of Aurobindo is similar to Puruṣottama of Svāminārāyaṇa. Supermind of Aurobindo is somewhat similar to Akṣarabrahman of Svāminārāyaṇa. Overmind of Aurobindo is somewhat similar to Īśvara of Svāminārāyaṇa. Mind (Psyche) of Aurobindo is similar to jīva of Svāminārāyaṇa.

Philosophy of Aurobindo aims at transformation of man into Divine man. It seeks to transform human beings into guastic beings. Its ultimate purpose is to establish a society of guastic beings.[1] For achieving this purpose, there must be a union of God and the world. But Mind cannot be a link between God and the world. Mind has certain fundamental limitations which render it unfit to serve as link between God and the world. Only Supermind can be the link between God and the world.[2] But mind, as it is, cannot have direct relation with Supermind. There must be a link between Mind and the Supermind, Overmind serves as the link between Mind and the Supermind.[3]

Like Aurobindo's Supermind, Svāminārāyaṇa's Akṣarabrahman serves as link between jīva and Puruṣottama. Just as Supermind is the elimination of Mind,[4] Akṣarbrahman is the elimination of Jīva. But in Aurobindo's philosophy, Overmind is the link between Mind and Supermind. Same is not the case with Īśvara. Īśvara does not serve as link between jīva and Akṣara. Jīva can directly realise itself as Akṣarabrahman. Then, in Aurobindo's philosophy, Overmind functions as Golden Lid and hides the greater Truth Consciousness.[5] Īśvara of Svāminārāyaṇa discharges no such function. Īśvara is as bound as jīva & therefore he cannot and does not hide any truth. Consciousness from jīva. There are certain striking similarities between Īśvara and Overmind. One, as seen, the knowledge of Īśvara is limited to the universe with which he is associated. Same is the case with Overmind.[6] According to Aurobindo, Overmind consciousness is global in its cognition.[7] It functions as a principle of cosmic truth.[8] Two, the body of Īśvara is constituted of twenty four elements.[9] These elements, which constitute the body of Īśvara, also function as substratum of the bodies of all living beings.[10] In other words, according to Svāminārāyaṇa, the body of Īśvara embraces the entire universe. Er gind the same idea expressed by Aurobindo in respect of Overmind. He says that Overmind embrances the totality of the universe.[11] According to Svāminārāyaṇa, Īśvara is dependent on God for his existence and activity. Īśvara cannot do anything without God.[12] In respect of Overmind Aurobindo speaks almost in similar terms. He ways that the dynamic movement of Overmind is not determined by it.[13] It merely wields the power of Supreme Reality.[14] Overmind energy proceeds through an indivisible all-comprehending unity.[15] Four, Aurobindo observes that "we can recognise in Overmind the original cosmic Māyā, not a Māyā of Ignorance, but a Māyā of knowledge."[16] In other words, according to Aurobindo, ignorance is the Māyā of Mind and knowledge is the Māyā of Overmind. Svāminārāyaṇa has made a similar observation regarding the Māyā of Jiva and Īśvara. Svāminārāyaṇa says that īśvara, at the time of dissolution can sever his connection with Māyā but jīva cannot sever its connection with it. Even in the state of dissolution jīva's connection with māyā (ignorance) continues.[17]

According to Aurobindo, what to mental reason are irreconcilable differences present themselves as coexistent correlatives; what to mental reason are contraries are to Overmind-intelligence complementariness.[18] Svāminārāyaṇa would say that a īśvara is omniscient for his universe, what are contraries to jīva are complementaries for īśvara.

REFERENCES

1. Plurality of Īśvaras

1. V.G.F.S. 7.
2. V.G.F.S. 63; V.G.M.S. 21.
3. V.G.F.S. 63; V.A.S. 5; V.J.S. 4; V.J.S. 5; V.G.L.S. 39.
4. V.L.S. 15.
5. V.G.M.S. 21.

2. Metaphysical Nature of Īśvara

1. V.G.F.S. 7.
2. V.S.S. 5.

3. V.L.S. 16.
4. V.G.F.S. 41.
5. V.G.F.S. 7.
6. V.G.M.S. 31.
7. V.G.F.S. 64.
8. V.G.F.S. 52; V.G.F.S. 64; Svāminārāyaṇa has said that nature of Īśvara is very similar to jīva; V.G.M.S. 31.

3. Three Bodies of Īśvara

1. V.G.M.S. 31.
2. V.K.S. 12.
3. V.G.M.S. 31.
4. V.G.F.S. 63.
5. V.G.F.S. 63.
6. V.V.S. 5; V.G.F.S. 12; S.P. 106.
7. V.G.F.S. 12.
8. V.G.M.S. 31.
9. V.K.S. 12.
10. V.V.S. 6.
11. V.K.S. 12.
12. V.K.S. 12.
13. V.V.S. 6.
14. V.K.S. 12; V.G.M.S. 31.

4. Three States of Īśvara

1. V.G.M.S. 31.
2. V.P.S. 2.
3. V.P.S. 2.
4. V.G.M.S. 21.
5. V.P.S. 2.

5. Four Forms of Speech of Īśvara

1. V.S.S. 6.
2. V.S.S. 6.
3. V.S.S. 6.
4. V.S.S. 6.
5. V.S.S. 6.
6. V.S.S. 6.
7. V.S.S. 6.

8. V.V.S. 6.
9. V.S.S. 6.
10. V.S.S. 6.
11. V.S.S. 6.
12. V.S.S. 6.
13. V.S.S. 6.

6. Parabrahman in Īśvara

1. V.G.F.S. 52; V.G.M.S. 31.
2. V.G.M.S. 10.
3. V.G.M.S. 31; V.G.M.S. 31; V.G.M.S. 31.
4. V.G.M.S. 1.

7. Birth, Death and Rebirth of Īśvara

1. V.G.F.S. 41.
2. V.G.F.S. 41.
3. V.G.F.S. 41.
4. V.K.S. 1; See also V.G.F.S. 41.
5. V.K.S. 1; V.G.M.S. 31; *See also* V.G.F.S. 41.
6. V.G.F.S. 12.
7. V.G.F.S. 12.
8. V.G.F.S. 12.
9. V.G.M.S. 31; *See also* V.G.F.S. 12.

8. Liberation of Īśvara

1. V.G.M.S. 31.
2. V.G.M.S. 31.
3. V.G.M.S. 31.
4. V.G.M.S. 31.
5. V.G.M.S. 31.
6. V.G.M.S. 31.

9. Similarities between Jīva and Īśvara

1. V.G.M.S. 31.
2. Īśāvāsya Upaniṣad 2.
3. V.G.M.S. 31.
4. V.P.S. 2.
5. V.K.S. 12.
6. V.P.S. 2.
7. V.G.M.S. 21.

8. V.G.M.S. 31.

10. Difference between Jīva and Īśvara

1. V.G.M.S. 69.
2. V.G.M.S. 31.
3. V.P.S. 2.
4. V.P.S. 2.
5. V.G.M.S. 21.
6. V.G.F.S. 7
7. V.P.S. 2.
8. V.P.S. 2.
9. V.P.S. 2; V.P.S. 2.
10. V.P.S. 2.
11. V.G.M.S. 31.
12. V.G.M.S. 31.
13. V.G.M.S. 31; V.G.M.S. 31; V.G.M.S. 31.
15. V.A.S. 3.

11. Relation between Jīva and Īśvara

1. V.S.S. 6.
2. V.S.S. 6.
3. V.S.S. 6.
4. V.G.M.S. 31.

12. Can Jīva become Īśvara?

1. V.G.M.S. 25; V.G.M.S. 25; V.G.M.S. 4.

14. Īśvara of Svāminārāyaṇa and the Overmind of Aurobindo

1. Aurobindo, Life Divine (1965), p. 856.
2. S.K. Maitra, An Introduction to the Philosophy of Sri Aurobindo (1965), p. 16.
3. *Ibid.*, p. 26.
4. *Ibid.* p. 19.
5. Aurobindo, Life Divine, p. 255.
6. Aurobindo, *Ibid.*, p. 256.
7. *Ibid.*, p. 256.
8. *Ibid.*, p. 259.
9. V.G.F.S. 12; V.G.F.S. 41.
10. V.P.S. 2.
11. Aurobindo, Life Divine, p. 256.

12. V.G.F.S. 52.
13. Aurobindo, Life, Divine, p. 256.
14. Aurobindo, *Ibid.*, p. 606.
15. Aurobindo, *Ibid.*, p. 256.
16. Aurobindo, *Ibid.*, p. 261.
17. *See above*, V.G.M.S. 31.
18. Aurobindo, Life Divine, p. 258.

CHAPTER 10

LAW OF KARMA

1. What is Karma?

The word "Karma" is derived from the Sanskrit root "Kṛ" which means to do or to perform an action. Thus, the etymological meaning of this word is "what is done" or "an action that is performed". And as an action may be either physical or mental, the broad sense of the word "Karma" includes both the physical and the mental activities.[1]

Stated very simply, Karma means action. According to Jainas, Karma is of material nature (Paudgalika). Karma, according to them is matter in subtle form. This Kārmic matter retards the radiance of soul and creates bondage (bandha). It does not leave the soul till final emancipation.[2]

According to Vaiśeṣika darśana, Karma means movement. It is an irreducible element of universe.[3] It is neither substance nor quality, but different from both. It is in itself an independent category (padārtha). Like quality, Karma (movement) subsists in substance. Both are, however, different in the sense that whereas quality is a permanent feature of substance, the association of Karma with it is only temporary.[4]

Svāminārāyaṇa does not accept the Jaina view of Karma. For him, Karma is not matter. He thinks that anything that is material must have a form. But, according to him, Karma has no form.[5] He says that those who say that Karma has form are atheists.[6] Svāminārāyaṇa does not accept Vaiśeṣika view of Karma fully. For him Karma means activity.[7] He accepts that Karma is some sort of movement; but he does not accept that Karma is only movement and nothing-else.

According to him, Karma is a voluntary action which may be either good or bad. Karma by itself does not produce any pleasant or painful result but God as Karmaphaladātā produces such result for the doer of the Karma.[8]

2. Kinds of Karma

The word "Karma" can be taken in two senses. One, in the sense of voluntary action. Two, in the sense of potency of bearing fruit or in the sense of force which brings about consequences. Karma in the second sense is variously classified.

According to the classification made by Svāminārāyaṇa, there are three kinds of Karmas : Sañcita, Prārabdha and Kriyamāṇa.[1] The usual meaning which is given to these three kinds of Karmas in the Indian Philosophical Systems is like this. Those Karmas which have begun to bear fruit or begun to give consequences are called prārabdha Karmas. Those Karmas which have not yet begun to bear fruit of give consequences are called Sañcita Karmas. The Karmas which we perform in this life are called Kriyamāṇa Karmas. Svāminārāyaṇa accepts the meanings given, as above, to the three Kinds of Karmas.[2] He says that self experiences happiness or misery according to its Karmas in the past life (Prārabdha) which have started bearing fruits.[3] According to him, self acquires different types of bodies in different births in accordance with their Karmas. He goes to the extent of saying that even nature, potency, health and appearance of the body depend on the deeds of self in the past life or lives.[4] According to Śaṅkara, the acquisition of a good or a bad body results from one's own actions.[5] The doctrine which Svāminārāyaṇa and Śaṅkara both accept has its roots in the Upaniṣads. Explaining this Upaniṣadic doctrine R.E. Hume has said that "according to one's good or bad actions in this life one passes at death into the body of a higher or lower being."[6] According to Svāminārāyaṇa, the causal body (Karaṇa śarīra) is constituted of sañcita Karma which have not yet started bearing fruits.[7] According to him, each self is having a beginningless association with this causal body.[8] In accordance with its Karma God places the self in such circumstances which will enable it to experience the fruits of its actions.

We find another classification of Karma in Indian Philosophy thought. According to this classification, the Karma are classified into three kinds : Vihita, Niṣiddha and Udāsīna. Vihita Karma are those which are enjoined in scriptures and are to be performed in accordance with the instructions contained therein. Vihita Karmas, again, are of two Kinds : Sakāma and Niṣkāma. Sakāma Karmas are those which are done with the desire for fruit and Niṣkāma ones are those which are done without any desire for fruit. Niṣiddha Karmas are those which are prohibited in scriptures and in the moral consciousness of society. Udāsīna Karmas are those which are neither Vihita nor Niṣiddha.[9] Svāminārāyaṇa accepts this classification. According to him, the devotee of God would always perform Karmas which are enjoined in scriptures and would never commit a breach of instructions contained therein.[10] He would never do anything which is against morality or public conscience.[11] With regard to Vihita Karma, Svāminārāyaṇa says that a true devotee of God would always perform Niṣkāma Karma and would never indulge in Sakāma Karma.[12]

There is once again a classification of Karmas which is made by Svāminārāyaṇa. According to this classification the Karmas are of three kinds : Sātvika, Rājasika and Tāmasika.[13] According to Svāminārāyaṇa, the Jīva's experiences of waking, dreaming and deep sleep are respectively of the fruits of its Sātavika, Rājasika and Tāmasika Karmas.[14]

According to him, the doer of Sātvika Karma goes to devaloka (the region of cosmic Gods), the doer of rājasika Karma goes to the madhyaloka (middle region) and the doer of the tāmasika Karma throws himself into the abyss of degradation.[15]

3. What is Law of Karma?

The root of Law of Karma lies in the conception of Ṛta

as found in Ṛg-Veda. The conception of Ṛta is of great importance. It anticipates Law of Karma. Ṛta is the moral law which pervades the entire universe.

The idea of Ṛta has shaped itself into the Mīmānsā conception Apūrva, the law that guarantees the future enjoyment of fruits of rituals performed now; into Nyāya-Vaiśeṣika conception of Adṛṣṭ, the unseen principle which sways even on material atoms and brings about objects and events; into Law of Karma. Law of Karma which has become a common feature of all the systems of Indian Philosophy. It is accepted by orthodox schools as well as by Jainas and Bauddhas. To put it very shortly, Law of Karma is a belief that every action, good or bad, produces its effect in this life or the next life. The apparent differences in the life of individuals demand an explanation for understanding them. The belief in Law of Karma provides such an explanation. We see that some men are unhappy without any deed in this life. We observe that certain actions produce good or bad effects in the present life. From this observation it can be reasonably maintained that all actions will produce their effects in this or next life. We feel that there is an inexorable law of relations between particular kinds of actions and their consequences. The law of this inexorable relationship between actions and their moral effects is generally known as Law of Karma. Karma is at once cause, effect and the law which equilibrates the two. It is Newton's third law of motion, that action and reaction are equal and opposite, applied to moral and all other realms of sentient life.[1] The Biblical expression of this law is found in the pronouncement that "for whatever a man soweth, that shall he also reap." When Jesus Christ on the Mount Said "Judge not that ye be not judged, for whatever judgment ye judge ye shall be judged"[2] he was pronouncing this inexorable law. The Law of Karma is the counterpart, in the moral world, of the law of causality in the physical world. W.Y. Evans-Wentz has said that "the doctrine of Karma happens to be scientifically conceivable and, therefore, acceptable, at least intellectually, for the average occidental, because he has become accustomed to it under its more familiar designation as the law of cause and effect.[3] Dr. S.N. Dasgupta has pointed out that "the Law of Karma is almost universally regarded as an ethical law by which each person was bound to reap the good and bad effects of his deeds."[4] In Yogavāsiṣṭha it is written that the fruits of good or bad actions performed by a person have got to be necessarily experienced by him. They will not wear out without experienced by him even in millions and billions of years.[5] Dr. Chandradhar Sharma observes that the Law of Karma is the general moral law which governs not only the life and destiny of all individual beings but even the order and arrangement of the physical world.[6] Of course, it is very difficult to understand the operation of the Law of Karma. According to Gītā the process of Law of Karma is very hard to comprehend.[7] Although we may have no idea how Law of Karma is functioning, we do have an inclination to regard it as self-evidently true.

Svāminārāyaṇa accepts the Law of Karma,[8] but he has his own reservations about it. We shall see later what reservations he has about the universal application of Law of Karma.

4. Law of Karma and Human Freedom

In the context of moral philosophy, two doctrines are well known : One, the doctrine of free will, the other the doctrine of determinism. The doctrine of free will postulates that man is free and is able to choose and act according to the dictates of his own will. The doctrine of determinism postulates that all events including human actions are predetermined.

Pāṇini, in clear terms, says that self in free.[1] Svāminārāyaṇa would completely agree with Pāṇini. According to Svāminārāyaṇa, self is free to choose good or bad.[2] One immediately gathers this impression on reading the pages of Vacanāmṛta. In Svāminārāyaṇa's view self can discriminate between good and bad.[3] In fact Law of Karma itself implies freedom of choice to do right (savalo Vicāra) or wrong (avalo

Vicāra). Self in Svāminārāyaṇism is an ontological reality[4] and its freedom lies in self-determination as opposed to determination by accumulated past Karmas.[5] It is true that past can never be eliminated,[6] but it is also true that past can be utilised. According to Svāminārāyaṇa it is sometimes possible to eliminate the influence of past factors which have made us what we are.[7] According to Svāminārāyaṇa, human will is generally free, but not absolutely free. Man has general freedom of choice, but he has no absolute freedom of choice. Then, the question arises, How much freedom does man have?

This question brings us to the paradox of human freedom in the philosophy of Svāminārāyaṇa. On one hand Svāminārāyaṇa says that self is completely free and has unlimited power (atisamartha) to do anything it chooses.[8] On the other hand he says that the self is bound (baddha) and has no power to do anything (asamartha)[9], this means that the self is both free and not free. Here we are reminded of the similar position that we find in Sartre's philosophy. Sartre also poses the paradox in similar terms that man is both free and not free.[10] It is very interesting to see that Svāminārāyaṇa anticipated Sartre, and even Heidegger, when he talked of human freedom.

In regard to human paradox Sartre is much influenced by Martin Heidegger. According to Heidegger, man's project is infinite and his existence is finite. The contradiction between man's project towards infinity (i.e. God) and his finitude as symbolised by death gives rise to human paradox which leads to utter absurdity of life. According to Heidegger man wants to attain perfection and be God-like. This is his project (desire). But possibility of becoming perfect and God like is contradicted by the supreme tragedy of death. Death puts an end to everything.[11] Neither Heidegger nor Sartre could solve this paradox. Svāminārāyaṇa has solved it. Let us see how he solves the paradox.

According to Svāminārāyaṇa, everything does not end with death. Only body dies. Self continues. It never dies. It is immortal (amar)[12] it exists eternally (anādi).[13] By declaring immortality and eternality of the self, Svāminārāyaṇa destroys the horror of death. According to Svāminārāyaṇa, the concept of finitude applies to empirical ego.[14] It has no application to the real individuality of self.[15]

Again the doctrine of liberation (mokṣa) as propounded by Svāminārāyaṇa is a complete answer to the problem of paradox passed by Heidegger and Sartre. Man wants something which takes him beyond his empirical ego. Liberation gives him what he wants. According to Svāminārāyaṇa, the self, in the state of mokṣa, retains its individuality and attains similarity (sādharmya) with God. According to Svāminārāyaṇa, death is not an end. It is only a stage in the journey of the self towards final goal which is to go to Akṣaradhāman and attain similarity with God. In the state of Mokṣa the self becomes God-like in form (ākāra), in beauty (rūpa) and in potency (samarthi).[17] According to Svāminārāyaṇa every soul is destined to be God-like. Some day or other, sooner or later, every soul will attain liberation and likeness of God.[18] What Heidegger and Sartre consider impossible of achievement, Svāminārāyaṇa makes it possible for every seeker (mumukshu). And this is how Svāminārāyaṇa resolves the paradox which haunts Heidegger and Sartre.

According to Svāminārāyaṇa, God is all powerful and self is eternally dependent (adhīna) on God.[19] It can do what it is enabled by God to do.[20] Not only that, it cannot, at its will and desire, experience the fruits of its Karmas. It can experience them only when it is enabled by God. But even with respect to exercise of one's free choice, Self depends on God. This is the general metaphysical dependence. It is in this sense that Svāminārāyaṇa describes self as asamartha. But according to him, self is Knower (jñātā) and consciousness, is eternal attribute.[23] Self is self-conscious (jñānasvarūpa)[23]. The self-conscious self has unlimited freedom of choice. So much so that the self has freedom to choose and do bad actions. God never suspends this freedom. Even though the self is bracketed on one side by Law of karma and divine sovereignty on the other, it has all the freedom either to choose the way of liberation (mokṣa) or the way of bondage (saṁsāra). The way of liberation is the way of blessedness. If the self chooses the way of blessedness, it attains release from the forces of māyā, becomes God-like and enjoys eternal bliss in communion with God. If it chooses the way of samsāra, it is tied up with the ever moving wheel of births and deaths and every time it has to experience the consequences of its good or bad Karmas. It is in respect of this freedom of choosing that Svāminārāyaṇa says that the self has unlimited power of choice (atisamartha).

It is evident from the above that Svāminārāyaṇa does not regard Law of Karma as implying a negation of human freedom which is the foundation of ethical values. According to Svāminārāyaṇa Law of Karma does not conflict with the reality of freedom. Karma does not fetter the self. Self is the master and can triumph over the forces of māyā which try to enslave it.[24] Self has the potency to act against the strongest desire. According to Svāminārāyaṇa, Law of Karma can be subjected to freedom of self.[25] But to say that Law of Karma can be subjected to freedom of self is not to say that Law of Karma is false. It should be noted that Svāminārāyaṇiya doctrine of Karma does not imply fatalism. It merely teaches that there is a correlation between moral acts and their consequences. In fact its implications are the very opposite of fatalism in that man by his free action can control the present and determine his future.

Sometimes the problem of human freedom is confused by drawing a distinction between the self and the will. Such a distinct in Svāminārāyaṇism is of no avail. According to Svāminārāyaṇa will is only the self in its active aspect and freedom of will essentially is the freedom of the self.[26] In fact it is determination by the self.

5. Law of Karma and God

Law of Karma occupies an important position in Svāminārāyaṇa's Philosophy. Svāminārāyaṇa emphasises it. From the emphasis of Svāminārāyaṇa one may argue that Law of

Karma is an independent principle and is not subject to the control of God. If the absolute God is obliged to take note of and act, according to Law of Karma He cannot be absolute. Law of Karma would mar the absoluteness of God. And, therefore, law of Karma is inconsistent with Svāminārāyaṇiya theism which envisages absolute God. If one argues like this, the argument will not be well founded. Svāminārāyaṇa would have no difficulty in exposing the infirmity of the argument.

According to Svāminārāyaṇa, God, no doubt, acts according to certain laws; but these laws are nothing but the expression of His will (Icchā)[1]. If Law of Karma is independent of the will of God, then God's absoluteness will be impaired. But to regard Law of Karma as independent of God will not be a correct view of Svāminārāyaṇa's idea of God. According to Svāminārāyaṇa, Law of Karma expresses the will of God. The order of Karma is set up by God who is the ruler of Karma (Karmādhyakṣa)[2]. Since the day of creation, God has so arranged the universe that it works without His interference.[3] This is in a sense "pre-established harmony." And the harmony established by God is so perfect and thorough going that there is law, order and uniformity every where in the physical realm. God has chosen Law of Karma as a means (kāla) of establishing order and harmony.[4] Since Law of Karma is the expression of God's will, God himself is regarded by Svāminārāyaṇa as rewarding righteous and punishing wicked.[5] According to Svāminārāyaṇa, God is the giver of fruits of actions (Karmaphalapradātā)[6]. He apportions happiness according to dessert. It is He who synthesises happiness with virtue and sufferings with vice.[7]

Again, according to Svāminārāyaṇa Law of Karma is unconscious. It is guided by all-intelligent God.[8] Without the guidance of all-intelligent God Law of Karma cannot perform the complicated task of bringing about the harmony between the different deeds of different persons and their appropriate fruition. Svāminārāyaṇa has viewed Law of Karma as operating, not by itself, but under the lordship of ominscient and omnipotent (sarvakartā) God.[9] Law of Karma is dependent on God[10]. God is above Law of Karma.[11] Law of Karma has to function according to the will of God. It cannot go beyond His will.[12] God is the cause of all causes.[13] He is the final cause.[14] He is above all (sarvopari).[15] He is all in all.[16]

6. The Eight Principles

According to Svāminārāyaṇa, Law of Karma is not the only principle at work. There are eight principles which are functioning in the universe, and Law of Karma is one of them. These eight principles are : Deśa, Kāla, Kriyā, Saṅga, Mantra, Dīkṣā, Dhyāna and Śāstra.[1]

Deśa means specific place or region. Deśa has always its qualities and peculiarities. There is a region where there is six months day and six months night. There are regions where there is too much cold and others where too much heat. Svāminārāyaṇa gives an illustration of Marwar region where the underground waters are found at very deep level. Wells in Marwar region have to be very deep. According to Svāminārāyaṇa the deep underground waters should come up for those who have done pious deeds and should have gone deeper for those who have done evil deeds. But this does not happen. The desert land does not respond favourably to the doers of good deeds and unfavourably to the doers of evil deeds. It creates the same kind of difficulties of getting water both for virtuous as well as vicious. Water at deep level is the peculiarity of the desert land. It is the law of nature. This natural law is not in harmony with the deeds of person inhabiting that region. In other words law of nature is not in harmony with the law of Karma.[2] The particular region does not give up its inherent character either for the pious or for the sinful.[3] According to Svāminārāyaṇa, in such cases, principle of Deśa predominates the principles of Karma.[4]

Kāla means time. According to Svāminārāyaṇa, time may be good or bad. The nature of time overcomes the efficacy of pious or sinful deeds. When there is predominance of good Kāla, it eliminates the morbid influence of evil deeds.

When there is predominance of bad time, famines, wars and epidemics prevail and millions of people die. But it cannot be said that all those who die in this way determined to die by Law of Karma. Thus, according to Svāminārāyaṇa, sorrow, suffering and death are not always the result of past deeds. We cannot say that they suffer and die because their good deeds are exhausted.[5] It is the evil nature of time that predominates Karmas and causes sorrows, sufferings and deaths.[6] Karmas at times lose potency before the power of time.[7]

Kriyā means Karma. We have seen above what it means.

Saṅga means company, association or attachment. According to Svāminārāyaṇa, as is the company, so is the character (antaḥkaraṇa) and as is the character, so is the man.[8] In this view, a devotee worshipping God with pure heart, will be vitiated, if he associates with a sinful person. The very touch of a sinner will pollute him. His good deeds will lose all efficacy in evil company. Evil company overrides past good deeds.[9]

Mantra, according to Svāminārāyaṇism means chanting the name of God or singing songs (Kīrtana) in the praise of God. According to Svāminārāyaṇa, if a man devotedly chants the name of God or sings Kīrtanas, his metaphysical understanding of his self as well as of God goes on increasing.[10] This means that, according to Svāminārāyaṇa, Mantra, if resorted to, can progressively impart greater and greater Knowledge of the greatness and glory of God. According to Svāminārāyaṇa, the effect of past Karmas can be eradicated by chanting the name of God or singing Kīrtanas.[11]

Dīkṣā means initiation into a holy order. A person who has taken Dīkṣā, lives in a different order of life. In law, it is called civil death. For a person, who has taken Dīkṣā, his past actions, which were performed by him in a different order or life, have no efficacy. He is dead for the order which he has left or renounced. Dīkṣā dominates Karma.

Dhyāna in Svāminārāyaṇa context means meditation on the form of God or meditational worship of God.[12] When the devotee is in rapturous meditation of God, he places himself beyond the reach of his past Karmas.

Śāstra means scriptures. Svāminārāyaṇa regards eight scriptures as authoritative and holds them in high significance. They are : four Vedas, Vedānta Sūtras by Vyāsa, Śrīmad Bhāgavata, Viṣṇusahasranāma, Bhagavad Gītā, Vidurnīti, Vāsudeva Mahātmya from Viṣṇukhaṇḍa of Skanda Purāṇa and Yājñavalkya Smṛti.[13] Svāminārāyaṇa regards tenth and fifth books of Śrīmad Bhāgavata as Bhaktiśāstra and Yoga Śāstra and Yājñavalkya Smṛti as Dharma Śāstra.[14] The man who has faith (viśvāsa) in the injunctions of scriptures performs acts enjoined therein and abstains from acts forbidden by them. He acts or abstains according to the instructions of the scriptures.[15] He acts or abstains on faith. Faith in scriptures promotes moral behaviour.[16] And faith is neither Karma nor cause. Faith is faith. According to Svāmiārāyaṇa Law of Karma is helpless before the faith in scriptures.

A parallel statement of principles made in Gītā may be recalled here. According to Gītā, there are five principles which are constituents of all human actions. They are : Adhiṣṭhāna, Kartā, Kāraṇa, Ceṣṭā and Daiva.[17] These five principles are at work in all the actions performed by man.

Adhiṣṭhāna means place of action. It is what Svāminārāyaṇa calls Deśa. Kartā means self which is the agent of all activity. It is what Svāminārāyaṇa calls Jīva. Kāraṇa means instrument with which action is performed by the kartā. There are three such instruments. They are body (Śarīra) which Svāminārāyaṇa calls Deha, Speech (Vāṅg) which Svāminārāyaṇa calls Mantra and thought which Svāminārāyaṇa calls Mana. Ceṣṭā means Kriyā. Kriyā means Karma. Karma means action. Svāminārāyaṇa does not use the word "Ceṣṭā". He uses either "Kriyā" or "Karma". Some times he uses the word "Kriyā" and sometimes "Karma". Daiva means destiny. Svāminārāyaṇa calls it prārabdha. Prārabdha, according to him, is constituted of past accumulated deeds.

Regarding these five principles Gītā says that whatever action a man performs by his body, speech or mind whether good or bad, is the result of these five principles acting together.[18] It is not difficult to see that all the five principles of human action laid down by Gītā are covered by the eight principles of Svāminārāyaṇa.

7. God and the Eight Principles

From the foregoing account of the eight principles it should be quite clear that these principles or any of them do not operate as limitation on the absolute power of God. If some physical or mental event can be explained by reference to any one of the eight principles under particular circumstances, it does not means that it creates a limitation on the power of God.[1] God's power is limitless and absolute. Inspite of these principles God remains all powerful. These principles in no way truncate the power of God. Since they are expressions of will of God, they are never derogatory of the power of God. Deśa, Kāla, Karma and other principles never operate independently of God. They always work under the control and guidance of God. They all are subject to the will of God. If any one of the eight principles enjoys preponderance, it is only at the will and pleasure of God.[2] They can never go against the will of God. None can predominate without divine sanction. They can never override divine will.[3] God is independent of them. They all are subordinate to and dependent on God for their existence and activities.[4] They have no power to disturb the teleological plan and purpose of God. Divine plan goes on in an undisturbed manner.[5]

8. Law of Karma and Law of Nature

What is law of nature?

According to Svāminārāyaṇa, God has created the world for the purpose of providing jīvas with opportunities to experience the sense objects and make endeavours for attaining the final emancipation (mokṣa)[1]. The world of nature created by God is governed by laws inherent in it. The laws of nature are expressions of God's will. The field for the operation of the natural laws is very vast and objective. The course of nature is determined not by the passions and prejudices of empirical selves but by the operation of natural laws. The universe is a law governed universe. It is lawful to the core.

Law of Karma is one of the eight principles which are at work in the universe.[2] Svāminārāyaṇa does not accept absolute predominance of Law of Karma. He does not believe that Law of Karma is the only principle which is instrumental for everything that happens to a man.[3] In fact he objects to the claim of Karmavādins that every thing is determined by previous Karmas. He is totally against the rigid application of Law of Karma.[4]

According to Svāminārāyaṇa, the principle of Karma may be at variance with the principle of Deśa or Kāla or other principle. It is not that Law of Karma always functions in harmony with other principles. As Dr. Yajnik has put it, "the field of the laws of nature being more general and objective, it cannot always be in complete harmony with the past deeds of the each of the jīvas working in given natural environment." Therefore, according to Svāminārāyaṇa, sorrows, sufferings and death are not always due to previous Karmas. This opens a possibility that if sufficient care and caution are extended and necessary steps taken, man can avert many difficulties of life.[6]

But, here Svāminārāyaṇa should not be misunderstood. He should not be understood to say that there is incompatibility between Law of Karma and other principles. According to him, there is no fundamental incompatibility between Law of Karma and Laws of Nature. Both flow from the same source, namely, God. Both are expressions of God's teleological will. And, therefore, one generally gets the natural environment according to one's past deeds. What Svāminārāyaṇa asserts is that Law of Karma is not the only principle which is predominant in human life.[7] It should not be supposed that only Law of Karma or any one of the eight principles always predominates.[8] Different principle may predominate at different time.[9] All human actions cannot be explained only by reference to the principle of Kāla or Karma or even by reference only to the will of God.[10] It would be foolish and dogmatic to explain every physical and mental event only in terms of one principle with total neglect of other principles.[11] It would be impossible to give a causal account of all human actions only in terms of past deeds. Jainas regard only the Karma as completely governing the life of jīvas[12], but, according to Svāminārāyaṇa they are absolutely wrong[13]. Those who accept predominance of Karmas only and disregard God as guider or inspirer (preraka), lack in spiritual wisdom.[14] Scriptures have mentioned prevalence of these principles by will of God.[15]

9. Area Where Law of Karma Operates

According to Svāminārāyaṇa, the area over which Law of Karma operates is limited. It is not that everywhere and in every field Law of Karma operates. The area of its operation is limited to the world of passions and desires. Law of Karma has applications to the actions performed in pursuance of some desire or interest. Where desires and interests are absent Law of Karma is powerless. It a SINE QUA NON of the application of Law of Karma that action must proceed from a desire for gain here or hereafter. It is not necessary that the gain aimed at should be attainable only in this world. According to Svāminārāyaṇa, even the desire for other-worldly gain will come within the ambit of Law of Karma.[1] Desireless and disinterested actions do not produce any binding effect.[2] Just as a fried seed has no potency to fruitify, in the same way disinterested action has no potency to produce binding consequences.[3] The true devotee of God has no interest in the worldly objects. For him bird or an animal or wood or stone or gold makes no difference. All are same for him.[4] Action performed by such a devotee causes no bondage to him.[5] Distinterested actions not only do not cause the binding effects, but help in destroying accumulated past deeds (Sañcita Karmas) which require to be exhausted for attainment of liberation.[6] All actions motivated by lust anger, greed, hatred, attachment or vanity cause bondage and come under the sway of Law of Karma. Pure action without any tinge of these qualities does not come under the binding power of Law of Karma. To the man, who has the knowledge of greatness and glory of God, actions do not bind.[7] According to Svāminārāyaṇa, Law of Karma has no jurisdiction over the man of such Knowledge.[8] Such person identifies the actions which are likely to cause bondage and keeps himself away from them and does not allow them to bind him.[9] It should be noted that when release is attained by the self, it rises above Law of Karma and enjoys real freedom. Release is always release from the bondage of Law of Karma.

10. Law of Karma and Social Service

Someone may argue that Law of Karma and social service cannot go together. He may amplify his argument by saying that if, according to Law of Karma, every man has himself to suffer the consequences of his previous deeds, then there cannot be any one to relieve him from them. No one can take away or share his burdens. According to the critic, such a position which results from Law of Karma rules out social service. To put it plainly, the question posed by the critic is, Is not the doctrine of Karma inconsistent with social service? The answer of Svāminārāyaṇa is No. Svāminārāyaṇa does not rule out social service in force of Law of Karma. According to him, Law of Karma and social service are not incompatible.[1] According to Svāminārāyaṇism, the problem of social service can be viewed from two standpoints: from the standpoint of one who receives the social service and from the standpoint of one who performs the social service. Looking from the first standpoint, it should be stated that Svāminārāyaṇa would not agree with the critic that there would be no one to relieve the person from the consequence of his previous deeds. According to Svāminārāyaṇa, if such a person remains in the holy company of a saintly man, his accumulated Karma (Prārabdha), howsoever bad they may be, will be destroyed and he will be free from the evil consequences thereof.[2] Thus, the social service and the Law of Karma are not inconsistent with each other. Looking from the second standpoint, it should be stated that actions performed in social service are not selfish. It is only selfish actions that are subject to Law of Karma. Selfless actions have no binding force. Selfless actions do not bind the doer of them.[3] It is not action as action that has faltering effect. Only selfish actions entail binding consequences. Selfless social work is not inconsistent with Law of Karma. Selfless work does not cling to self.[4] In fact it is necessary for attaining early emancipation.

11. Law of Karma and Grace of God

According to Svāminārāyaṇa, God is merciful.[1] He has nothing against any Jīva. He is kind to all. He is essentially a redeemer. He creates the universe for a redemptive purpose. He maintains it out of compassion for Jīvas. Even when he destroys the universe, His purpose is redemptive.[2]

God is the moral governor of the universe. He judges jīvas in accordance with their deserts, But this does not mean that He is a merciless judge. He is not cruel. His justice is always tampered with mercy. God of Svāminārāyaṇa has no interest in torturing and tormenting Jīvas. He has perennial interest in the emancipation of jīvas. All His activities are directed towards this eschatological purpose. Any and every Jīva can hope to attain final emancipation. Any and every jīva can hope to receive His grace (Kṛpā).

According to Svāminārāyaṇa, man can attain the grace of God, if he bears intense love for Him, wholeheartedly worships Him and lives a moral life of Ekāntika as Nirvāsanika.[3] God is lover of His devotees (Bhaktavatsala).[4] However sinful his past actions may be, if he devotedly loves and worships God and makes a total surrender to Him, he becomes worthy of His grace.[5]

It is an important feature of Svāminārāyaṇa's philosophy that grace and law of Karma are not treated as opposed to each other. According to Svāminārāyaṇa, Law of Karma is nothing but the expression of the will of God. And therefore, grace is not inconsistent with Law. Grace is not without law. And law is not without grace. Both stand together. Both converge in God. But, it should, however, be noted that it is not easy to attain grace of God. One has to sincerely try for attaining it. One has to be very steadfast in one's devotion to God. God does not arbitrarily grant grace. He grants only to him who deserves it.[6]

REFERENCES

1. What is Karma?

1. R.S. Naulakha, Śaṅkara's Brahmavāda, (1964), p. 239.
2. R.I., p. 319.
3. R. II (1979), I.P. p. 208.
4. K. Narayana, The Outline of Madhva Philosophy, (1962), p. 92.
5. V.K.S. 2; V.K.S. 2.
6. V.K.S. 2; V.K.S. 6.
7. See above V.K.S. 2.
8. V.G.F.S. 13; V.G.F.S. 34.

2. Kinds of Karmas

1. V.G.M.S. 20.
2. V.S.S. 14; V.G.L.S. 13.
3. V.S.S. 14.
4. V.V.S. 6; V.G.L.S. 13.
5. Śaṅkara Bhāṣya on Bhagavat Gītā 2.51.
6. R.E. Hume, Introduction to his Translation "Thirteen Principal Upaniṣads", p. 51.
7. V.V.S. 6.
8. V.V.S. 6.
9. K. Narayana, An Outline of Madhva Philosophy, (1962), p. 93.
10. V.G.M.S. 26.
11. V.S.S. 14.
12. V.G.F.S. 43; V.G.L.S. 5.
13. V.G.F.S. 65; V.G.M.S. 45.
14. V.G.F.S. 65.
15. V.G.M.S. 45.

3. What is Law of Karma?

1. Christmas Humphrey, Buddhism, Penguin, (1958), p. 100.
2. Gospel of John, 7.1.
3. W.Y. Evans Wentz, Tibetan Yoga and Secret Doctrines, (1974), p. 46.
4. Dr. S.N. Dasgupta, Indian Idealism (1933), p. 3.
5. Yogavāsiṣṭha, 3.95.33.
6. Chandradhar Sharma, Indian Philosophy (1952), p. 16.
7. Gītā 4.17.
8. V.G.L.S. 13; V.S.S. 8; V.G.F.S. 18; V.S.S. 6; V.S.S. 14; V.G.F.S. 65; V.G.L.S. 20.

4. Law of Karma and Human Freedom

1. Pāṇini 1.4.54.
2. V.L.S. 8.
3. V.G.F.S. 16.
4. V.G.F.S. 7.
5. V.G.F.S. 16.
6. V.G.F.S. 13.
7. V.L.S. 8.
8. V.G.F.S. 57.
9. V.G.M.S. 31; V.G.F.S. 64.
10. Mary Warnock, The Philosophy of Sartre.
11. Peter Koestenboum, Religion in the Tradition of Phenomenology, in Religion in Philosophical and Cultural Perspective, Edited by J. Clayton Feaver and William Horosz (1967), p. 182.
12. V.V.S. 4; V.S.S. 12.
13. V.G.F.S. 7.
14. V.K.S. 12.
15. V.G.F.S. 8; V.J.S. 2.
16. V.L.S. 13.
17. V.K.S. 1; V.G.M.S. 67.
18. V.G.F.S. 21.
19. V.G.F.S. 64.
20. V.G.F.S. 52.
21. V.G.F.S. 65.
22. V.G.L.S. 39; V.G.F.S. 38.
23. V.S.S. 12.

24. V.G.F.S. 57.
25. V.G.F.S. 59; V.G.F.S. 58.
26. V.G.M.S. 23; V.G.M.S. 23; V.K.S. 4.

5. Law of Karma and God

1. V.G.M.S. 2.
2. Śvetāśvatara Upaniṣad, 6. 11.
3. V.G.F.S. 65.
6. S.P. 107; V.G.F.S. 65.
7. V.S.S. 14; V.G.L.S. 13.
8. V.G.M.S. 21.
9. V.G.M.S. 21.
10. V.G.M.S. 21.
11. V.V.S. 2.
12. V.G.M.S. 21.
13. V.G.L.S. 38.
14. V.L.S. 2.
15. V.G.L.S. 38.
16. S.P. 107; V.G.F.S. 64; V.G.M.S. 21.

6. The Eight Principles

1. V.G.F.S. 77; V.G.F.S. 78.
2. V.G.F.S. 78.
3. V.G.F.S. 78.
4. V.G.F.S. 78.
5. V.V.S. 6.
6. V.V.S. 6.
7. V.V.S. 6.
8. V.G.F.S. 18.
9. V.G.F.S. 18.
10. V.S.S. 17.
11. V.S.S. 17.
12. V.G.L.S. 5.
13. S.P. 93, 94, 95; V.V.S. 18.
14. S.P. 99; V.G.M.S. 64.
15. V.S.S. 13.
16. V.S.S. 13.
17. Gītā 18: 14.

18. Gītā 18: 15.

7. God and the Eight Principles

1. V.G.M.S. 21.
2. V.G.M.S. 21.
3. V.G.M.S. 21.
4. V.G.F.S. 64; V.G.M.S. 21.
5. V.G.F.S. 34.

8. Law of Karma and Law of Nature

1. V.P.S. 1.
2. V.G.F.S. 77; V.G.F.S. 78.
3. V.G.F.S. 78.
4. V.G.F.S. 78; *See also* V.V.S. 6.
5. Dr. Yajnik, The Philosophy of Śrī Svāminārāyaṇa, p. 78.
6. V.G.F.S. 78; S.P. 153-154.
7. V.V.S. 6.
8. V.G.F.S. 21.
9. V.V.S. 6.
10. V.G.F.S. 21.
11. V.G.M.S. 21; *See also* JAY, p. 79.
12. V.V.S. 6.
13. V.V.S. 6.
14. V.G.M.S. 21.
15. V.G.M.S. 21; S.P. 153-154; In the event of famine, or harassment from the wicked or tyranny of a King, which is likely to harm one's prestige or wealth or even one's own life, my followers should in such circumstances quit that place at once, even if it be their native place, and migrate to some other place where there is no such harassment; V.G.F.S. 78; V.G.F.S. 78.

9. Area Where Law of Karma Operates

1. V.G.F.S. 43.
2. V.G.F.S. 43.
3. V.K.S. 12.
4. V.G.M.S. 1.
5. V.G.M.S. 66.
6. V.A.S. 4.
7. V.G.M.S. 28.
8. V.G.F.S. 37.

9. V.G.F.S. 16.

10. Law of Karma and Social Service

1. V.G.F.S. 31.
2. V.G.F.S. 58.
3. V.V.S. 17.
4. Īśāvaśya Upaniṣad 2.

11. Law of Karma and Grace of God

1. V.G.F.S. 61.
2. V.K.S. 1.
3. V.V.S. 11; V.G.F.S. 61.
4 V.G.F.S. 61.
5. V.G.F.S. 58; V.G.F.S. 61; V.G.F.S. 61.
6. V.G.F.S. 61; V.S.S. 11.

CHAPTER 11

THE DOCTRINE OF REBIRTH

1. Meaning of Rebirth

The doctrine of rebirth is as old as human thought. It is also known as transmigration of soul. Sanskrit term for it is punarjanma (again birth). The doctrine of rebirth runs through the entire course of Vedic, Aupaniṣadic and Paurāṇika thought.

Rebirth means birth after death. It indicates life after death. The act of embodying oneself in flesh again is called reincarnation in modern language. In ancient language of Sastras it is called Saṁsārayātrā which means passing of the individual soul from one life to another repeatedly.[1] Rebirth viewed as Saṁsārayātrā means life after life. Here we should recall Dr. Raymond A Moody. He does not like the expression "Life after death." He prefers the expression "Life after Life." In his view, rebirth is not life after death, but it is life after life. Therefore he names his book as "Life after Life" and not "Life after death."[2]

2. Idea of Rebirth Follows from Law of Karma

According to Svāminārāyaṇism, Law of Karma gives rise to three postulates : One God; two, permanent self; three, rebirth. God as giver of fruits of actions (Karmaphalapradātā) is an inevitable postulate of law of Karma. Now, unless permanence is acceded to self, God as Karmaphalapradātā and law of Karma as expression of God's will lose all their significance. If there is no permanent existence of the individual self, there cannot be any possibility of future life, after death. According to Law of Karma, our enjoyments and sufferings, our pleasures and pains, of this life are consequences of our actions in previous life or lives. This obviously means that we must have existed prior to this life. It also means that we must continue to exist even after the death of our physical bodies to experience consequences, good or bad, of our deeds in this life.[1]

3. Rebirth Explained

The truth of this doctrine cannot be proved beyond all possible doubting. But in view of law of Karma it is immensely reasonable to believe it. Idea of rebirth is an echo of man's inner being. It is not difficult to grasp that all acts re-act. They-act via universe. They act upon the doer with a force commensurate with his own. This re-action is rebirth.

As we have seen, the causal body, according to Svāminārāyṇa, is inseparably associated with the self since beginningless time.[1] The causal body is rarefied subtle matter which surrounds the self in the form of covering.[2] Every thought and deed produce their effects on this covering by making it either more or less gross. These effects so made on the subtle covering get accumulated and become, as it were, a part of the self. When the physical body dies, the self leaves the body with this covering and is born in another body in the same or lower species according to grossness or otherwise of the covering. If the self can, by removing by necessary Sādhanā, succeed in purifying the self,[3] it becomes free from the cycle of birth and death (Saṁsārayātrā) and attains liberation.[4]

How does the self find a new body? The mechanism of rebirth is very difficult to know, but not impossible to conceive. Simply because we do not understand the process, we cannot deny the fact. At physical death, only outer body perishes. The self remains in-tact.[5] Rebirth is only re-forming of the gross body. In each successive birth, self is not a new entity. Self is the same. Rebirth is nothing but passing from one situation to another.[6] Life continues, life is perpetual going on. On rebirth self merely takes a new gross body.

4. Kinds of Gross Bodies

According to Svāminārāyaṇa, rebirth is for the purposes of purifying the self and ultimately attain salvation. But this is a long-drawn process and requires a long time and graded course of Sādhanā extending over many lives in many bodies. According to Svāminārāyaṇa, there are four kinds of gross bodies : (Sthūla śarīra) through which an individual soul passes in the course of its evolution till it attains liberation. They are : Udbhija that is, plant organisms such as plants and creepers; Svedaja, that is, insect organisms such as mosquitos, flies, bee and so on; aṇḍaja, that is, ovi-born organisms such as birds, fishes, reptiles and so on born of eggs; and jarāyuja, that is vivi-born organisms such as beasts and human beings born of wombs.[10] It will be interesting to compare Svāminārāyṇīya position on gross bodies with that of Sāṅkhya. According to Sāṅkhya Sūtra, there are only six kinds of gross bodies : Uṣmaja, aṇḍja, jarāyuja, udbhija, saṅkalpaja and sānsidhika.[11]

As pointed out by J.N. Sinha,[12] the nature of these six gross bodies has been explained in Sāṅkhyapravacanabhāṣya of Vijñānabhikṣu. According to Radhakrishnan, Sāṅkhyapravacanabhāṣya is the most important work on Sāṅkhyapravacanasūtra of Kapila.[13] According to Sāṅkhyapravacanbhāṣya, Uṣmaja are bodies generated from moisture. Aṇḍaja are those born of eggs like birds, serpents and the like. Jarāyuja are those born of wombs like men and others. Udbhija are born of soil like plants. Saṅkalpaja are born of will. Sānsiddhika are born of miraculous powers of penance, mantras and the like.[14] Out of these six kinds of gross bodies Svāminārāyaṇa has accepted only four : Uṣmaja, aṇḍaja, jarāyuja and udbhija. Uṣmaja is the same thing svedaja. What is called Uṣmaja by Sāṅkhya Sūtra is called Svedaja by Svāminārāyaṇa. Svāminārāyaṇa has not accepted saṅkalpaka and sānsiddhika kinds of gross bodies.

According to Svāminārāyaṇa, the self generally passes from the lowest towards the highest.[15] But that is not always so. If regressive factors develop on account of some fault committed by the self, then the self is reborn in a body in the lower species. Svāminārāyaṇa explains this position with the help of the illustration of Bharataji who developed attachment for a deer and consequently by had to take birth in the body of a deer in the next life.[16] God gives the self body according to the merits of its deeds.[17]

5. Life in Rebirth

What will be the kind of life in rebirth? According to Svāminārāyṇa, the kind of life in rebirth cannot be totally different from the present one. The event of death, which separates the self from the gross physical body, does not introduce profound changes in the life of the self. No self takes birth in a body which is incongruous to its evolved traits and qualities. When the self is reborn in body, it is reborn with all the characteristics and qualities it had in the previous life. The self rebirth is the same as it was in the former body.[1]

6. Rebirth in Indian Philosophy

Except Cārvāka materialism, all the systems of Indian philosophy admit the doctrine of rebirth. Jainas do not believe in God, but they do believe in rebirth. Buddhas do not believe either in God or in permanent self. And yet they believe in rebirth. Svāminārāyaṇa believes both in God as well as permanent self. Like many ancient religions of the world, Svāminārāyaṇism believes in the rebirth of the individual soul after the death of the physical body.[1] Svāminārāyaṇa does not attempt to prove the doctrine of rebirth. He accepts it as too obvious to need proof. According to Svāminārāyaṇa, we all have to die and be born again and again till we attain liberation (mokṣa).[2]

7. Radhakrishan's Arguments for Rebirth

Radhakrishnan maintains the doctrine of rebirth. According to him, the doctrine of rebirth has had a long and influential history.[1] He advances powerful arguments to establish the doctrine.

According to Radhakrishnan, the emergent view of the self makes the doctrine of rebirth a reasonable one.[2] He says that throughout the nature, life is preserved and continued through incessant renewal. According to him life is a perpetual going on, always straining forward for something that has not been but should be.[3] Elaborating his argument, he says that if everything in nature arises from something continuous with it, the self need not be an exception to the general scheme. In support of his argument he cites Kaṭhopaniṣad wherein it is stated that like corn the mortal grows; like corn is born again.[4]

Radhakrishan argues that the self aims at fulfilment of function or development of individuality. It can grow indefinitely in depth, richness and comprehensiveness. In his view, we cannot exercise all the powers we possess or exhaust all the values we strain after. The capacity of the self for endless improvement point to a future where the self's "withheld completions" obtain a chance.[5]

Basing his argument on science, he says that it is an admitted principle that if we see a certain stage of development, in time, we may infer a past to it. It is not true that we "brought nothing in this world." In his view, the self enters this life with a certain nature and inheritance. We commonly speak of talents that are inherited. So, says he, the self must have had a past history here and elsewhere, We cannot believe that the rise of the self with a definite nature is simply fortuitous.[6]

According to Radhakrishnan, the life of the human self does not centre in the body though it uses the latter for the promotion of its purposes. Therefore, the death of the physical body does not mean dissipation of the self. In support of his argument he quotes from Chāndogya Upaniṣad wherein it is stated that it is the body which dies when left by the self.[7] In view of Radhakrishnan, if the self wakes up after a dreamless sleep and feels its continuity with the self that went to sleep, death need not mean discontinuity.[8]

Radhakrishnan says that the ancient theory of finer ethereal body seems to receive some support from psychical research. According to him, there is enough evidence to justify the belief that apparitions are due to the action of the dead persons whose bodies they represent.[9] According to Radhakrishnan self is not altogether discarnate, it is invested in a finer vehicle, the subtle body (sūkṣma śarīra). The necessary physical basis is secured by the subtle body. He points out that it is this subtle body, which accompanies one throughout one's empirical existence, is the form on which physical body is moulded.[10] At physical death, only the gross, outer form perishes. The rest of the self is not disturbed. According to Radhakrishnan, rebirth is only the renewal of the instrument through which the self works. The self is not at birth a new entity, but a continuous process. A transition is conceived from one situation to another at physical death.[11]

Radhakrishnan has pointed out that in the Hindu Scriptures dying thought has been accorded great significance for the next life. The thoughts at death represent the culmination of the process of self-development. The dying thought resumes in itself all thoughts and states that went before. It is the sum-total of its predecessors, the inheritor of its past and the point for the future growth.[12] According to Radhakrishnan, we are born in the families where the qualities we possess and seek to embody are well developed. In rebirth the deciding factor is the nature of the self and not the parents of the body.[13]

A common objection is urged against the doctrine of rebirth. The objection is that the self lacks the memory of the past. And therefore, it could not be in the past. According to Radhakrishnan this objection cannot be sustained. In his view death may destroy the memory of our deeds but not their effects on us. The metaphysical question of continuity of self is not in any way affected by the discontinuity of memory. Radhakrishnan says that the nature of each individual is moulded by the experiences of the past. Every state is conditional by the prior and leads on to another. Radhakrishnan argues that simply because we do not have a memory of early phases of our life or of our existence in the mother's body. We do not deny them. Even in this life we forget ever so much.[14]

Radhakrishnan says that death is a change within a general structural progression. Death is not an unique event in our progress. It is a part of a continually recurring rhythm of nature marking a crisis in the history of the individual.[15]

Sounding an optimistic note Radhakrishnan says that the children of God in whose eyes a thousand years are as a day need not be disheartened if the goal of perfection is not attained in one life.[16] The individual has appeared and disappeared times without number, in the long past and will continue to be dissolved and reformed through unimaginable centuries to come. According to Radhakrishnan, the bodily life is just an episode in the larger career of the individual soul which proceeds birth and proceeds after death.[17]

Svāminārāyaṇa would endorse all the arguments advanced by Radhakrishnan for establishing the doctrine of rebirth.

8. Rebirth in Gītā

In Gītā the doctrine of rebirth is very well expounded. According to Gītā, self is immortal and life is continuous existence. It is declared in Gītā that death is certain of that which is born and birth is certain of that which is dead.[1] Death is not the end of soul's life, but only a stage in its career for change of bodies. Just as a man casts off worn out garments and puts on new ones, so the embodied soul casts off worn out bodies and enters into new ones.[2] As are childhood, youth and old age of this body to the embodied soul, so also is attaining of another body.[3] According to Gītā, rebirth is as certain as death. But the nature of rebirth depends on the quality of Karmas which the self has performed in the former life. A yogi who falls from yoga is reborn in the house of pure and prosperous,[4] or in the family of the enlightened yogi.[5] Such a yogi regains the knowledge acquired by him in his previous body.[6] The yogi, perfected through many births, reaches the supreme goal.[7] God says, "on reaching me, there is no rebirth."[8] Svāminārāyaṇa would completely agree with the theory of rebirth expounded in Gītā.

In passing it may be noted that the Bṛhadāraṇyaka Upaniṣad gives a detailed description of the manner in which the man dies and is born again.[9] Svāminārāyaṇa, would fully agree with the above-mentioned ideas expressed in Gītā and in Bṛhadāraṇyaka Upaniṣad.

9. Rebirth in Western Philosophy

The doctrine of rebirth finds a wide expression in the history of western religion and philosophy. Pythagoras, Plato, Empedodes, Bruno, Lissing and Herder seriously believe in this doctrine.[1] For them pre-existence and survival stand or fall together.

In the myth of ER by Plato, we find a story of a Greek Soldier whose name is ER. He was killed in the war. His dead body was laid on the funeral pyre. He revived and described how his soul went out of the body and what he had seen in his journey to the realms beyond.

According to Plato, the wise man turns away from the world of senses and keep his inward and spiritual eye ever directed to the world of eternal idea, and if only the pursuit is maintained, the individual becomes freed from the bonds of sensualism, and after death his released spirit slowly mounts up higher and higher until at last it finds it way back to the home of the eternal light.[2] Emmanuel Swedenborg says that "man, when he dies, only passes from our world into another."[3] Svāminārāyaṇa would fully endorse the views of Plato and Swedenborg.

In his book "Karma and Rebirth" Christmas Humphreys gives a long series of quotations from Western writers who accept the doctrine of rebirth.[4]

10. Rebirth in Bible

In the old as well as New Testaments we find ample references to the belief in rebirth. In Isaiah it said "the dead man shall live awake and sing, ye that dwell in dust."[1] In

Daniel a reference is found to the same effect. "And many of them that sleep in the dust of earth shall awake."[2] In Corinthians it is said, "But some men will say, How are the dead raised up?"[3] In Titus it has been written, "Not by works of righteousness which we have done, but by the washing of Regeneration and Renewing of the Holy Ghost."[4]

Doctrine of rebirth is clearly present in some parts of Christ's teachings. In the Gospel of John we find that when Jesus was passing by, he saw a man who was blind from his birth. His disciples asked him, "who did sin, this man or his parents?"[5] Here we find a tacit reference to the previous life of the blind man. But "rebirth" finds a Specific mention in the conversation Jesus had with Nicodemus. Jesus said to Nicodemus, "Except a man be born again, he cannot see kingdom of God."[6] On being asked by Nicodemus whether man could be born again, Jesus said, "Marvel not that I said unto thee, ye must be born again"[7] One may dispute about the meaning of the word "rebirth" in this conversation. Whatever the symbolic meaning of the word may be, but literal meaning of it indicates that belief in rebirth was prevalent in those days.

In the Gospel of Mathew we are told there were rumours that Christ was the incarnation of Jeremiah or Elias.[8] Even the king Herod believed that Jesus was John the Baptist "risen from the dead". Herod said, "It is John whom I beheaded : he is risen from the dead."[9]

Svāminārāyaṇa would fully agree with the doctrine of rebirth as expressed in old and New Testaments.

11. Rebirth in Quran

In Quran also we find ample references to the belief in rebirth. There are certain texts in Quran which may be interpreted as meaning that man lives and dies repeatedly even as worlds are created and destroyed repeatedly. According to Dr. Bhagawan Das some sufi sects of Islam believe that Mohammad was Abraham reborn and Abraham's two sons were reborn as Ali and Ali's son Husain.[1]

We shall now quote from Quran to prove the belief in rebirth in Islam. Let us take a text like this. Summa basma-Kunla alla-kun tushkurun. It means, "I (God) gave you birth Again after you died that you may think of Me with gratitude".[2] We shall quote another text from Quran to show that Islam embodies belief in repeated births until final day. The text is this "Minha Khalaquakun Wa fi ha naido-kun eta ta' atin-ukhra". It means, From out of earth have I (God) now given birth to you, and I will send you into it Again and bring you forth from it Again, Again repeatedly until the end.[3] We have still another text which gives a very clearly evidence for rebirth in Quran. "Kaifa takfuruna billahe wa Kuntum anvatan fa ahyakum summa yahgikum summa ilaiha tarja un". It means, How can you make denial of your God who made you live Again when you had died, will make you dead Again, Again alive until you go back finally to Him?[4]

Maulana Jalaluddin Rumi was a great Islamic poet. He has written his famous Masnawi in Persian language. Masnawi is generally accepted in Islam as next to Quran in holiness. In this long poem Maulana Rumi may be regarded as commenting on the above mentioned texts when he says in the first half of his couplet that "Ham cho Sabza Baraha royidah am". It means, like grass I have grown over and over again.[5]

According to both Svāminārāyaṇism and Islam, there would be repeated births till the "end." According to both, when the "end" is reached, the self becomes free from the cycle of births and deaths. However, the word "end" does not possess the same meaning in both the system. It possesses different meanings. According to Svāminārāyaṇism, "end" means end of bondage. It means release from the entanglements of forces of Māyā. Such a release can be attained even during embodied existence. A liberated self, on the death its physical body, goes to Akṣaradhāman where it eternally enjoys the bliss of nearness and sernitude of God. In Islam "end" means the day of judgement (Roz-e-Hashar). On the day of judgement the self shall receive from God either reward (jaza) or punishment (saza) in accordance with its good or bad deeds. A soul that received punishment shall eternally suffer the torments of hell (jahauṇum). It will be eternally condemned to hell. A soul that receives reward shall go to heaven (Jannat) and there with the inmates of heaven shall enternally reside and enjoy bliss. According to Quran when man attains salvation or release (najat) from his sinful life, God rewards him with eternal life of bliss in heaven.[6]

Svāminārāyaṇa would endorse the doctrine of rebirth in Quran. Svāminārāyṇa would also endorse the doctrine of eternal life of blissful residence in heaven on salvation. But, Svāminārāyṇa would not accept the doctrine of eternal condemnation. According to Svāminārāyṇa, every soul is eligible for final emancipation (ātyantika mokṣa).

12. Rebirth as Moral Value

The idea of rebirth, according to Svāminārāyaṇa, is of great moral value. It inspires man to do virtuous deeds in the hope that he will be happier in the life to come. It prevents man from doing evil deeds in the apprehension that if he performs them, he will have to suffer painful consequences.[1] According to Kant also immorality of soul, in the sense of rebirth, is a postulate of morality. If rebirth is a postulate of morality and if morality is prescribed by all religions, it follows that rebirth is accepted by all religions either implicitly or explicitly. Svāminārāyaṇa has not only explicitly accepted the doctrine of rebirth, but has also shown its relevance to morality.

REFERENCES

1. Meaning of Rebirth

1. Yatīshwarānanda, Reflections on Hinduism (1969), p. 100.
2. Raymond A. Moody, Life After Life (1977).

2. Idea of Rebirth Follows from Law of Karma

1. V.G.M.S. 59.

3. Rebirth Explained

1. V.V.S. 6.
2. V.K.S. 12.

3. V.G.L.S. 20.
4. V.G.M.S. 11.
5. V.S.S. 1.
6. V.G.F.S. 37; V.G.F.S. 21; V.G.M.S. 11.

4. Kinds of Gross Bodies

1. V.G.F.S. 13.
2. Sāṅkhya Sūtra 5. 111.
3. J.N. Sinha, A History of Indian Philosophy, Vol. II (1952), p. 22.
4. Radhakrishnan, Indian Philosophy, Vol. II (1977), p. 256.
5. Sāṅkhyapravacanabhāṣya, 5. 1. 112; J.N. Sinha, A History of Indian Philosophy, Vol. II, p. 22.
6. V.G.F.S. 21.
7. V.G.F.S. 42.
8. V.G.F.S. 13.

5. Life in Rebirth

1. V.G.L.S. 20.

6. Rebirth in Indian Philosophy

1. V.G.M.S. 18; V.G.L.S. 39; V.G.F.S. 37; *See also* V.G.M.S. 11, and V.J.S. 4.
2. V.G.M.S. 11.

7. Radhakrishnan's Arguments for Rebirth

1. Radhakrishnan, An Idealist View of Life (1947), p. 286.
2. *Ibid.*, p. 287.
3. *Ibid.*, p. 287.
4. *Ibid.*, p. 288.
5. *Ibid.*, p. 288.
6. *Ibid.*, p. 289.
7. *Ibid.*, p. 291.
8. *Ibid.*, p. 291.
9. *Ibid.*, p. 291-292.
10. *Ibid.*, p. 295.
11. *Ibid.*, p. 295.
12. *Ibid.*, p. 295.
13. *Ibid.*, p. 296.
14. *Ibid.*, p. 299.
15. *Ibid.*, p. 288.
16. *Ibid.*, p. 289.
17. *Ibid.*, p. 289.

8. Rebirth in Gītā

1. Gītā 2.27.
2. Gītā 2.22.
3. Gītā 2.13.
4. Gītā 6.41.
5. Gītā 6.42.
6. Gītā 6.43.
7. Gītā 6.45.
8. Gītā 8.16; *See also* Gītā 8.15.
9. Bṛhadāraṇyaka Upaniṣad, 4.3.37 and 38.

9. Rebirth in Western Philosophy

1. Dr. J.A. Yajnik, The Philosophy of Śrī Svāminārāyaṇa, p. 111.
2. Radhakrishnan, An Idealist View of Life, p. 122.
3. Compendium of the Theological and Spiritual Writings of Emmanuel Swedenborg, Corsby and Nicholas (1853), p. 160.
4. Christmas Humphreys, Karma and Rebirth (Wisdom of East Series) 1958.

10. Rebirth in Bible

1. Isaiah 26.19.
2. Daniel 12.2.
3. Corinthians 15.35.
4. Titus 3.5.
5. John 9.1 and 9.2.
6. John 3.3.
7. John 3.7.
8. Matthew 16.13 to 16.
9. Mark 6.14 to 16.

11. Rebirth in Quran

1. Dr. Bhagwana Das, Essential Unity of All Religious (1955), p. 224.
2. Quran, Sur-i-Bakra, Chapter 2, verse 56.
3. Quran, Sur-i-Taha, Chapter 20, verse 55.
4. Quran, Sur-i-Bakra, Chapter 2, verse 28.
5. Maulana Jalaluddin Rumi, Masnawi, Book III, Kanpur Edition, p. 334.
6. Surah Zalzalah 99. 5.6-8.

12. Rebirth as Moral Value

1. V.G.F.S. 13; *See also* V.G.M.S. 59.

PART FOUR

LIBERATION

CHAPTER 12

MEANS OF LIBERATION

1. Principle Means of Liberation

According to Svāminārāyaṇa, there are four principle means of self-realisation, God-realisation or liberation. They are Dharma (morality), Jñāna (metaphysical understanding), Bhakti (intense love for God) and Vairāgya (non-attachment).

Svāminārāyaṇa regards Dharma, Jñāna, Bhakti and Vairāgya not only as the principle means of liberation, but as very important aspects of religious life also. He has amply discussed them in Vacanāmṛta and has pointed out their efficacy in attaining the Ultimate goal. The Svāminārāyaṇist view of these four means of liberation has been very well worked out by Dr. J.A. Yajnik in Chapter 16 of his book "The philosophy of Svāminārāyaṇa". We have, therefore, not elaborated here the Svāminārāyaṇist views on these four principal means of liberation.

2. Auxiliary Means of Liberation

In addition to the above four principle means, Svāminārāyaṇa has pointed out twelve auxiliary means of liberation. They are : Śraddhā (respectful faith), Indriyanigraha (control of senses), Ahiṁsā (non-violence), Brahmacarya (abstinence), Satsanga (holy company), Santoṣa (contentment), Nirdambhapaṇam (non-hypocrisy), Dayā (compassion), Tapa (austerity), Gurubhāva (respect for seniors), Śiṣyabhāva (sympathy towards juniors) and Mitrabhāva (friendliness).[1] We shall deal with them one by one and attempt to bring out real connotation of each of them in accordance with the principles of Svāminārāyaṇist philosophy.

3. Śraddhā

Śraddhā occupies all important place in the religious life. Śraddhā usually means respectful faith in the assertions of scriptures learnt through one's teacher. In Svāminārāyaṇism Śraddhā has a special connotation. In Svāminārāyaṇism Śraddhā connotes a firm conviction (niścaya) in the divine form and personality of God. In other words in Svāminārāyaṇism, Śraddhā means ākāraniścaya. According to Svāminārāyaṇa, by having faith in the pronouncements of scriptures, one's conviction in the form and personality of God becomes firm.[1] Unless the devotee has such a conviction, he cannot love God. According to Svāminārāyaṇa, when the devotee has such a conviction, he establishes relation with God.[2] And when he establishes relation with God, he imbibes divine attributes of God.[3] According to Svāminārāyaṇa, unless the devotee has intense and undivided love for God, complete surrender to God is not possible. Intense and undivided love for God makes absolute surrender (āsaro) possible.[4] According to Svāminārāyaṇa, without absolute surrender to God, liberation is not possible.[5] Svāminārāyaṇa has said that by complete surrender the devotee attains the grace of God.[6] And therefore, Svāminārāyaṇa, has regarded complete surrender to God as the highest means of liberation.[7] Thus we see that it is by Śraddhā that love for and surrender to God is possible. Therefore, Svāminārāyaṇa has said that it is necessary for the development of religious life that one should ever have a renewed Śraddhā.[8] Renewed Śraddhā renews the man.

The importance of Śraddhā in religious life has been recognised by Gītā. In Gītā, apart from stray discussions on Śraddhā in other chapters, one full chapter has been devoted to the discussion of the nature and kinds of Śraddhā.[9] According to Gītā, man is of the nature of his Śraddhā. What his Śraddhā is that verily he is.[10] Gītā says that a man of faith attains spiritual knowledge.[11] In other words, according to Gita, faith is a source of knowledge. Svāminārāyaṇa would agree with this view of Gītā and would support it by saying that faith is "evidence of things unseen."[12]

According to Gītā a man who has faith in God will attain release from the Kārmic forces.[13] Svāminārāyaṇa fully agrees with this idea of Gītā. Svāminārāyaṇa says that if a man has firm faith in the form and personality of God, all his passions, cravings and desires, which constitute an impediment in his way of self-realisation and God-realisation, will come to an end.[14] In a philosophy like that of Desecrates which is founded on doubt, faith can have no legitimate place. But Indian religious thinkers in general, and Svāminārāyaṇa in particular, have held faith as a necessary condition of spiritual life. Svāminārāyaṇa teaches faith that seeks and finds its fulfilment in actual experiences. Its purpose is to serve the aspirant as a speedy guide to his ultimate goal.

In Western Philosophy also the importance of faith has been very well recognised. Neo-scholastics believe that faith, like reason, is a way of coming to knowledge of God. According to them, faith is one of the ways by which knowledge of God can be attained. According to them faith can be a source of knowledge.[15] Svāminārāyaṇa would certainly accept faith as a source of knowledge.

In "Critique of Pure Reason" Kant determined the rules and limits of human reason. After a thorough examination of reason, he came to the conclusion that the principles which can extend only to the objects of possible experience cannot be applied to objects which lie beyond this sphere. He, therefore, declared that "I must........abolish reason to make room for belief."[16] It is, therefore, evident that the logic of religion is precisely what Saint Paul said, "We live by faith, not by scientific thought."[17] Svāminārāyaṇa would completely agree with Saint Paul on this point.

Radhakrishnan has pointed out that "to live without faith is impossible. If nature has horror of a vaccum, the human soul has fear of emptiness."[18]

And what is our common experience? Every moment we do not make use of reason. Every time we do not insist that what is presented before us should be proved by the rules of logic. By and large we live on faith. The Svāminārāyaṇist standpoint on faith is borne out by our every day experience. What Svāminārāyaṇa insists is only this that the faith which one exercises in every day affairs should not halt there. It should go beyond every day life and reach God. In Svāminārāyaṇa's view when one exercises faith one reaches God.

4. Indriyanigraha

Indriyanigraha means controlling the sense organs. A seeker of final emancipation (ātyantika Kalyāṇa) is required to withdraw his senses from their objects. In Śaṅkara Vedānta the withdrawal of senses from their objects, when effected, is called Uparati and the withdrawer of senses is called Uparata. Svāminārāyaṇa would have no objection in accepting the terms "Uparati" and "Uparata" for "Withdrawal" and "Withdrawer" respectively.

Svāminārāyaṇa has laid great emphasis on the control of senses. In his view sense control is an important ingredient of Sādhanā to be performed by the devotee for the purpose of attaining self-realisation and God-realisation. If sense organs are allowed to have a free play with their objects, they will prove to be a source of mental distraction. When senses are allowed to indulge in sense objects, they corrupt the conscience (antaḥkaraṇa).[1] In Svāminārāyaṇa's view a true devotee of God should control all senses, especially the palate.[2] Svāminārāyaṇa says that man normally consumes different varieties of food with different tastes. Different kinds of food produce different effects on the psycho-physical organism of man. When food is consumed by man, its essence affects his antaḥkaraṇa (conscience).[3] The impure food would make the conscience impure. Svāminārāyaṇa says that the devotee of God should be a conqueror of taste (Nisvādi).[4] According to Svāminārāyaṇa each sense has its own peculiar food. And for maintaining the purity of conscience the purity of the food for each sense should be maintained. Purity of food generates purity of conscience.[5] Svāminārāyaṇa, therefore, maintains that extreme purity of food should be maintained.[6] According to Svāminārāyaṇa, the devotee, who desires to please God and attains His Grace, should never think of enjoying the pleasures of flesh.[7] He should withdraw his senses from the objects of sensuous enjoyment. Svāminārāyaṇa has said that the devotee of God should establish complete control over senses.[8] According to Svāminārāyaṇa when the desire to enjoy sensuous objects comes to an end, the control of senses becomes complete.[9]

The question is, how to control external senses? Answering the question Svāminārāyaṇa has said that the external senses can be controlled by observing scriptural precepts, control of diet, suffering cold, heat, hunger and thirst and by engaging in religious songs (Kīrtana) and talks of greatness and glory of God and sitting in a fixed posture.[10] Another question that can arise is, can we control antaḥkaraṇa by controlling senses or can we control senses by controlling antaḥkaraṇa? The answer of Svāminārāyaṇa is that senses cannot that controlled by controlling antaḥkaraṇa, but antaḥkaraṇa can be controlled by controlling senses.[11]

Gītā says that control of senses is necessary for acquiring serenity of mind.[12] Gītā further says that one, who has control over senses, attains the ultimate goal of God-realisation.[13] Svāminārāyaṇa would fully agree with the idea of sense-control expressed in Gītā.

According to Gītā, external control of senses must be accompanied by the internal control of mind. A man who externally controls sense organs and internally craves for the objects of sense is a hypocrite. Such a man is deluded.[14] Svāminārāyaṇa completely endorses this view of Gītā. According to Svāminārāyaṇa, control of mind is of prime importance in religious life. According to him, a man of true detachment (vairāgya) is one who has mentally renounced the objects of sense.[15] According to Svāminārāyaṇa the renouncement of the sensuous objects must be external as well as internal. Physical renouncement must be accompanied by mental renouncement.[16]

5. Ahiṁsā

Ahiṁsā is one of the important features of Svāminārāyaṇism. Svāminārāyaṇa has given it an important place in his scheme of religious life. Not only that. He has regarded it as a means of liberation.

Ahiṁsā means non-violence. In its actual meaning it means non-injury. It is non-killing. But Svāminārāyaṇa has not restricted its meaning to mere non-injury or non-killing. In his view ahiṁsā would mean abstinence from inflicting injury, from falsehood, theft and avarice. In his broad interpretation it is abstinence from malice towards all living creatures. He says man should completely uproot from his mind anger, hatred and revenge.[1] He should not have malice towards any one either in thought or in speech or in action.[2] Nor should he ever make use of language which may cause insult or annoyance to any one.[3] According to Svāminārāyaṇa ahiṁsā is a supreme virtue to be cultivated not only by the householders, but by sādhus (hermits) also.[4] Ahiṁsā is a high moral principle and is helpful in attaining final emancipation.[5]

Yoga enjoins the practice of restraints (Yama). One of the five restraints enjoined by Yoga is ahiṁsā. The other four are : Satya (truthfulness), asteya (non-stealing), Brahmacrya (sexual abstinence) and aparigraha (non-acceptance of gifts)[6]. According to Yoga, three yamas are of universal validity regardless of differences of caste country, age and condition.[7] No exceptions are allowed to these yamas which are absolute in their character. These are negative virtues. The chief of them is ahiṁsā and all other virtues are rooted in it. In Yoga non-injury is considered as the root of other negative (Yama) and positive (niyama) virtues. Svāminārāyaṇa would completely agree with this view of Yoga. According to Svāminārāyaṇa, ahiṁsā is absolutely necessary if one desires to attain liberation.[8] Again in Yoga ahiṁsā has been interpreted as abstinence from malice towards all living beings in every way and at all times.[9] In view of Yoga ahiṁsā is not only non-injury, but non-hatred also.[10] Svāminārāyaṇa would have no hesitation in accepting this view of Yoga. In Gītā ahiṁsā has been recognised as an austerity of body.[11] It is regarded by Gītā as a divine quality (daivī Sampat).[12] Svāminārāyaṇa would agree with this view of Gītā regarding ahiṁsā as a divine quality. In Śrimad Bhāgavata it is stated that life is the life of life.[13] Although Svāminārāyaṇa has great regard for Śrimad Bhāgavata and holds it as an authoritative scripture,[14] he would not agree with this statement which negates ahiṁsā.

Mahatma Gandhi was a great advocate of ahiṁsā. While discussing the central teaching he has said that the central teaching of Gītā is not hiṁsā, but ahiṁsā. Hiṁsā is important without anger and hatred and Gītā strives to carry us beyond a state that excludes anger and hatred.[15] Mahatma Gandhi has also said "Non-violence is a perfect state. It is a goal towards which all mankind moves naturally, though unconsciously."[16] He has also said; "We pretend to believe that retaliation is the law of our being. Whereas in every scripture we find that retaliation is nowhere obligatory. It is restraint that is obligatory. Restraint is the law of our being. For highest perfection is unattainable without highest restraint".[1] Svāminārāyaṇa would fully endorse the ideas of Mahatma Gandhi expressed herein. Svāminārāyaṇa would also endorse the principle of ahiṁsā expounded by Buddha and Mahāvīra.

6. Brahmacarya

Brahmacarya means abstinence from sexual act. It is a sex restraint. It consists in restraining sex organ and all other sense-organs with regard to the object of sex-gratification.

Brahmacarya is one of the five external restraints (yama) enjoined by Aṣṭāṅga Yoga.[1] It has been regarded by Gītā as a bodily austerity (Śarīra tapa).[2] Sexual continence has been considered as an important aspect of religious life by all Indian religionists. Svāminārāyaṇa regards it as an essential condition of religious life. Not only that, He also regards it as a means of liberation. Svāminārāyaṇa has invested Brahmacarya with the status of being a means of self-realisation and God-realisation.

According to Svāminārāyaṇa, the lack of brahmacarya causes intense distraction in mind. A man who takes to sexual indulgence becomes depraved.[3] He has, therefore, exhorted his sādhus to be Brahmacari.[4] According to Svāminārāyaṇa, if a man observes strict and infallible sex restraint, it will very greatly help him in the realisation of his ultimate goal which is God-realisation.[5]

7. Santoṣa

Santoṣa means contentment. It has been regarded by Svāminārāyaṇa as a high quality to be possessed by a man who wants to lead religious life.[1] To Santoṣa Svāminārāyaṇa has given the status of being a means of liberation.[2] In view of Svāminārāyaṇa santoṣa dwells in him who has no worldly carvings.

In religious life santoṣa signifies full contentment with bare means of bodily sustenance. A religious man is happy with what he has and what he gets. He has always a feeling of fulness when he gets even a little of what he needs. He neither grumbles nor complains. He is ever satisfied and cheerful. A man of santoṣa is always in a poised state of mind. If a man is always dissatisfied with his surroundings and with what he has, his mind remains in constant tension and suffers from the agitations of conflicting desires. Such a man cannot meditate on the personality of God. A man of contentment always enjoys inner peace and can easily take to undivided meditation of God. According to Svāminārāyaṇa, Santoṣa is necessary for higher life of contemplation. Now a days we hear a cry of raising the standard of living. Raising standard of living means nothing more than increasing wants and acquiring more things. But wants are insatiable. Things can never bring contentment (santoṣa). Desires have no end. If you try to satisfy one, ten will arise. Svāminārāyaṇa would say "make your life rich by making your wants few. Be contented." According to Svāminārāyaṇism, minimising wants is a sure way to contentment.

8. Tapa

Tapa means austerity. Svāminārāyaṇa has not given a definition of tapa. But it largely connotes a capacity for sustained efforts in connection with a desired goal. It involves performance of asceticism. Svāminārāyaṇa regards tapa as a useful means (Sādhanā) of liberation.[1] One, who aspires to attain liberation, should practice it regularly. Tapa gives strength and sturdiness to body and courage and confidence to mind. It is a necessary ingredient of spiritual life. Svāminārāyaṇa says that one should endeavour to attain the grace of God by steady practice of tapa.[2] Steadfastness in tapa is considered Sat in Gītā.[3]

Tapa is one of the five observances (niyama) enjoined by Aṣṭāṅga Yoga for attainment of Kaivalya (liberation).[4] Svāminārāyaṇa would have no objection in accepting tapa as niyama. Gītā regards tapa as a divine quality (daivī sampat)[5]. In the seventeenth chapter of Gītā, namely, Śraddhātrayavibhāgayoga, tapa is considered of three Kinds : śarīra tapa (bodily austerity), Vāṅmaya tapa (oral austerity) and Manas tapa (mental austerity). Continence (brahmacarya) and non-violence (ahiṁsā) are regarded as the austerities of body.[6] Pleasant, truthful and beneficial speech and practice of sacred recitation are regarded as the austerities of speech.[7] Serenity of mind (prasāda), gentleness (saumyatva), silence (mauna), self-control (ātmavinigraha) and purity of disposition (Bhāvasanśuddhi) are considered mental austerities.[8] Svāminārāyaṇa would endorse the division of tapa into three kinds made by Gītā. Svāminārāyaṇa would say that all the three instruments, that is, body speech and mind, should be utilised in the manner indicated by Gita for the purpose of attaining final emancipation (ātyantika Kalyāṇa).

According to Svāminārāyaṇism, tapa should be accompanied by Upāsanā. Svāminārāyaṇa has regarded Upāsanā as an important ingredient of spiritual sādhanā. At the first sight Bhakti and Upāsanā may appear to be the same. But that is not so. Svāminārāyaṇa has made a distinction between them. According to Svāminārāyaṇa, Bhakti and Upāsanā are two different things.[9] He has pointed out that there are nine ways of worshipping God. They are Śravaṇa, Kīrtana, Smaraṇa, Pādasevana, Arcana, Vandana, Dāsya, Sakhya and Ātmanivedana.[10] According to Svāminārāyaṇa, Bhakti means worshipping God in any of the nine ways.[11] According to him, Upāsanā means firm conviction and undivided concentration on the divine form of God.[12] According to Svāminārāyaṇa Upāsanā should necessarily be of the divine form of God.[13] There cannot be any Upāsanā of the formless. Upāsanā must be of a Being that possesses no empirical attributes, but divine attributes. According to Svāminārāyaṇa, God possess infinite number of divine attributes which are supremely marvellous. According to Svāminārāyaṇa, one who performs Upāsanā, that is, one who meditates upon the divine form of God realises God and attains similarity with Him in Akṣaradhāman.[14]

In Svāminārāyaṇa's view Upāsanā is not merely a prop to mind. He views Upāsanā as the way in which the self can discover its own depth and realise what it is in itself and what it is in relation to God.

9. Nirdambhapaṇa

Nirdambhapaṇa means non-hypocrisy. It connotes unpretentiousness. It is an important moral principle. Svāminārāyaṇa has considered it as a means of liberation. It is opposite of Dambha. Dambha means hypocrisy. It is a hollow showmanship. According to Svāminārāyaṇa, bhakti is not a matter of making show. It is a matter of realising the ultimate goal which is self-realisation and God-realisation. Svāminārāyaṇa has said that one should worship God without making any show.[1] A true devotee would worship God and do service of saints without indulging in hypocrisy.[2] Not only that One should, also not make any exhibition of one's metaphysical understanding.[3] Hypocrisy is not compatible with true worship of God.

In Gītā unpretentiousness has been considered as an important aspect of self culture.[4] According to Gītā, one who is given to pretentiousness and hypocrisy (dambha) is impelled by the forces of lust and attachment.[5] Svāminārāyaṇa would completely agree with this view of Gītā. In Svāminārāyaṇa's view Nirdambhapaṇa should be accompanied by

Nirmamapaṇa (egolessness). According to Svāminārāyaṇa to be same in honour as well as dishonour is a great spiritual achievement.[6] A man, who aspires to attains self-realisation and God-realisation should be above honour and dishonour.[7] According to Gītā, one who is above honour and dishonour is very dear to God.[8] Svāminārāyaṇa would completely endorse this view of Gītā. According to Svāminārāyaṇa an aspirant should never seek honour.[9] Svāminārāyaṇa has said that the devotee of God should be away from egoity.[10] According to Svāminārāyaṇa, self conceit is worse than cupidity.[11] It gives rise to jealousy and anger.[12] Egoity is a great evil.[13] According to Svāminārāyaṇa it constitutes an obstacle in the path of liberation. The seeker of liberation should always remain free from egoity.[14]

10. Dayā

Dayā is karuṇā. It means compassion. It involves co-suffering. It connotes sympathetic sorrow. Svāminārāyaṇa has emphasised the practice of dayā, not only as a moral principle, but as a means of liberation also. When the sight of a man in distress draws out sympathy and fellow feeling, it is a mark of compassion to that man. When one has a feeling of compassion for other, one identifies with the other. When we feel compassion for some one, we feel one with that one. A truly religious man, in view of Svāminārāyaṇa, would put himself in the place of the lowest of his fellow human beings and would be compassionate for them. According to Svāminārāyaṇa, the moral aspirants should practice compassion for distressed creatures.

In Gītā dayā is considered as a divine quality (daivī sampat).[1] Svāminārāyaṇa would agree with this view of Gītā. Svāminārāyaṇa takes this Gītā-view further and places dayā in the rank of the means of liberation. Like Buddha and Mahāvīra. Svāminārāyaṇa is a great advocate of dayā. He describes himself as full of compassion (dayālu).[2] He asked two boons from his spiritual teacher (guru) Rāmānanda Svāmī that he should have capacity to free his disciples from the miseries and that if any one of his disciples were to suffer any ailment, such ailment should fall upon him.[3]

Svāmī Vivekānanda has said that mercy should not for men alone, but should go beyond and embrace the whole world.[4] Svāminārāyaṇa would completely agree with this view of Vivekānanda. Svāminārāyaṇa says that he is so full of compassion that he would not even pluck a green leaf.[5] In view of Svāminārāyaṇa one should have compassion for all the living beings of the human, animal and plant world. Buddhism,[6] Jainism[7] and Yoga[8] enjoin the cultivation of love and compassion for all living beings. Svāminārāyaṇa would fully endorse the standpoint of these three philosophical systems, Svāminārāyaṇism enjoins upon all the members of the society the cultivation of this virtue.

It should be noted that Mahāyāna school of Buddhism was founded upon the doctrine of Great Compassion (Mahā-karuṇā).[9]

11. Satsaṅga

Satsaṅga means holy company. According to Svāminārāyaṇa, so is a man as is his company. The conscience of man becomes good in good company and bad in bad company.[1] Svāminārāyaṇa, therefore, lays great emphasis on pious company (satsaṅga). He has regarded satsaṅga as a means of liberation. He has gone to the extent of saying that no means of liberation can stand on parity with satsaṅga.[2] Satsaṅga is superior to all other means of liberation.[3] According to Svāminārāyaṇa, if the disturbing thoughts and agitations of mind cannot be tranquilised by any other means, satsaṅga can tranquilise them.[4] It is highly conducive to religious life. It produces piety in the life of man[5].

According to Svāminārāyaṇa, love for God becomes steadfast in the company of holy persons.[6] As the devotee goes on imbibing the virtues of the saintly men in their company, his devotion and adoration for God goes on increasing.[7] According to Svāminārāyaṇa without satsaṅga even a man knowledge and erudition degenerates.[8] In the company of holy saints, even a dog-like man becomes a religious man, and attains desirelessness.[9] A true saint inspires even a sinful man to lead a life of Dharma, Bhakti and Vairāgya.[10] According to Svāminārāyaṇa a true saint is one whose mind remains steady in all conditions, good or bad.[11]

According to Svāminārāyaṇa, saints are the pillars of society.[12] When a man devoutly loves and serves a holy saint, he raises his self to the level of that saint.[13] True love for a saint becomes a means of self-realisation[14] and God-realisation.[15] Svāmịnārāyaṇa has said that saint is not necessarily a tyāgī who has renounced the world. According to him, even a householder can possess saintly qualities.[16]

12. Gurubhāva and Śiṣyabhāva

According to Svāminārāyaṇa, gurubhāva means respect for seniors who abound in virtues.[1] When one respects the seniors for their virtues, one imbibes those virtues. According to Svāminārāyaṇa, Śiṣyabhāva means loving sympathy towards juniors in pupillage.[2] Svāminārāyaṇa acted as a teacher towards all those who constituted his fellowship (satsaṅga). He described himself sometimes as guru,[3] sometimes as ācārya[4] and sometimes as Bhagavān[5]. He described his disciples as his āśrita (dependent). It is for them that he had written Śikṣāpatrī, the Gospel of Ethics.[6] His love and spiritual concern for his disciples are manifest on the pages of Vacanāmṛta. He answered every question of his disciples and solved their metaphysical difficulties. He answered the questions on the authority of his own direct personal experience.[7] This reminds us of the Upaniṣadic teachers who had direct experience of reality and who attempted to convey the substance of their experience to their disciples. In the Śānti stanzas of Upaniṣads we find that both the teacher and the disciple sincerely wished and prayed that they should see and hear nothing but auspiciousness. They were very keen to see that their spiritualism was not defiled by worldly forces. Hence the great prayer of the Vedic teachers that they should see and hear only goodness and purity.[8] Both the teacher and the disciple attempted together to bring perfection in the ethical life of the community.[9] Svāminārāyaṇa would fully endorse the spirit of these Śānti stanzas.

According to Svāminārāyaṇa, the cardinal function of guru is to work for the spiritual uplift of his disciples.[10] Speaking of the duties of disciples, Svāminārāyaṇa, has said that the disciples should never insult his teacher.[11] He should always respect his teacher. When the teacher comes, he should honour him by rising up and bowing to him.[12] Svāminārāyaṇa has said that the disciple should always abide by the precept of his teacher.[13] He should never violate the ethical principles taught by the teacher.[14]

According to Svāminārāyaṇism, "gurubhāva and śiṣya-bhāva" have a direct reference to Śravaṇa, Manana and Nididhyāsa. According to Svāminārāyaṇa, śravaṇa means listening to the truths of the scriptures from the lips of the teacher (guru). It is receiving instruction from the teacher.[15] Śravaṇa entails the study of scriptures under the guidance of a competent teacher. The teacher should not only be learned, but should have realised the truths through meditation.

After receiving the instructions, the students have to achieve intellectual conviction of what is taught by the teacher. In order to arrive at intellectual conviction, the student has independently to reflect upon the instructions received from the teacher. In Svāminārāyaṇa's view the independent reflection of the student for the purpose of arriving at intellectual conviction is called Manana. Svāminārāyaṇa says that, from the instructions of the teacher, the student should accept only those ones which carry conviction with him. According to Svāminārāyaṇa this discriminatory reflection is called Manana.[16]

Nididhyāsa means constant and uninterrupted meditation with a view to transform the instructions received from the teacher into an immediate experience.[17]

According to Svāminārāyaṇa, mere study of scriptures and instructions from the teacher are not enough for the purpose of self-realisation and God-realisation. After receiving the instructions from the teacher, the student has to constantly and uninterruptedly reflect and meditate upon the truth contained in those instructions. He has to do this day in and day out. According to Svāminārāyaṇa, this every day act of constant and continuous reflection and meditation is called Nididhyāsa. If he performs Nididhyāsa, he will attain self-realization and God-realisation. It he does not perform it, he will never attain self-realisation and God-realisation, even though he may study the scriptures and receive instructions for the whole of his life.

13. Mitrabhāva

Svāminārāyaṇa has emphasised mitrabhāva as a means of attaining liberation which is the highest goal of human life. According to Svāminārāyaṇa, mitrabhāva is a feeling of friendliness towards equals.[1] In view of Svāminārāyaṇa mitrabhāva is an important aspect of religious life. Mitrabhāva cannotes good-will and love.

It is very well known that hatred operates as a very great obstacle in the progress of spiritual life. Hatred generates hatred. A harsh word excites a harsh word. Therefore, hatred should be conquered by love which is contained in mitrabhāva. The cultivation of mitrabhāva or friendliness produces cheerfulness and serenity of mind.

What is called Mitrabhāva by Svāminārāyaṇa is referred to as maitry in Yoga sūtras of Patañjali. The importance of maitry in the progress of religious life has been accepted by Yoga, Jainism and Buddhism also. According to Yoga, Jainism and Buddhism, the moral aspirant should observe good-will and friendliness towards all living creatures. Svāminārāyaṇa would completely endorse this idea.

14. God's Grace as the Ultimate Means of Liberation

According to Svāminārāyaṇa, liberation is not a mere matter of attainment. It is a matter of God's gift (Kṛpā) also. Liberation cannot be attained only by human efforts. Grace of God is indispensable for it. There can be no liberation without grace of God.[1] Svāminārāyaṇa believes that man's salvation is dependent on God's grace. Two facts are to be noted about grace. One, grace is something which we cannot earn by our efforts. It is a free gift of God. Even in Old Testament this principle is accepted.[2] Two, it is not a matter of right to receive grace. There is no vested right in the grace of God. The grace is not a matter of contract between soul and God.

According to Śaṅkara, mokṣa is native (nitya) and not derivative (prāptavya) to human soul. In Svāminārāyaṇism the position is other way round. In Svāminārāyaṇism mokṣa is derivative and not native. Mokṣa is not the birth right of man, it is a gift from God. This view has found expression in the Upaniṣads and in the Gītā. In Kaṭha Upaniṣad it is said that the ātman (self) cannot be gained by the study of Vedas (pravacana) nor by intellect (medhā) nor even by much learning (bahuśrutatva). It may be gained only by him whom God chooses.[3] In Gītā Arjuna says that "My delusion is destroyed. I have regained my memory by your grace."[4]

If according to Svāminārāyaṇa, attainment of mokṣa is dependent on the grace of God, a question would naturally arise. Is it that there is nothing to be done on the part of man to attain liberation? The answer of Svāminārāyaṇa, would be in the negative. According to Svāminārāyaṇa, total surrender to God is necessary to attain grace of God.[5] Svāminārāyaṇa has observed that complete surrender to God is the most effective means of securing God's grace.[6] He says that our conduct should be such that God would be pleased with it and would bestow His grace upon us.[7] How should a devotee behave to become eligible to receive grace of God? Svāminārāyaṇa says that the devotee should follow Ekāntika Dharma,[8] which consists of four virtues : religious conduct (dharma), right knowledge (jñāna), detachment (vairāgya) and devotion (bhakti) to God.[9] The devotee should worship God in deep devotion and profound sense of service.[10] According to Svāminārāyaṇa, only those who are desireless (nirvāsaṇika) and have qualified themselves by their single devotion (ananya bhakti) to God would be shown grace by

God and none else.[11] One becomes Ekāntika bhakta only when grace is shown by God.[12] God's grace can be reached only by those who take refuge in Him and develop excessive and exclusive love and devotion to Him.[13] Thus, if a man is having dharma, jñāna and vairāgya, but not having bhakti, he will fail to secure the ultimate end of God-realisation and complete release from forces of māyā, for this end is achieved only through the grace of God and this results only from the love of God (bhakti).[14] There is nothing that can buy the grace of God except total giving up of self, a complete self-opening to God. In Gītā also it is said that "Seek refuge in Him alone with all your heart. By His grace you will gain supreme peace and the enternal abode."[15]

Thus, according to Svāminārāyaṇa, liberation is both an attainment as well as grace of God. A question would arise : What are the roles of human efforts and divine grace in attainment of mokṣa? How much does the realisation depend on efforts and how much on grace? As Shri P.N. Shrinivasachari has said, "It is a holy mystery which cannot be resolved by logic, but can only be resolved by direct experience."[16] However, on this point, we find a controversy going on in some theistic schools. Notably, there are two schools : Northern School (vaḍagalais) and Southern School (teṅgalais). Northern School advances "Monkey Theory" (markaṭa nyāya) and the Southern School "Cat theory" (mārjāra nyāya). According to monkey theory, the cub of a female monkey has to make efforts in holding fast to its mother to travel to a safe place. Similarly, the mumukṣu has to make efforts to get himself qualified for the grace of God. For realisation of mokṣa human efforts and grace both are necessary. According to cat theory, the female cat holds fast to her kitten and puts it to a safe place, without kitten making any effort for travelling. Similarly, the mumukṣu has simply to surrender himself to God, and do nothing, for attaining liberation. Self-surrender (prapatti) is all that is necessary for realisation of mokṣa. Divine Grace is the sole means, Sola Gratia, of liberation. Svāminārāyaṇa would agree with the Northern School.

15. Relation of Auxiliary Means to Principle Means

From the description of the twelve auxiliary means, one can see that none of them is opposed to the rest nor are they opposed to one another. All the twelve means are complementary to one another. As a matter of fact, all the sixteen means, that is four principle and twelve auxiliary, are complementary to one another. All of them have a common goal-the self-realisation and God-realisation. All the sixteen means function on the basis that the self of man is essentially divine and is distinct from the mind-body organism with which it is wrongly identified.

These twelve auxiliary means, if they are earnestly adopted, would make the four principle means highly efficacious. Thus, according to Svāminārāyaṇa, there are, in all, sixteen means of attaining final emancipation. Svāminārāyaṇa has said that if man, who is desirous of gaining liberation, zealously adopts these sixteen means, he would surely gain it. He would unfailingly go to Akṣaradhāman in the eternal service of God.[1]

According to Svāminārāyaṇism before a man sets out on the path of liberation, he must satisfy these twelve essential conditions. In other words, these twelve means are spiritual qualifications for a man who is aspirant of Mokṣa and who desires to adopt the four principle means. Svāminārāyaṇa attaches very great importance to the possession of these spiritual qualifications of religious life. In view of Svāminārāyaṇa the practice of these twelve auxiliary means would favour the development of Dharma, Jñāna, Vairāgya and Bhakti which are principle means of liberation.

It is interesting to note that most of the auxiliary means fall in the category of dharma, which is one of the four principle menas of liberation. Svāminārāyaṇa has defined dharma as moral conduct enjoined by scriptures.[2] In other words, according to Svāminārāyaṇa, dharma means morality. Now, when we relate the auxiliary means to dharma, we find that except Śradhhā and Guruśiṣybhāva, all of them turn out to be moral virtues. And as moral virtues they are included in dharma. This means, except śraddhā and guruśiṣyabhāva, all the auxiliary means are included in the principle means. In a way these sixteen means are sixteen different aspects of religious life. All of them are interrelated. No one is complete by itself. Each one of them requires to be supplemented by the rest. According to Svāminārāyaṇa, all of them are absolutely necessary.[3] Principle means require to be supplemented by the auxiliary means. One who is desirous of attaining the final emancipation cannot afford to miss any one of them. According to Svāminārāyaṇa, a harmonious synthesis of all the sixteen aspects is absolutely necessary for attaining self-realisation and God-realisation.[4] According to Svāminārāyaṇism, one in whom all the sixteen aspects are synthesised is a person of highest spiritual attainment and such a one is called Ekāntika Bhakta. Unless one becomes an Ekāntika Bhakta, one cannot enter God. In other words, Ekāntikapaṇa is absolutely necessary for the attainment of liberation. According to Svāminārāyaṇa, the highest form of religious life can be seen in the life of an Ekāntika.[5] Svāminārāyaṇa says that such Ekāntika Bhaktas can nowhere be found except in his satsaṅga.[6]

16. Social and Moral Significance of Some of the Auxiliary Means

As shown above except Śraddhā and Guruśiṣyabhāva, all the auxiliary means are moral virtues. These means in religious life are primarily a matter of individual concern, but they, as moral principles, have far reaching implications. According to Svāminārāyaṇism, moral virtues have great social significance. Svāminārāyaṇa's philosophy is not divorced from social life. Although spiritual motive dominates his philosophy, it has an important social context. It aims at a sociospiritual reformation of the community. Svāminārāyaṇa's life-work was to organise a moral community on the basis of spiritual life. According to Svāminārāyaṇism, what makes a community a moral community is the practice of dharma (morality) by the members of that community. Svāminārāyaṇa has given foremost importance to the performance of duties and cultivation of virtues. As pointed out by Manilal Parekh, Svāminārāyaṇa has made the principles of righteousness as essential element in the life and discipline of his Sampradāya.[1] He has enjoined his followers to act always in accordance with the rules of morality with utmost vigilance and enthusiasm.[2] Svāminārāyaṇa has made the observance of moral rules obligatory on his followers. He has said that one who does not follow the moral rules has no place in his organisation (sampradāya).[3] Thus we see that the obligatoriness of moral rules occupies a central place in Svāminārāyaṇa's philosophy. Ekāntika Bhakti, advocated by Svāminārāyaṇa, must be positively ethical and holy. Svāminārāyaṇa has regarded Dharma as much important as Bhakti. According to Svāminārāyaṇism, no man can be socially acceptable unless he acts in accordance with moral rules.[4] This clearly shows that Svāminārāyaṇa was primarily interested in moral practice and social reconstruction. Apart from religious context, even in secular activities, moral laws have foremost importance. From the humanist point of view, one may not call Svāminārāyaṇa's philosophy as Dharma-Bhakti Mārga or Jñāna-Bhakti Mārga, but one would certainly call it Dharma Mārga.

REFERENCES

2. Auxiliary Means of Liberation

1. V.G.L.S. 24.

3. Śraddhā

1. V.S.S. 13.
2. V.G.F.S. 62.
3. V.G.F.S. 62.
4. V.G.F.S. 33.
5. V.P.S. 2.
6. V.G.F.S. 33.
7. V.G.F.S. 33.
8. V.G.F.S. 15.
9. Chapter 17, Gītā, Śraddhātrayavibhāgayoga.
10. Gītā 17:3.

11. Gītā 4:39.
12. Hebrews 11.1.
13. Gītā 3:3.
14. V.S.S. 5.
15. T.F. Ross, Religion in the Neo-Saholastic Tradition in Religion in Philosophical and Cultural. Perspective (1971) by Clayton Feaver and Others, p. 117.
16. Kant, Critique of Pure Reason, Preface to Second Edition, translated by J.M.P. Meiklejohn (1978), p. 18.
17. 2 Corinthians 5:7
18. Radhakrishnan, Recovery of Faith (1955), p. 42.

4. Indriyanigraha

1. V.G.F.S. 18.
2. S.P. 189.
3. V.G.F.S. 18.
4. V.K.S. 2.
5. V.G.F.S. 18.
6. V.G.F.S. 18.
7. V.G.F.S. 78.
8. V.G.L.S. 24.
9. V.S.S. 1.
10. V.L.S. 5.
11. V.L.S. 5.
12. Gītā 2:64.
13. Gītā 12:4.
14. Gītā 3:6.
15. V.G.F.S. 38.
16. V.G.F.S. 38.

5. Ahimsā

1. V.G.F.S. 69.
2. V.G.F.S. 69.
3. V.S.S. 2; V.G.F.S. 62.
4. V.G.F.S. 69.
5. V.G.F.S. 69.
6. Yoga Sūtra 2:30.
7. Yoga Sūtra 2:31.
8. V.G.F.S. 69.

9. Yoga Bhāṣya 2:30.
10. Yoga Sūtra 2:35.
11. Gītā 17:14.
12. Gītā 16:2.
13. Śrīmad Bhāgavata Purāṇa 1:13:46.
14. *See also* S.P. 93.
15. Young India, November 13, 1925.
16. Young India, March 9, 1920.
17. Young India, March 9, 1920.

6. Brahmacarya

1. Patañjala Yoga Sūtra 2:30.
2. Gītā 17:14.
3. V.G.F.S. 8.
4. S.P. 188.
5. V.G.M.S. 33.

7. Santoṣa

1. S.P. 89.
2. V.G.L.S. 24.

8. Tapa

1. V.G.L.S. 24.
2. V.K.S. 10.
3. Gītā 17:27.
4. Patañjala Yoga Sūtra 2:32.
5. Gītā 17:27.
6. Gītā 17:14.
7. Gītā 17:15.
8. Gītā 17:16.
9. V.G.F.S. 40.
10. V.G.F.S. 40.
11. V.G.F.S. 40.
12. V.G.F.S. 40.
13. V.G.F.S. 64.
14. V.G.F.S. 64.

9. Nirdambhapaṇa

1. V.G.F.S. 47.
2. V.G.F.S. 47.

3. V.G.L.S. 26.
4. Gītā 13:8.
5. Gītā 17:5.
6. V.G.F.S. 27.
7. V.G.L.S. 12.
8. Gītā 12. 18 and 19.
9. V.G.L.S. 12.
10. V.G.F.S. 56.
11. V.G.L.S. 27.
12. V.G.L.S. 27.
13. V.G.L.S. 27.
14. V.G.L.S. 12.

10. Dayā

1. Gītā 16:1-3.
2. V.G.M.S. 28.
3. V.G.F.S. 70.
4. Vivekānanda, Rājayoga, (1966), p. 20.
5. V.G.M.S. 60.
6. Sutta Nipāta, 149, 150.
7. मैत्रीप्रमोद कारुण्यमाध्यस्थानि।
   सत्त्वगुणाधिकक्लिश्यमाना विनेयेषु।।
   Tattvārthasūtra-VII.6.
8. Patañjala Yoga Sūtra 1:3.
9. Christmas Humphreys, Buddhism (1958), p. 159.

11. Satsaṅga

1. V.G.F.S. 18.
2. V.G.F.S. 30.
3. V.G.F.S. 54.
4. V.G.F.S. 30.
5. V.S.S. 9.
6. V.G.F.S. 8.
7. V.G.F.S. 58.
8. S.P. 114.
9. V.G.F.S. 58.
10. V.S.S. 18/238.
11. V.G.M.S. 23.

12. V.G.F.S. 27.
13. V.G.F.S. 78.
14. V.S.S. 11.
15. V.S.S. 11.

12. Gurubhāva and Śiṣyabhāva

1. V.G.L.S. 24.
2. V.G.L.S. 24.
3. V.S.S. 18.
4. V.S.S. 18.
5. V.G.L.S. 31; V.G.L.S. 38; V.A.S. 6
6. S.P. 2.
7. V.G.M.S. 13.
8. Māṇḍūkya Upaniṣad, Śānti Mantra.
9. सहनाववतु। सहनौ भुनक्तु।
   सहवीर्यं करवावहै।
   Kaṭhopaniṣad
10. V.G.L.S. 24.
11. S.P. 35.
12. S.P. 69.
13. V.G.F.S. 16.
14. V.G.M.S. 51.
15. V.S.S. 3.
16. V.S.S. 3.
17. V.S.S. 3.

13. Mitrabhāva

1. V.G.L.S. 24.

14. God's Grace as the Ultimate Means of Liberation

1. V.S.S. 11; F.W.W. 11.
2. Eph. 2:8.
3. Kaṭha Upaniṣad 1:2:23.
4. Gītā 18:73.
5. V. Vad. S. 10; V.G.F.S. 33; V. Vad. S. 5; V. Vad. S. 10.
6. V.G.F.S. 33.
7. V.G.M.S. 45.
8. V.S.S. 11 *See* above.

9. V.L.S. 6; V.G.F.S. 19; V.G.F.S. 19.
10. V.G.M.S. 35.
11. V.S.S. 11.
12. V.S.S. 11.
13. V.G.F.S. 38.
14. V.G.F.S. 19.
15. Gītā 18:62.
16. P.N. Shrinivasachari, Viśiṣṭādvaita, p. 174.

15. Relation of Auxiliary Means to Principle Means

1. V.G.L.S. 24.
2. S.P. 103.
3. V.G.L.S. 24.
4. *See above* V.G.L.S. 24.
5. V.G.L.S. 13.
6. V.G.M.S. 21.

16. Social and Moral Significance of Some of the Auxiliary Means

1. Bhai Manilal Parekh, Śrī Svāminārāyaṇa, (1936), p. 239.
2. S.P. 206.
3. S.P. 207.
4. V.G.M.S. 21.

CHAPTER 13

CONCEPT OF LIBERATION

1. Concept of Liberation (Mokṣa)

According to Svāminārāyaṇa, Jīva in its essential nature is pure and blissful. However, it is eternally wrapped in Māyā (avidyā). The Karaṇa Śarīra (causal body) is Māyā attached to Jīva. The Karaṇa Śarīra evolves into Sūkṣma Śarīra (subtle body) and Sthūla Śarīra (gross body). These three bodies, permanently attached to Jīva, constitute its Māyā.[1] Due to permanent attachment of these bodies, Jīva remains away from its true self (Ātma). The influence of Māyā obliterates its real nature. Mokṣa consists in becoming completely free from entanglements of Māyā and its evolute, that is, the physical organism of twenty four elements.[2] As Dr. J.A. Yajnik has pointed out, what is called Vivekajñāna in Sāṅkhya philosophy is the minimum condition of Mokṣa.[3] Though this is minimum and necessary condition of mokṣa, it is by no means sufficient condition. For, according to Svāminārāyaṇa, Mokṣa consists in realisation of one's self as distinct from these three bodies and identification of self with Akṣarabrahma and dedicated devotion to Parabrahma (Puruṣottama) as one's Lord.[4]

2. Plurality of Liberated Souls

Svāminārāyaṇism believes in the plurality of the liberated souls. According to Svāminārāyaṇa, liberated souls are infinite in number.[1] As seen above, the liberated souls maintain their separate individuality. Qualitatively all the liberated souls are different.[2] Svāminārāyaṇa has accepted the doctrine of difference in the degree of Knowledge of God possessed by different muktas. According to Svāminārāyaṇa, no two liberated souls are alike.

Rāmānujācārya, Sāṅkhyas and the Jainas accept the plurality of souls, but they do not admit any distinction between different souls in the state of liberation. Their pluralism only applies to empirical egoes. It go without saying that so long as there is conjunction between the soul and the body, plurality of empirical egos cannot be gainsaid.

Rāmānuja believes in the plurality of the liberated souls, but he does not admit qualitative distinctions among them. All the souls are of the same quality. There are no distinctions among them as regards Knowledge and enjoyment of bliss. Svāminārāyaṇa does not accept this view of Rāmānuja. Radhakrishnan suggests that, if all the liberated souls are alike, there would be overlapping in them. He asks a straight question: "What is it that distinguishes these souls from one another?"[3] Svāminārāyaṇa's answer to this question is very clear. The released souls are distinguished from one another by the different degrees of knowledge of God possessed by them. The unfathomable nature of God makes room for the infinite differences in the degrees of his Knowledge possessed by different released souls. Therefore, the question of "Overlapping of these souls" would never arise.

In Sāṅkhya system also, there is plurality of liberated souls. Liberated souls (puruṣas) are infinite. In the state of liberation the souls are of the same type. There are no distinctions among them. All are alike. Each one attains isolation (Kaivalya) for itself. Sāṅkhyas believe that puruṣa (soul) is only conscious in the state of liberation. It does not enjoy the bliss. Sāṅkhya system being atheistic, we do not get a society of the liberated souls with God at the top. All the liberated souls have eternally scattered existence. As against Sāṅkhya, in Svāminārāyaṇism, we get a society of liberated souls with Puruṣottama (God) as its all powerful Head. In Svāminārāyaṇism no two souls are alike. In liberation they enjoy graded bliss in accordance with their degrees of knowledge and realisation of God.

Jainas also believe in the plurality of liberated souls. According to them, the souls are infinite in number, not only in the state of bondage (bandha), but also in the state of liberation (mokṣa). The liberated souls (siddhas) maintain, through all eternity, their separate entity. They possess separate entity, but no separate individuality. This plurality is only quantitative. Inherently and quantitatively, all liberated souls are alike. Question of "overlapping" would arise here. Such a plurality is phenomenal (vyāvahārika naya) and not final. It is not real. In fact it is a noumenal unity (suddha naya) of the souls.[4]

As against Jainism, plurality in Svāmināyaṇism is real and final. In Svāmināyaṇism souls are eternally different from one another. No two souls were ever alike and would never be alike. Moreover, Jainism does not try to synthesise the plurality of liberated souls in some unitary system like Brahmaloka or Akṣaradhāman as in Svāmināyaṇism with God as Supreme Head. In absence of an Absolute Supreme Head, Siddhaśīla (abode of final rest for liberated souls) cannot give us a picture of a society of liberated as we get in Svāmināyaṇism.

Madhvācārya also believes in the plurality of the liberated souls. According to him, souls are infinite in number. He believe in the qualitative pluralism of liberated souls. He admits qualitative distinctions among them. These distinction (bheda) are eternal. The souls retain their individuality in the state of liberation. According to Him, each individual soul has a particular capacity for the development of Knowledge, devotion and enjoyment of bliss. The bliss of enjoying the vision and nearness of God is graded according to knowledge and realisation of God. It differs with each released soul. Svāmināyaṇa would fully agree with this doctrine of Madhva.

The position of Svāmināyaṇa is in sharp contrast to that of Śaṅkarācārya. According to Śaṅkara, there is no plurality of liberated souls. As a matter of that there is no plurality of any thing. The liberated souls merge in Parabrahma. There is only unity of Parabrahma. It is one without second. According to Svāminārāyaṇa, plurality is real and final.

It may also be noted here that Svāminārāyaṇa holds a middle position between Śaṅkara and Rāmānuja. He does not agree with Śaṅkara in holding that the souls realises itself to be Parabrahma and that there is no difference between It and the soul. He does not agree with Rāmānuja in holding that all souls are alike and that there are no distinctions in the enjoyment of bliss (Brahmānanda) among liberated souls.

The position in respect of plurality of liberated souls, as stated above, can be taken as correct position of Svāminārāyaṇism. However, Svāminārāyaṇa has said at one place that differences (bheda) in souls are not inherent, but are due to their actions.[5] This observation of Svāminārāyaṇa might appear contrary to what has been said above. One can, from this observation, argue that, according to Svāminārāyaṇa, the differences are in empirical egos only and not inherent in souls. In other words, differences are phenomenal as in Jainism and not real as in the philosophy of Madhva. But this would not be a correct statement of Svāminārāyaṇiya position for two reasons: (i) Svāminārāyaṇa has all throughout emphasised not only the eternal differences between God and souls, but between souls and souls also. This solitary observation cannot be taken to alter the uniform position of Svāminārāyaṇism in this context; (ii) according to Svāminārāyaṇa, each liberated soul is busy with the activity of knowing and having communion with God. The nature of this constant activity as conceived by Svāminārāyaṇa is such that no two souls can be said to be identical with respect to this activity. Thus, though each soul is essentially of the same nature, no soul will be exactly like another with respect to its activity. Of these two reasons, the second one is obviously fundamental.

3. No Sakāma Mukti

According to Svāminārāyaṇa, there are two types of

liberation: one, liberation with desire for liberation (sakāma mukti) and the other, liberation without any desire for liberation (niṣkāma mukti). Svāminārāyaṇa prefers the latter.[1]

Following the Vedāntic theism Svāminārāyaṇa makes another classification and says that there are four categories of liberation (mukti): One, Sālokya; two, sāmīpya; three, sārūpya; and four, sāyujya. Sālokya mukti means living in the city of God. Sāmīpya mukti means enjoying the nearness of God. Sārūpya mukti means attaining a form similar to that of God. And sāyujya mukti means acquiring lordship equal to that of God.[2] Svāminārāyaṇa says that the devotee of God should not have the slightest desire to attain all or any of the four types of mukti.[3] The devotee, who desires all or any of the four types of mukti, is called desirous devotee (sakāma bhakta) and the devotee, who does not desire such mukti, called desireless devotee (niṣkāma bhakta)[4]. Svāminārāyaṇa maintains that after realising one's' own self one should be desireless devotee.[5]

According to Gītā, there are four types of devotees: one, man in distress (ārta); two, man seeking knowledge (jijñāsu); three, man seeking wealth (arthārthi); and four, man of spiritual wisdom (jñāni).[6] In view of Svāminārāyaṇa, desireless devotee (niṣkāma bhakta) is one who is described as a man of spiritual wisdom (jñāni) in Gītā. In the same way a desirous devotee (sakāma bhakta) is one who is described as a man seeking wealth (arthārthi) in Gītā.[7]

Svāminārāyaṇa says that there are devotees who apparently seem to be desireless, but in their inner hearts cherish a secret desire to have the vision of one's own soul and attain celestical objects irrespective of the desire for God. Such a devotee is called a sakāma bhakta. When a sakāma bhakta leaves the body and goes to the other world, he does not attain the bliss of a very high type, but attains a bliss of lesser type.[8] Then, there are devotees, who apparently seem to be sakāma, but in their hearts desire nothing but the beatific vision of God. Such a devotee is called a niṣkāma bhakta. When a niṣkāma bhakta leaves the body and goes to the other world, he attains a very high type of bliss.[9] Such a devotee attains the Divine Abode of God. God would not allow such a devotee to occupy an intermediary position.[10]

Svāminārāyaṇa says that although a Sakāma bhakta devotedly worships God, worldly desires do not leave him. When such a sakāma bhakta meets with his physical end, he is taken to Indra Loka or some such place where he enjoys various heavenly objects in the company of divine damsels. But these realms of davii-gods are as good as hell compared to the Divine Abode of God. And the enjoyment of these heavenly objects, in comparison to the enjoyment of bliss in the Divine Abode (Akṣaradhāman), as good as hell like.[11] According to Svāminārāyaṇa a sakāma bhakta at the most can become a deity. Nothing more. And a deity cannot go to the Divine Abode. To go to the Divine Abode of God the deity has once again to became a human being and make efforts to become a niṣkāma bhakta. It is only when he becomes a niṣkāma bhakta, he can go to the Divine Abode. It is true that a sakāma bhakta is not condemned to move round the cycle of births and deaths like an unbeliever (vimukha).[12] Thus, according to Svāminārāyaṇa, a Sakāma bhakta is better than the unbeliever.

This means that Svāminārāyaṇa would agree with the ṛṣi of Praśṇa Upaniṣad who says that those who do Sakāma bhakti would go to the realm of fore fathers (Pitṛloka) and stay there as long as the fruits of their good acts are not exhausted. When they have enjoyed the fruits of their good acts, they are bound to come down to earth and be born again.[13]

According to Svāminārāyaṇa, a niṣkāma bhakta prefers sevā even in the liberated state.[14] To such a devotee nothing is dearer than God.[15] Nothing else than God would satisfy him. Even the four-fold liberation (caturdhā mukti) would not be acceptable to him without the service of God.[16] The theism of Svāminārāyaṇa is based on the doctrine of eternal service of God in Akṣaradhāman rather than just on the attainment of self-realisation (ātmasattā). To Svāminārāyaṇa mere self-realisation without the content of God is meaningless.

According to Svāminārāyaṇa, a niṣkāma bhakta is he who has destroyed all of his desires and passions and has made a total surrender of himself to God.[17] Gītā, says that he who has destroyed all of his desires and passions and has become free from them, will attain peace.[18] A man of complete detachment realises the Supreme.[19] In the same spirit and words, Svāminārāyaṇa says that God is never away from the man who is of firm detachment.[20]

4. Arcimārga

According to Upaniṣads, there are two paths by which the departed soul proceeds to enjoy the fruits of its acts (Karma) which it performed during its life time on earth.[1] One is called Arcimārga (the path of Light) and the other is called Dhūmamārga (the Path of Darkness). Arcimārga is also known as Devapatha (the Path of Gods) or Brahmapatha (the Path of Brahman)[2]. It is also known as Devayāna (the Vehicle of Light)[3]. It is also known as Uttarāpatha or Uttarāyaṇamārga (Northern Path).[4] Dhūmramārga is also known as Pitṛmārga (the Path of Forefathers). It is also known as Pitṛyāna (the Vehicle of Forefathers). It is also known a Dakṣiṇāpatha (Southern Path).[6]

The Arcimārga leads to Brahmaloka or Satyaloka through different regions (Loka) of Sūrya (sun), Varuṇa (water), Agni (fire), Vāyu (wind), Indra and Prajāpati. For him, who goes to Brahmaloka through this path, there is no return.[7] Pitṛmārga leads to Candraloka (region of moon) through different spheres of smoke and night. He, who goes to Candraloka through this path, after enjoying the fruits of his good acts, comes back to earth and is born again.[8] The Upaniṣadic distinction between the two paths is acceptable to Svāminārāyaṇa, for he has said that a true devotee (Ekāntika Bhakta) of God, through Arcimārga, goes to Divine Abode (Akṣaradhāman) where he, in eternal bliss, serves God and never returns therefore.[10]

According to Vedānta Sūtra, after the fall of the gross body starts the spiritual journey of the soul to Brahmaloka.

The first thing which happens is that his function of speech merges into mind. Then gradually the functions of all the organs merge into mind. Then the mind itself merges in prāṇa (vital airs). Then prāṇa merges into individual soul. After this the soul of the knower of God (jñāni) enters the vein Suṣumnā and then goes out of the body and takes the path of Gods.[11] According to Svāminārāyaṇa, the form of the body is like the form of the universe.[12] Anything that is contained in the universe is also contained in the body, but it is in the miniature form.[13] Just as there are veins in the body there are rivers in the universe.[14] There are three veins in the body: Idā, Piṅgalā and Suṣumnā.[15] The veins in the body function in unision with the reverse in the universe.[16] Out of the three, according to Svāminārāyaṇa suṣumnā is very important. It resides in the heart and is extended up to Brahmarandhra in the region of head known as Sahasrāra. When one controls Suṣumnā, one controls the Fire Vaiśvānara which resides in Sisumāra Cakra. Then the path of light (arcimārga), starting from Brahmarandhra and extending beyond Prakṛti-Purusa stands revealed before him.[17] That path of light is Suṣumnā.[18] According to Svāminārāyaṇa, arcimārga is nothing else than the Suṣumnā of the universe. This Suṣumnā functions as a vein in the body and as a path in the universe.[19]

5. Soul's Entering into God

On liberation the released soul enjoys the bliss of self-realisation and God-realisation.[1] When this state is attained by the devotee, he is said to have "entered into" God. Svāmi-nārāyaṇa says that when the single-minded devotee (ekāntika bhakta) leaves the body, he enters into the divine form of God.[2] But Svāminārāyaṇa makes it clear that this entering is not like entering of water into water or fire into fire[3], because the devotee who enters into God does not merge in God. He does not lose his separate existence. He retains his peculiar individuality. Then, what is this entering into (Praveśa)? Svāminārāyaṇa compares the devotee's entering into God with the entering of a miser into money. He further says that this entering of devotee is similar to the entering of a lover into his beloved. This entering is also comparable to the entering of a childless wealthy father into his son, if he gets one.[4]

According to Svāminārāyaṇa this "entering into" only means that the devotee, who had reached the state of God-realisation, loves God so much that he is lost in Him. He remains in uninterrupted, continuous and loving touch with God. In boundless love he is singularly attached to God only. Without Him, he would feel that the miseries of the whole world had fallen upon him.[5] In Gītā it is said that by loving devotion the devotee knows God in truth and having Known Him in truth he forthwith enters into Him.[6] The unknown becomes progressively more and more knowable to the true lover. The devotee understands God well because he sees Him with the eye of love. The more he understands God, more he loves Him. The released soul looks only on the form of God, sings His glory and contemplates only on Him.

Svāminārāyaṇa illustrates the point and says that one, who is addicted to opium-eating, would not give it up, even though it is bitter in taste and even though he is given a large amount of money, because he has lost himself in the addiction of opium-eating. Svāminārāyaṇa gives another illustration and says that a person, who is habituated in taking alcoholic drink, would not give it up. Eventhough it is pungent in taste and eventhough he is offered a large amount of money, because he has become one with his drink. Similarly, one, who is addicted to love and devotion of God, cannot give it up, even if he finds himself in evil surroundings, because he has become one with God. A person, who is in such devotional love of God, is said to have entered into God.[7] A person, who has entered into God, is never attached to any object of the world.[8] He sees nothing but God. He wants nothing but God.[9] He is sunk in His divine presence.

Explaining the point further Svāminārāyaṇa says that we should love God in the same way as lover his beloved.[10]

Out of extreme devotion and love for God the devotee loses awareness of himself[11] and remains aware only of God and nothing else. This view of Svāminārāyaṇa is supported by Bṛhadāraṇyaka Upaniṣad which says that "as a man embraced by his beloved wife knows nothing that is without or within, similarly the self when embraced by the Supreme Self knows nothing without or within.[12] In Rāma Carita Mānasa Tulsīdās echoes the same idea when he says that we should love God like a lover who loves his beloved and like a miser who loves his money.[13] This is the essence of Rāma Carita Mānasa and with this Tulsīdās closes his text.

It should be evident from what has been said above that the soul "entering into" God attains divinity, but retains its individuality.

REFERENCE

1. Concept of Liberation (Mokṣa)

1, V.K.S. 12
2. V.G.F.S. 12
3. Dr. J.A. Yajnik, The Philosophy of Śrī Svāminārāyaṇa, (1972), p. 111.
4. S.P. 116; S.P. 121.

2. Plurality of Liberated Souls

1. V.G.F.S. 21; V.G.F.S. 63; V.G.F.S. 71; V.G.F.S. 18; V.L.S. 1; V.G.M.S. 67.
2. V.S.S. 17.
3. Radhakrishnan, Indian Philosophy Part-II (1977), p. 719.
4. Radhakrishnan, Indian Philosophy Part-I (1977), p. 308, 338 See also, Chandra Dhar Sharma, Indian Philosophy, (1952), p. 81
5. V.L.S. 10.

3. No Sakāma Mukti

1. V.G.F.S. 43.
2. V.G.F.S. 43.
3. V.G.F.S. 43.
4. V.G.F.S. 43.
5. V.G.F.S. 21.

6. Gītā, 7.16.
7. V.G.F.S. 43.
8. V.G.L.S. 5.
9. V.G.L.S. 5.
10. V.G.L.S. 7.
11. V.S.S. 4.
12. V.S.S. 4.
13. Praśṇa Upaniṣad 1.9.
14. V.G.F.S. 43.
15. V.G.M.S. 57.
16. V.G.L.S. 33; Śrīmad Bhāgavata 3.29.13.
17. V.G.F.S. 21
18. Gītā 2.71.
19. Gītā 3-19.
20. V.G.M.S. 33.

4. Arcimārga

1. Bṛhadāraṇyaka Upaniṣad 6-2-2; Chāndogya Upaniṣad 4–15-4.
2. Chāndogya Upaniṣad 4-15-4.
3. Kauśītakī Upaniṣad 1-3.
4. Praśṇopaniṣad 1-9.
5. Bṛhadāraṇyaka Upaniṣad 6-2-2.
6. Praśṇopaniṣad 1-9
7. Chāndogya Upaniṣad 4-15-4; Gītā 15.16; Gītā 9.21.
8. Praśṇopaniṣad 1-9; Kauśītakī Upaniṣad 1-3-; Gītā 8-15 (6-41); Gītā 8-16; Gītā 9.21.
9. V.G.F.S. 21.
10. V.G.F.S. 21.
11. Vedānta Sūtra, 4-2-1 to 7.
12. V.G.F.S. 65.
13. V.G.F.S. 65.
14. V.G.F.S. 65.
15. V.G.F.S. 65.
16. V.G.F.S. 65.
17. V.G.F.S. 65.
18. V.G.F.S. 65.
19. V.G.F.S. 65.

5. Soul's Entering into God

1. V.G.M.S. 62.
2. V.G.M.S. 38; V.G.L.S. 33.
3. V.G.M.S. 38.
4. V.G.M.S. 38.
5. V.G.L.S. 33; V.G.M.S. 38.
6. Gītā 18:55.
7. V.G.L.S. 33.
8. V.G.L.S. 33.
9. V.G.L.S. 5.
10. V.L.S. 14.
11. V.S.S. 1.
12. Bṛhadāraṇyaka Upaniṣad 4:3:21.
13. Śrī Rāma Carita Mānasa by Tulsīdās, Uttarakāṇḍa, 130.

CHAPTER 14

STATE OF LIBERATED SOUL IN AKṢARADHĀMAN

1. Stuff of Soul's Body in Akṣaradhāman

The soul in its embodied existence in this world possesses a body which is made up of matter (prakṛti). In other words the stuff of the body of the embodied soul is matter. Even the subtle (sūkṣma) and causal (Karma) bodies are of material stuff (māyā)[1]. In the state of liberation the individual soul is freed from all the three material bodies. As said above, when the devotee of God leaves the material body and goes to Divine Abode, God gives him a divine body. Svāminārāyaṇa calls this divine body "bhagavati tanu", as already seen.

Now, the question arises as to what is the stuff of this divine body? Svāminārāyaṇa has not said anything specific about it. But he has given certain indications from which we can have some idea of the stuff of the divine body of the individual soul residing in Akṣaradhāman on attaining liberation.

"Bhagavati" is an adjective derived from "Bhagavat". It means "God-like". So "bhagavati tanu" means "God-like body." God-like body means a body similar to the body of God. The indication here is that the stuff of the divine body of the individual soul is similar to the stuff of the body of God.

We are told by Svāminārāyaṇa that God always has a human form.[2] God has always two-handed and two-legged human form.[3] And this is His original form[4]. This means God always has a body similar to human body.

Then, what is the stuff of God's body? According to Svāminārāyaṇa God is fundamentally different from matter (māyā); and therefore body of God, obviously, cannot be of matter. Svāminārāyaṇa says that the body (mūrti) of God is extremely luminous. The lustre of the body of God is equivalent to the light of the millions of suns.[5] The luminosity emanating from His body is extremely white.[6] This means that the body of God consists of some substance which emanates extremely white luminosity. What is that substance? Can we know it? In clear terms Svāminārāyaṇa says that the substance, qualities, beauty and powers of God are unfathomable and inexhaustable. But this only means that God or anything about God cannot be known completely. No one can ever know God fully and completely.[7] This does not mean that there is a blanket ban on the Knowability of God. This only means that we cannot know everything about God, but we can Know something about God. Svāminārāyaṇa would prefer to say that we can have some knowledge of God on the basis of śruti. In Chāndogya Upaniṣad God has been described as the highest light (param jyoti)[8]. Therefore without hesitation we can take it that the body of God is made up of pure (śveta) light.

Now, when the body of God is made up of pure light and the body given to the liberated soul in Akṣaradhāman is similar to the body of God, the latter should also be made up of light. So, from the indications given by Svāminārāyaṇa we can take it that the stuff of body of the liberated soul is pure light.

In the very first discourse of Vacanāmṛta, Svāminārāyaṇa says that when the devotee of God leaves his physical body and goes to Divine Abode, he gets an effulgent body (Brahmamaya deha).[9] Svāminārāyaṇa has clarified that Brahman is nothing but the light of God (Puruṣottam Bhagavān)[10] This makes it clear that the stuff of the body of the liberated soul is light. When Brahman is light of God and when released soul's body is Brahmamaya, the stuff of released soul's body must be nothing but light. According to Chāndogya Upaniṣad, the liberated soul (samprasāda) having approached the highest light (God) manifests itself in the body of light.[11] The conclusion, therefore, is that the body of the released soul in Akṣaradhāman is of the same stuff of which the body of God is and that stuff is pure divine light. However, the nature of this divine light is beyond our comprehension.[12]

2. No Merger in Release

According to Svāminārāyaṇa, in the state of liberation, the soul does not lose itself. This idea of Svāminārāyaṇa is contrary to the idea of Śaṅkara who holds that in the state of liberation the soul merges in Brahman. It loses itself in Brahman. According to Śaṅkara, he who has attained liberation, becomes one with Brahman.[1] According to Svāminārāyaṇa, liberation is not disappearance of self, but its release from limiting barriers. Merger of self in Brahman is nothing less than destruction of self.

According to Svāminārāyaṇa, the five-fold ontological differences between Jīva, Īśvar, Māyā, Brahman and Parabrahman are real. These are five reals. They are eternally different.[2] What is different cannot be identical. According to Svāminārāyaṇa, the jīva on attaining liberation does not lose itself in Parabrahman, but it persists in Akṣarabrahma as Parabrahma's body.

Liberation is one of the four ideals of human life as recognised by Indian Philosophy.[3] From the standpoint of Svāminārāyaṇism, the ideal is not worthy of pursuit, if the pursuer does not survive, after realisation of it. Svāminārāyaṇa emphatically maintains that the individuality and identity of jīva remains in-tact in the state of liberation. In liberation the separate existence of jīva is never lost.

As Svāminārāyaṇa believes in the separate existence of jīva even in mokṣa, he does not like the philosophy of Advaita Vedānta as propounded by Śaṅkara.[4] The reason why he does not like Śaṅkara's philosophy is that it is disrepresented by the modern followers of Śaṅkara.[5] He describes then as "Śuṣka Vedāntins." Explaining the difficulties in which śuṣka Vedānta is involved Svāminārāyaṇa says that if jīva is Brahman, then there is nothing for jīva to adore and worship. Śuṣka Vedānti admits that so long as jīva is the bondage, it is subject to periodical birth and death. Now, when jīva is subject to periodical birth and death and when jīva is Brahman, Brahman would also be subject to periodical birth and death.[6] So when Śuṣka Vedāntins assert the identity (aikya) between jīva and Brahman, they falsify their own doctrine of liberation.[7] On their own doctrine, when Brahman itself becomes subject to periodical birth and death, there can never be liberation of self. Under this condition of Brahman, jīva can never hope to attain liberation. In this situation jīva would eternally remain subject to periodical birth and death. In other words, jīva would eternally remain in bondage, and would never attain liberation. Such a doctrine is obviously a false doctrine and propounders of this doctrine (Śuṣka Vedāntins) are ignorant (ajñāni)[8]. Svāminārāyaṇa calls these Śuṣka Vedāntins great sinners. He says that they will never attain emancipation. Svāminārāyaṇa places Nāstikas and Śuṣka Vedāntins on the same level and says. that they are sacrilegious and people should stay away from them.[9]

Svāminārāyaṇa admits that merger of individuality is a form of mukti.[10] But he does not regard it to be the highest.[11] In the highest condition of mokṣa, the freed spirit possesses its own individuality in Akṣarabrahman. The highest state is dwelling in Akṣarabrahman in the nearness of God. Those who have attained it are freed from rebirth. Thus in Svāminārāyaṇism, release is not the obliberation of individuality, but a state of blissful freedom of soul with a distinct existence in the presence of God. God in Gītā declares that "my devotees come to me"[12] This means that the author of Gītā, like Svāminārāyaṇa, seems to believe in the continuance of individuality in liberation.

3. Similarity with God

According to Svāminārāyaṇa the released soul does not become God, but attains similarity (Sādharmya) with God.[1] Svāminārāyaṇa says that the devotee, who attains the knowledge of God, becomes like God.[2] In Gītā also God says that "he who acquires such knowledge, attains similarity with me."[3] According to Svāminārāyaṇa, Sādharmya means similarity (Samānadharmatā) and not identity (tadrūpatā). Mokṣa means elevation of soul to God like existence. The liberated soul attains the nature of God, but not identity with God. On liberation the soul becomes omniscient and acquires the intuition of God. It is egoity, and not individuality, that is opposed to liberation. As Radhakrishnan has put "in liberation we do not cease to be selves, but deepen on our selfhood.[4]

Viṣṇu Purāṇa says that the view of identity of the liberated soul with Brahman is wrong, because any substance which is different from another substance cannot acquire the character of that other substance. The iron gets magnetised when it is rubbed with magnet. Similarly the ātman becomes only similar with Brahman when it enjoys nearness (sāmīpya) with Him, but it does not itself become Brahman.[5] The liberated becomes similar to God (Puruṣottama). It does not become identical with Him. According to Svāminārāyaṇa, the knower of God attains the highest. He attains all the auspicious qualities of God.

Svāminārāyaṇa says that when the devotee, who acquires the knowledge of the glory, greatness, bliss and charm of God, leaves his body and goes to Divine Abode (Akṣaradhāman), he attains the glory, greatness, bliss and charm similar to those of God.[6] The devotee of God becomes similar to God.[7] Just as God is autonomous, the released soul also becomes autonomous.[8] Just as God is beyond time, Law of Karma and forces of māyā, so is released soul completely beyond time, Law of Karma and forces of māyā.[9]

In Muṇḍaka Upaniṣad it is stated that one who is freed from māyā, attains similarity with Brahman.[10] On the authority of this statement of Śruti, Svāminārāyaṇa maintains that the liberated soul becomes similar, only similar, to God and not identical with Him.[11]

However, according to Svāminārāyaṇa, this similarity is not absolute. It is with regard to glory, greatness, bliss, charm and enjoyment and not with regard to powers.[12] The powers of creation, preservation and destruction of the world and imparting grace to the souls are reserved by God only for Himself. The released soul reaches its autonomy in the state of release, but this autonomy does not encroach upon the powers of God. The similarity with God means similarity in enjoyment of bliss, glory and greatness and not similarity in cosmic functions of God. Infinite number of released souls have attained such similarity with God, but God transcends them all in glory, greatness, bliss and charm.[13] Svāminārāyaṇa says that powers and excellence of God are infinite and unfathomable and the devotee can never reach them. No one can ever have the same powers and excellence of God.[14] No one can ever become like God.[15]

As in other Indian Philosophical systems, mokṣa in Svāminārāyaṇism is conceived as freedom from mundane existence. But Svāminārāyaṇism has also conceived the possibility of reaching supramundane sphere (Akṣara brahman) and there enjoying the highest bliss in the presence of God.

When the devotee of God leaves the body and goes to Divine Abode, God gives him a divine body (Bhagavati Tanu) and with this divine body he resides there.[16] Even if the devotee has physical disability like blindness, leprosy, lameness, deafness, agedness and ugliness here, he gets a perfect divine body there.[17] In other words, on attaining liberation, the material body (Prākṛta tanu) of soul is replaced by perfect divine body.[18] Here it should be noted that release in Svāminārāyaṇism does not mean a disembodied state of soul as it does in some other philosophical system. As in the philosophy of Rāmānuja, in Svāminārāyaṇism the liberated soul enjoys an embodied existence. With the perfect non-prakṛtic body, the soul in Divine Abode enjoys the highest bliss in the presence of God.

4. Distinction between God and Liberated Souls

A question might arise here. When the bodies of the

liberated souls are similar to the body of God, how can God and the liberated souls be distinguished? This was exactly the question which was asked by Svāmi Nityānanda to Svāminārāyaṇa.[1] Svāminārāyaṇa has clearly answered this question. According to him, it is very easy to distinguish between God and the emancipated souls. He says that moon and stars all shine, and yet we are able to distinguish between moon and the stars. Both are distinct in their luminosity. The disc of the moon is greater than those of the stars. Besides various medicinal herbs flourish only in moon shine. The darkness of the night fades away when moon shines. The King and the King's servants are alike in their frame, and yet the King is above his servants because of his power, position and dignity, howsoever great a servant my be. The things which can be done by the King cannot be done by his servant. There is a distinction between the King and his servants. Similarly there is a distinction between God (Nārāyaṇa) and the released souls (muktas). What God can do the liberated souls cannot do. God is extremely beautious, all-powerful and the supreme cause and controller of all[2]. If He so desires He can by His divine power obliterate all the released souls of Akṣaradhāman[3] including Akṣaradhāman itself.[4] Such is the divine power and greatness of God. God is one without second. No one can attain greatness and power of God.[5] Even Akṣarabrahman cannot equal God.[6] As Dr. J.A. Yajnik has put it "the muktas go beyond māyā and become divine like God, but there remains a substantial and imbridgable gulf between their value and power."[7] God is fundamentally different from souls, either bound or released. Even though the liberated souls attain the similarity of form with God, soul remains soul (puruṣa) and God remains God (puruṣottam)[8] God reigns supreme. He is the Lord of all and the object of worship of all.[9] The distinction between God and the liberated souls is all very obvious.

5. Graded Knowledge of God

In Svāminārāyaṇism soul's knowledge of God in Akṣaradhāman is direct. The released soul directly knows

God. But this direct knowledge of God is not uniform for all the released souls. All released souls do not have the knowledge of God in the same proportion. Their knowledge of God is graded. Their capacity to know God and the proportion of their knowledge are different. Each soul's knowledge of God is proportional to its receiving capacity.[1] But this capacity can develop further. Svāminārāyaṇa has admitted growth in this capacity. Radhakrishnan has said that "Hindu thought believes in the evolution our knowledge of God. We have to vary continuously our notions of God."[2]

According to Svāminārāyaṇa the released soul's capacity to know God grows in accordance with the growth in its knowledge of glory and greatness of God. As this capacity admits of further development, there always remains a possibility of progress in the soul's knowledge of God[3]. But the infinite nature of God is never fully known by the released soul,[4] inspite of the fact that there is a continuous growth in its knowledge of God. Svāminārāyaṇa says that the released soul goes on knowing more and more about the greatness and glory of God, and with this the inexhaustible character of God's Being becomes more and more evident to it.[5] According to Svāminārāyaṇa the capacity of the released soul to know God as well as knowledge of God go on increasing simultaneously and infinitely. With the growing knowledge of glory and greatness of God, the soul's state of emancipation (muktapaṇa) goes on rising higher and higher.[6] According to Svāminārāyaṇism, the soul is always in evolutionary movement. It seeks to increase continuously in its realisation. It grows always. It grows more. It seeks to grow more and more towards highest possible reach. It progresses into a more luminous and dynamic union with God. There is a constant accession to new truths and new lights. The soul rises to higher and higher planes of spiritual existence. There is a continuous process of development, and it follows a regular gradation. The principle of graded knowledge of God is accepted in Gītā wherein it is said that God reveals to the devotee His greatness and glory in proportion to the intensity of his seeking.[7]

Thus we see that there are distinctions in the status of released soul's knowledge of God.[8] These are distinctions of spiritual illumination that the souls attain. It is difficult for our intellect to grasp these spiritual distinctions. And even if we get a hazy notion about it, it cannot be satisfactorily expressed in language.

6. Activism of Liberated Soul

The state of liberation is a state where the released souls dwell in Akṣaradhāman enjoying the bliss and glory of God, but this does not mean that souls remain eternally dormant, doing nothing. Aristotle says that "endless duration makes good no better and white no whiter."[1] Liberation is not eternal idleness. According to Svāminārāyaṇa the state of liberation is not a state of inaction. It is a state of profound activism. The liberated soul remains in the uninterrupted service of God.[2] With Akṣarabhāva the liberated soul worships God.[3]

According to Svāminārāyaṇa the liberated soul does not seek to merge in God as water merges in water. Svāminārāyaṇa would agree with Śri Aurobindo when he says that an absorbed and immersed bliss, and wideness of actionless peace, a release of self-extinction of self-drowning in the Absolute is not our aim."[4] The released soul does not seek to lose its individuality. It retains its individuality and seeks to lose itself in the deep ecstasy of His divine presence, It is not the bliss of unity, but the ecstacy of union. Reaching Akṣaradhāman is not all. The liberated soul seeks more and more ecstasy. For attaining ever increasing ecstasy, progress in spiritual life is essential. The released soul keeps on growing. It seeks to know more and more of God's glory and greatness.

It seeks to become more and more God-like. It seeks to grow into higher and higher spiritual existence. The more and more it attains the knowledge of God's glory and greatness, the higher and higher it realises the state of its liberation.[4] So there would be greater and greater activism towards greater and greater awareness of God's glory and greatness, and towards greater and greater delight of His divine presence. The state of liberation is perpetual activism on the part of the released soul for total seeing and serving God. It is essentially a state of unimpeded activity of enjoying more and more the beatific vision of God. Svāminārāyaṇa would thus fully endorse the view of A.E. Taylor who says that "In heaven there would be no longer progress towards fruition, there might well be progress in fruition". Life "there" would be as life "here" is not, living by vision as contrasted with living by faith and hope; but might not the vision itself be capable of ever increasing enrichment?[5]

7. Svāmī-Sevaka Bhāva

According to Svāminārāyaṇa, the relation between God and the released soul is that of master (svāmī) and servant (sevaka). God is Divine Master and the soul is Divine Servant. The devotee loves God and serves Him. The detached devotee (niṣkāma bhakta) prefers service (sevā) in the state of emancipation. The theism of Svāminārāyaṇa is based on the doctrine of love and eternal service of God. The released soul serves Him in Akṣaradhāman and on earth when He incarnates. For a devotee, who has realised unity with Akṣarabrahman, to serve God is liberation. Svāminārāyaṇa has said that those who do not believe in the truth of this statement are in error.[1] The sevya-sevak-bhava, that is, the master-servant relation is an essential ingredient of Svāminārāyaṇist emancipation.

The theism of Svāminārāyaṇa is not aimed at mere attainment of pure consciousness (ātmasattā). Pure consciousness without love and service of God would hinder the path of total redemption. The devotee, who has realised identity with Akṣarabrahman, would always serve God with great love and reverance.[2] The released soul perpetually remains in the service of God. God (puruṣottama) resides in His Divine Abode (Akṣarabrahman) surrounded by infinite number of released souls who serve Him.[3]

According to Svāminārāyaṇa, we should always feel that we are the servants of God who is our Master, and we should submit to His will which is always good for us. We should always have an absolute sense of servitude to God and in the sense of such servitude we should uninterruptedly engage our selves in His devotional worship.[5] Svāminārāyaṇa says that although the devotee realises oneness with Akṣ arabrahman and continuously remains in Brahmabhāva, even then he does not leave the servitude of God. On the contrary, he becomes more and more service-minded and in intense devotion serves God.[6] Svāminārāyaṇa further says that even when the devotee attains similarity with God, he continues in service of God.[7]

Svāminārāyaṇa says that the devotee, who has realised pure consciousness, acquires great spiritual power (bala). But there is better way of acquiring greater spiritual power and it is this that the devotee should engage himself, with intense dedication, in the service of God.[8] Thus, it is very clear that he who wants to make his self powerful, should serve God in absolute dedication? According to Svāminārāyaṇa, as the released soul goes on knowing more and more about the greatness and glory of God, the unfathomable character of God's power and value become more and more evident to it. And with this, the liberated soul's sense of servitude of God goes on intensifying ad infiniture.[10]

Svāminārāyaṇa says that it is not easy to be a really devoted servant of God, who surrenders himself to Him. It is very difficult to imbibe servitude of God. The reason is that unless the devotee realises that body is not real and that only soul is real, he cannot be a true and devoted servant of God. The true servant of God would never behave as a body, but body would always behave as soul.[11]

In Yoga Vāsiṣṭha it has been stated that the state of Upasana is conducive to the attainment of liberation (Nirvāṇa-kari).[12] In this world we find that the body and the soul appear to be mixed up. But really it is not so. Body is body and soul is soul. Both are fundamentally different. When we realise the difference between them, the agitations of mind become quiet. A state in which the agitations of mind become quiet is called Upaśama Daśā.[13]

According to Svāminārāyaṇa, it is only in Upaśama Daśā that Svāmi-Sevakabhāva is possible. The question would arise, How to attain Upaśama Daśā? According to Svāminārāyaṇa, the devotee, who realises the greatness and glory of God and serves Him with faith, love and devotion, attains to the state known as Upaśama Daśā.[14]

Eulogizing the service of Uddhavji, Svāminārāyaṇa says that he served Lord Kṛṣṇa with great devotion and, therefore, he has been declaimed as Great Devotee of God (Parama Bhāgavata), and has been recognised as such in scriptures and held in high esteem by the people.[15]

As seen above, the relation of the released soul with God is that of master and servant. What is the basis of this relation? Is it fear? Svāminārāyaṇa would answer the question in the negative. Svāminārāyaṇa would say that fear would enter into relationship of master and servant, and even of father and child, but that would be only when they stood on sub-human level. Control, subjection and punishment figure predominantly in such human relationships. But in Svāminārāyaṇism the Divine Master does not punish, does not threaten, does not force obedience. There is no compulsion on the released soul to serve God. It freely and voluntarily serves Him. It serves God in love. It serves God, not out of fear, but out of love to Him neither fear not force, but love alone is the basis of this relation. Love is inconsistent with fear. God is full of love and sympathy for the devotee (śaraṇāgatavatsala). The devotee feels himself utterly worthless without service of God. Apart from God he feels that he is nothing. He loves God and seeks to love Him more and more. To his love is his eternal life. In Nārada Bhakti Sūtra devotion (bhakti) has been defined as the supreme love for God (Paramapremarūpa).[16] Svāminārāyaṇa has also defined bhakti as love.[17] The devotee is totally turned towards God in love. He gives himself over entirely to Him. He wants nothing. He demands nothing. He is all over filled with devotion. Nobody else. Nothing else. No one else, but puruṣottama Nārāyaṇa total love only for Him for no one else, this is the attitude of the devotee. He is in exclusive love (ananyaprema) of God. And it is this exclusive love which is the basis of Master-Servant relation. In other words, ananyaprema is the basis of Svāmi-Sevaka Bhāva. As Aurobindo has put it, the essential relation will be that of love from which all things flow, love passionate, seeking a hundred facets of joy of union[18]. To Svāminārāyaṇa, he who loves God never perishes. In Gītā also the voice of God declares that "this is My word of promise what he who loves Me shall never perish."[19]

According to Svāminārāyaṇa, the released soul remains in eternal servitude of God. A question might arise. Is this a regrettable position? Dr. J.A. Yajnik encounters the question with a big No. He says that "this is by no means a regrettable situation for the released soul, because the increase in the knowledge of the infinity beautiful and blissful being of God also means the increase in joy, which the released soul derives from His communion."[20]

8. Bliss of Liberated Soul

It is an important feature of Svāminārāyaṇa doctrine of liberation that the liberated souls experience the type of bliss as is enjoyed by God. An objection is some times raised that the enjoyment of bliss will bind the Jīva to the wheel of birth and death. But the objection is not well-founded. The objection arises from the erroneous conception of the nature of the objects of enjoyment by liberated souls. It is to be remembered that what binds the Jīva is not enjoyment as such, but the earthly (māyic) character of the objects of enjoyment. In the state of mokṣa in Akṣaradhāman the nature of the objects of enjoyment is not material, but divine. The enjoyments of the emancipated souls are absolutely unearthly and celestial.[1] The nature of enjoyment is similar to that of God. And, therefore, the enjoyment of bliss in Akṣaradhāman does not subject the jiva to transmigratory existence.

A Question may be raised, How is enjoyment possible for the liberated soul without a body? This question is clearly answered by Svāminārāyaṇa that on attaining liberation the

Jīva acquires a divine body similar to that of God. An objection can also be raised that the concept of having a body is always associated with the idea of pain; And, therefore, even in the state of mokṣa Jīva cannot be free from pain. Embodied existence, even in Akṣaradhāman, is bound to be painful. The objection is fallacious. The fallacy of the objection is this that it assumes that all bodies are necessarily associated with pain. According to Svāminārāyaṇism, this is not so. The idea of pain associated with earthly bodies cannot be so associated with divine bodies. If the idea of pain is associated with divine body, then God Himself, who has divine form and personality, would become unhappy and miserable. But that is not so. According to Svāminārāyaṇa, God is all joy, all bliss, and all ecstacy. A divine body can never be subject to pain.

9. No Fall from the Akṣaradhāma

Once the individual soul attains emancipation and reaches the supreme abode of God (Akṣaradhāma), there is no fear of his return to this world.[1] In Akṣaradhāma the liberated soul remains in the eternal service of God.[2] He enjoys the eternal bliss of nearness of God. The emancipated soul looks upon God as his all. Nothing else than God does he want. Nothing else than God can satisfy him. He loves God beyond measure. Having attained this position of highest bliss in the abode of God, no one ever returns to the worldly existence. Nothing will separate him from God.[3] One, who has acquired saving knowledge of the divine form of God, will have no attraction for any object of the world.[4] Gītā says the same thing. In Gītā God says in clear terms that "having come to me, the great souls do not again take birth in the world which is transitory and the abode of miseries; for they have reached the highest perfection".[5] At another place God says "having gone there, they do not return. That is my Supreme Abode."[6]

Svāminārāyaṇa has categorically asserted that a liberated soul never returns to the world of Prakṛti and its evolutes. In the challenging spirit he asks : Can you point out to me a single instance of an individual who has fallen back to the world after having reached Akṣaradhāma?[7] And he himself answers that a liberated soul never comes back.[8] Svāminārāyaṇa goes to the extent of saying that even if God wants him to be away from God's abiding shelter (caraṇāravinda), he would not do so.[9]

10. Future of the Liberated Soul

According to Svāminārāyaṇa, soul (jīva) is an ultimate ontological category. It never ceases to be. It is eternal.[1] it does not die with the body. It survives death.[2] But survival is not immortal life. Immortality is different from survival. On liberation the soul gets immortality or eternal life (Akṣaradhāman) until eternal life is gained, the soul remains bound up with the weary wheel of endless births and deaths.[3]

Unlike Christianity, Islam and Madhvācārya, Svāminārāyaṇa does not believe in the theory of eternal damnation of soul. According to him, every soul is destined, sooner or later, to gain eternal life.[4] In this sense liberation is the birth right of every soul. But it does not know when. According to him, the purpose of the descent (avatāra) of God on earth is to help souls to gain eternal life.[5]

What is the future of a liberated soul in Svāminārāyaṇism? One can answer the question by saying that eternal life is the future of a liberated soul. But really speaking the question and answer both are redundant. They can be said to be misconceived. For the question has a meaning only from worldly standpoint and not from transcendent standpoint.

The worldly (māyika) existence involves time process. The wheel of endless births and deaths (lākha chorāshi) is an expression of the time process. "Future" is an aspect of this time process. So long as we are moving in the time process, that is, so long as we are tied up with the wheel of births and deaths, the term "future" has a meaning and significance. But the moment we are out of the time process, the term loses its meaning and significance. To be out of the time process means to be free from the wheel of births and deaths (bhavacakra). Freedom from this wheel is nothing but liberation (mokṣa). In other words, liberation means freedom from time process. And where there is no time process, there is eternal life. Life beyond time process is eternal life. Liberation means eternal life. In eternal life concept of "future" has no place. It is simply not relevant. There is no future there. There is only eternal now. However, we can, for the convenience of finite logic, speak about the future of enternal life or liberated soul in order to rationally understand the nature of liberation or eternal life. According to Svāminārāyaṇa, the released soul dwells in the city of God (Akṣaradhāman). There it directly knows God. But its knowledge of God is proportionate to its knowing capacity.[6] Svāminārāyaṇa has admitted growth in this capacity. According to Svāminārāyaṇa the liberated soul's capacity to know grows in accordance with the growth in its knowledge of glory and greatness of God.[7] As this capacity admits of further and further growth, there always remains the possibility of progress in the souls knowledge of God. But the infinite nature of God is never fully known by the liberated soul, inspite of the fact that there is a continuous growth in its knowledge of God.[8] This means that eternal growth in the capacity to know God is the future of the liberated soul. The liberated soul will know more and more. It will grow more and more. Eternal growth is the future of the liberated soul. It will become more and more God-like. It will attain more and more knowledge of God's greatness and glory. The more it attains the knowledge of God, the higher and higher it realises the state of its liberation.[9] To put it summarily, growth in the knowledge of the greatness and glory of God, growth in the joy of nearness of God,[10] growth in the bliss of service of God, growth in the capacity to know and enjoy, growth in the God-likeness,[11] growth in the over all enjoyment of bliss,[12] and to take birth in humanity at the will of God,[13] is the future of the liberated soul.

11. Birth of the Released Soul

A question can be raised, as was raised by Svayamprakāśānand Svāmi before Svāminārāyaṇa, in respect of the birth of the released soul : is it possible for the released soul to return to the earthly existence? Svāminārāyaṇa has answered the question in the affirmative. Svāminārāyaṇa has admitted the possibility of the birth of the released soul in humanity. He says that on liberation, when the liberated soul goes to the divine abode (Akṣaradhāman), he becomes similar to God[1] and therefore he has power to take birth. This power, however, is exercised only at the will go God.[2] It the released soul takes birth on earth, he does so as independently as God does, and like God, he is immune to the influence of time (kāla), action (karma) and matter (māyā).[3] In other words, if the rclcased soul takes birth, he consciously controls the becoming of his body and remains completely beyond the forces of māyā.[4]

It is said that sages like Apantartamas, though liberated, returned to bodily existence. Such liberated souls do so in fulfilment of a mission for the good of the world. When their mission is completed, their individual existence terminates and they go to the Divine Abode. Their mission may well be to help those in bondage to attain liberation. The liberated "cave dweller" in Plato goes again into the cave to liberate others who are in bondages.[5] According to Radhakrishnan, the freed soul, so long as cosmic process continues, participates in it and returns to embodied existence not for its sake but for the sake of the whole. He has a feeling of Kinship with all (Sarvātmabhāva).[6] At another place Radhakrishnan has said that even after gaining insight into reality, we may take an interest in the world, though our return to it of the nature of a visit and not habitation.[7] As Dr. Yajnik has put it "the birth of a released soul is similar to that of an avatāra."[8] This is exactly the Svāminārāyaṇist position regarding the birth of a released soul.

REFERENCES

1. Stuff of Soul's Body in Akṣaradhāman

1. V.K.S. 12.

2. V.G.M.S. 13; V.L.S. 2.
3. V.L.S. 4; V.G.L.S. 38; V.G.M.S. 13.
4. V.K.S. 8.
5. V.G.M.S. 13; V.G.L.S. 38; V.G.F.S. 66; V.G.F.S. 71.
6. V.G.M.S. 13.
7. V.G.L.S. 37; V.G.M.S. 67.
8. Chāndogya Upaniṣad, 7:26:2.
9. V.G.F.S. 1.
10. V.G.F.S. 45.
11. Chāndogya Upaniṣad 7:26:2.
12. V.G.L.S. 37; V.G.M.S. 67.

2. No Merger in Release

1. Brahma Sūtra, Śaṅkara Bhāṣya, 1:1:4.
2. V.G.F.S. 7; V.G.M.S. 31.
3. Dharma, Artha, Kāma, Mokṣa.
4. V.L.S. 14.
5. V.L.S. 14; V.G.M.S. 18.
6. V.G.M.S. 18; V.G.M.S. 18.
7. V.G.M.S. 18.
8. V.G.L.S. 28.
9. V.G.M.S. 18.
10. Dr. J.A. Yajnik, Philosophy of Śrī Svāminārāyaṇa (1972), p. 101.
11. *Ibid.*, p. 11.
12. Gītā 4:9; Gītā 8:23; Gītā 9:25.

3. Similarity with God

1. V.G.M.S. 67; V.L.S. 13; V.G.L.S. 39; V.G.M.S. 67; V.S.S. 11.
2. V.K.S. 1.
3. Gītā 14:2.
4. Indian Philosophy, Radhakrishnan Pt. I (1977), p. 577.
5. Viṣnu Purāṇa 7:30.
6. V.G.M.S. 67.
7. V.S.S. 11.
8. V.S.S. 11.
9. V.G.M.S. 67.
10. Muṇḍaka Upaniṣad 3:1:3.

11. V.K.S. 1.
12. V.G.M.S. 67.
13. V.G.M.S. 67.
14. V.G.M.S. 67.
15. V.K.S. 8; V.L.S. 13; V.G.L.S. 37; V.G.L.S. 39; V.G.L.S. 39.
16. V.S.S. 14.
17. V.L.S. 18.
18. V.K.S. 1.

4. Distinction between God and Liberated Souls

1. V.L.S. 13.
2. V.L.S. 13.
3. V.L.S. 13.
4. V.L.S. 13.
5. V.L.S. 13.
6. V.L.S. 13.
7. The Philosophy of Śrī Svāminārāyaṇa by Dr. J.A. Yajnik (1972), p. 112.
8. V.G.L.S. 37.

5. Graded Knowledge of God

1. V.G.F.S. 24.
2. The Hindu View of Life, by Radhakrishnan (1965).
3. V.S.S. 17.
4. V.G.L.S. 37.
5. V.S.S. 17.
6. V.S.S. 17.
7. Gītā 4:11.
8. V.S.S. 17.

6. Activism of Liberated Soul

1. Quoted by Radhakrishnan, 5, An Idealist View of Life (1947), p. 208.
2. V.G.M.S. 66.
3. V.L.S. 12; V.G.M.S. 67; V.G.L.S. 24.
4. The Synthesis of Yoga by Śrī Aurobindo (1971), p. 647.
5. V.S.S. 17.
6. The Faith of a Moralist (1931) I pp. 407-408 Quoted by Radhakrishnan in An Idealist View of Life (1947), p. 309.

7. Svāmī-Sevaka Bhāva

1. V.A.S. 1.
2. V.G.F.S. 64.
3. V.G.F.S. 21; V.G.L.S. 7; V.G.F.S. 21.
4. V.G.F.S. 74; V.G.F.S. 74.
5. V.K.S. 10; V.G.L.S. 9.
6. V.L.S. 1; V.G.M.S. 67.
7. V.G.M.S. 67.
8. V.G.M.S. 63.
9. V.G.M.S. 63.
10. V.S.S. 17.
11. V.G.F.S. 14.
12. Śrī Yoga–Vāsiṣṭha 5:1:1.
13. *Ibid.,* 5:5:20.
14. V.A.S. 3.
15. V.S.S. 3.
16. Nārada Bhakti Sūtra 1:2.
17. S.P. 103.
18. Aurobindo, The Synthesis of Yoga (1971), p. 577.
19. Gītā 9:31.
20. Dr. J.A. Yajnik, The Philosophy of Śrī Svāminārāyaṇa, p. 113.

8. Bliss of Liberated Soul

1. V.A.S. 6; V.G.F.S. 11.

9. No Fall from Akṣaradhāma

1. V.G.M.S. 10.
2. V.G.F.S. 21.
3. V.L.S. 17.
4. V.A.S. 2.
5. Gītā 8:15.
6. Gītā 15:6.
7. V.S.S. 14.
8. V.S.S. 14.
9. V.L.S. 17.

10. Future of Liberated Soul

1. V.G.F.S. 7 *See also* V.G.M.S. 31; V.G.L.S. 10.
2. V.G.L.S. 39.

3. V.G.F.S. 21; V.G.L.S. 39.
4. V.G.F.S. 21.
5. V.G.F.S. 71.
6. V.G.F.S. 24.
7. V.S.S. 17.
8. V.G.L.S. 37.
9. V.S.S. 17.
10. V.P.S. 1.
11. V.G.M.S. 67.
12. V.P.S. 1.
13. V.S.S. 14.

11. Birth of the Released Soul

1. V.G.L.S. 37.
2. V.S.S. 14.
3. V.A.S. 2.
4. The Philosophy of Śrī Svāminārāyaṇa by Dr. J.A. Yajnik, (1972), p. 113.
5. Plato's Republic.
6. An Idealist View of Life, by Radhakrishnan (1947), p. 306.
7. Indian Philosophy, by Radhakrishnan, Part-II (1977), p. 644.
8. Dr. J.A. Yajnik, The Philosophy of Śrī Svāminārāyaṇa.

CHAPTER 15

MYSTICISM AND JĪVANMUKTI

1. Concept of Jīvanmukti

The summun bonum of life is the attainment of final release in an embodied state (Jīvanmukti). Svāminārāyaṇa has admitted the possibility of Jīvanmukti. He says that mukti is attainable even in the embodied condition.[1] The holding of a physical body is not incompatible with the release of the soul. According to Svāminārāyaṇa, even during the embodied state one can experience the bliss which one would experience when one reaches the divine abode (Paramapada).[2] Jīva in its true nature is pure being (Sattāmātra).[3] The bliss of the unitive consciousness of sattāmātra self can be derived after sublating the empirical self. And to sublate the empirical self, it is not necessary to be physically disembodied. Svāminārāyaṇa promises Mukti here and now in this very life.

Śaṅkarācārya is a staunch advocate of Jīvanmukti. He emphatically maintains that release (mukti) is possible during embodied life. He believe that liberation is not inconsistent with embodiment. Rāmānuja vehemently criticises Śaṅkara's conception of Jīvanmukti. Rāmānuja asks the question : What is the definition of embodied release? And then he himself answers the question. According to him, only definition of such release can be "Release of a soul while still in the embodied condition." But, says he, this definition is self contradictory. According to Rāmānuja, the bondage means being associated with a body, while liberation means freedom from the body. In his view, to say that I have attained Jīvanmukti is like saying that my mother is a barren woman.[4]

Rāmānuja's criticism is based on the assumption that embodiedness itself is bondage. Svāminārāyaṇa does not accept this position of Rāmānuja. According to Svāminārāyaṇa, the root cause of bondage is ignorance (Avidyā) of the true nature of the self. One has to be free from the Avidyā, if one is desirous of attaining liberation.[5] Svāminārāyaṇa says that ignorance can be removed by knowledge. According to Svāminārāyaṇa, knowledge means the realisation that Parabrahma (Puruṣottama) always has a divine form and that he is the cause and support of Prakṛti, Puruṣa and Akṣara, and transcends them. By such knowledge final release can be attained.[6] So far as the knowledge-the-means-of-liberation is concerned, the position of Svāminārāyaṇa is similar to that of Śaṅkara who maintains that knowledge alone is the means of Mokṣa. Svāminārāyaṇa would agree with Śaṅkara when the latter says that knowledge itself is Mokṣa. But there is a vital difference between the position of Śaṅkara and that of Svāminārāyaṇa. According to Śaṅkara, Brahma is the supreme reality and Jīva is Brahma itself. According to him, knowledge that Jīva is Brahma is Mokṣa. In Svāminārāyaṇism, although Jīva is essentially Brahman, supreme reality is Parabrahma. The position of Svāminārāyaṇa is significantly different from that of Śaṅkara. According to Svāminārāyaṇa, Jīva can realise brahmanhood, but cannot be Parabrahma (Puruṣottama). Jīva is Brahma or to use Svāminārāyaṇa's term, Akṣarabrahma. Jīva can never become Parabrahman.[7] According to Svāminārāyaṇa, knowledge that Jīva is Akṣarabrahma is Mokṣa and it is possible to attain this state even during one's worldly life span. Thus both Śaṅkara and Svāminārāyaṇa admit Jīvanmukti.

2. Jñāni Mukta and Mahā Mukta

Svāminārāyaṇa classifies the released souls into two categories.[2] One, Jñāni mukta and the other Mahāmukta.[2] This classification is made on the basis of another classification in which Svāminārāyaṇa classifies the state of liberation into two kinds : One, savikalpa and the other nirvikalpa.[3] A soul in the savikalpa state of emancipation is called jñāni mukta by Svāminārāyaṇa and the one in the nirvikalpa state of emancipation is called mahāmukta.[4] Svāminārāyaṇa has clearly explained the difference between the two categories of the emancipated souls and the two kinds the state of emancipation.

The released souls who are in the savikalpa state of liberation can visualise Jīva, Īśvara, Māyā and Brahman as separate, like a man who, standing on the mount Meru, can see clearly and separately other mountains, trees and the surface of the earth. He sees mountains and trees as separate from each other.[5] Again a man, who is standing on the highest peak of mount Lokayata, visualises the mountains, trees and all else as earth only, but not separately.[6] Similarly the released souls who are in the nirvikalpa state of liberation cannot visualise Jīva, Īśvara, Māyā and Brahman clearly and separately. The visualise Jīva, Īśvara and Māyā as Brahman only. They do not see them separately. They see no difference between them.[7]

The result is that the souls in the nirvikalpa state pronounce that Brahman alone exists, because they speak from their vision of oneness of all entities even though these entities exist separately. Therefore they declare that Brahman alone is the ultimate truth. Svāminārāyaṇa says that this declaration is not false. It is true in accordance with their vision. They call other entities like Jīva and Māyā as unreal and false because from their nirvikalpa state of liberation they do not see these entities separately.[8] Again the theory the Jīva, Īśvara, Māyā and Brahman exist separately is also true because the souls who are in the savikalpa state of liberation can see them separately.[9] Svāminārāyaṇa says that the released souls who have attained nirvikalpa state pronounce everything except Brahman as false, by reason of their nirvikalpa state wherein the differences are not seen. But the differences are eternally there, and are rightly observed by the released souls who are in the savikalpa state. In short, nirvikalpa state denies the differences and the savikalpa state asserts them. Svāminārāyaṇa has very critically observed that those philosophers who argue for or against the truth or falsity of ultimate ontological difference without having realised any of these states, savikalpa or nirvikalpa, are absolutely mistaken and deserve to be condemned for their folly.[10]

3. Nature of Mystical Experience

Philosophy of Svāmināràyaṇa has a mystical flavour. Mysticism is throughout interwoven in his Philosophy. In fact mysticism is the soul of his philosophy. According to Svāmināràyaṇa, Philosophy is not intellectual gymnastics. For him, it is a matter of realisation of self and God.

Svāmināràyaṇa was a great mystic. He had direct intuitive apprehension of God. He always enjoyed communion with God. His view regarding the means of liberation and the manner of describing them clearly spell out his mystical vision and experience of God. He has vividly described his own experience of the vision of God.[1]

Svāmināràyaṇa makes a difference between dhyāna[2] (meditation) and Sākṣātkāra[3] (realisation). Dhyāna is Upāsanā. Dhyāna is mental configuration of God which Upāsaka derives from his study of scriptures[4] and keeps before his mind even in the highest state of meditation.[5] Sākṣātkāra is direct vision of God. The form of God meditated in dhyāna is a mental construct, while the one visualised in Sākṣātkāra is actual revelation of God. In Sākṣātkara, sādhaka is face to face with God.[6] Such a state of direct apprehension of God is called Brāhmic state.

Svāmināràyaṇa has vividly described the nature of brāhmic state (brāhmi sthiti). He has also described the process by which it is reached. One who has realised one self as Akṣ arabrahman through knowledge and meditation is said to have attained Brāhmic state. Brāhmic state is state in which the devotee realises that he is one with Akṣarabrahman. And it is only when the devotee is one with Akṣarabrahman, he becomes eligible for the worship and service of God.[7]

Describing the process of reaching Brāhmic state, Svāmināràyaṇa says that the thought (vicāra) which is of the nature of knowledge (jñānasvarūpī) plays an important role. It is constitutive of the idea that soul and body are not one. This thought stands between the soul on one hand and the body (deha), senses (indriyas), internal organs (antaḥkaraṇa), three qualities (guṇas), five objects of senses (pañcaviṣaya) and all evolutes of Māyā on the other.[8]

This thought remains steady between the soul and the senses like the flame of a lamp which remains steady in a place where wind is not blowing.[9] It does not allow the body, the senses and the internal organs to be one with soul nor does the thought become one with the soul.[10] But, when, by knowledge and meditation, this thought of soul's distinctness from body becomes really powerful and most effective, the Sādhaka loses all worldly desires. When all worldly desires are absolutely uprooted, the causal body stands destroyed.[11] With the destruction of the causal body, the above mentioned thought gets merged in the soul and heart becomes pure. In the purity of heart shines forth the light of self-heart is flooded with illumination. In the brilliance of that illumination, says Svāmināṛāyaṇā, the devotee visualises his self as Akṣarabrahman. He becomes Akṣarabrahman. That is, he attains Brāhmic state. His self (ātmā) is Brahmanised. And in his Brahmanised self he visualises Parabrahman (God).[12] He is face to face with God. He becomes full of divine bliss. He feels one with God. He realises that he is Akṣarabrahman and God eternally dwells in him.[13] He settles himself in firm realisation that he is nothing else, but Akṣarabrahman itself.[14] He attains Brahmabhāva or, what Svāmināṛāyaṇa calls, Siddhadaśā. Here it should be made clear that, according to Svāmināṛāyaṇa, mystic is one, not identical, with God.

Describing the state of the devotee who has attained such a Brāhmic state (siddhadaśā), Svāmināṛāyaṇa says that he sees God everywhere and in all immovable (sthāvara) and movable (Jaṅgama) objects. For him even an atom is not devoid of God.[15] In the similar vein Gītā says that one who has become Brahmanised (Brahmabhūta) neither grieves nor desires. He establishes equanimity in his mind by which the great and the small, the good and the bad, are all same to him. A devotee with a Brāhmic state obtains highest devotion (parābhakti) of God.[16] Such is the state of self-realised and God-realised soul. Having reached it he overcomes delusion. And established in this state, even at the last moment when he is leaving his body, he attains final emancipation (Brahma-nirvāṇam).[17]

4. Supernormal Powers

Supernormal powers are those powers which are not normally exercised by human beings. These powers lie hidden in every human being. They require to be developed. Svāminārāyaṇa believes in the possibility of the development of supernormal powers.

According to Svāminārāyaṇa, one who has perfected his sādhanā by spiritual discipline acquires supernormal powers.[1] Such a person can see his own self. He can also the divine personality of God residing in his self.[2] Not only this, He can see the selves of other beings.[3] He can enter into the body of any being and through that body can see and hear everything.[4] He can see the past, present and future of any place or being.[5] He can project his astral body and enter anywhere he likes.[6] Quoting the scripture Svāminārāyaṇa says that Śukaji could enter the tree and speak therefrom.[7] Such a person can hear any speech or dialogue taking place in any part of the universe.[8] He can know everything in the universe from where he is.[9] Thus he acquires the powers of clairvoyance and clareaudience. Modern science indicates this possibility by the expression "extension of faculty", and clairvoyance and telepathy have been proved by psychical research conducted by the well known scientists like J.B. Rhine.

It should, however, be noted that Svāminārāyaṇa does not favour the exhibition of supernormal powers. In fact he is against their exhibition[10]. It should also be noted that a man having supernormal powers appears like an avatāra, but in fact he is not. He is merely a realised soul.

5. Jīvanmukta and Morality

The liberated person (Jīvanmukta) realises the distinction between the field (kṣetra) and the knower of the field (Kṣetrajña). He realises that Kṣetra consists of three bodies, namely, gross (sthūla), subtle (Sūkṣma) and causal (Karaṇa) and three states, namely, waking (Jāgrata), dreaming (Svapna) and deep sleep (Suṣupti). He realises that the Kṣetra is impure (Malina), non-sentient (Jaḍa) and Perishable (Nāśavanta). He experiences that he is free from the influence of the Kṣetra and feels that the characteristics of the Kṣetra are not within him. He is the knower of the Kṣetra (Kṣetrajña) and absolutely pure (Atiśuddha), formless (Arūpa) sexless (Aliṅga) and sentient (Cetana). He feels that he is distinct from three bodies and three states. With this realisation he worships God.[1]

Outwardly there is no difference between the liberated man and the man in bondage. But inwardly both are quite different. Outwardly the liberated appears to be like an unliberated man, but inwardly he feels no attachment to his body. He knows that he is not the body. He is separate from the body. He feels that he is Akṣarabrahma itself and Para-brahma Puruṣottama is perpetually present in him.[2] He believes that he is pure Brahma who transcends both Prakṛti and Puruṣa. He is steadfast in his belief that Brahma is the only truth and all the evolutes of Prakṛti are false.[3] He realises that God is the sole cause and support of everything.[4] God is the Prime Mover.[5] Without His will nothing can be done.[6] He realises that all the activities done by his body are nothing but guṇas acting upon guṇas, and he is a mere passive observer. He feels that it is only God who is acting through his body and his body is simply an instrument for the activities of God. He is not moved by the objects of the world. Even the most enchanting objects cannot attract him. He is not after objects. He is away from them. He would accept only the most essential objects which might be necessary to sustain his body, but he would never get entangled in them. He would never be a slave of objects. He would ever be master of them.[7]

According to Svāminārāyaṇa, the self is bound only by those actions which are performed with the sense of egoity and attachment.[8] The liberated person has the mystical experience of self-realisation and God-realisation; and therefore, he goes beyond the sense of egoity and attachment.[9] And thus, when he is bereft of such egoity and attachment, both of gross and subtle bodies, he is not bound by the actions performed through these two bodies, because he behaves purely as a soul.[10] A liberated person is self-realised soul (Ātmajñānī). And he, who has realised his self, is not bound by his actions.[11]

Gītā calls Jīvanmukta a man of steady wisdom (Sthitaprajña). A very nice description of the characteristic features of the inner life of Sthitaprajña is given in verse 56 of chapter 2 of Gītā. Here, the Shtitaprajña has been described as one whose mind is not shaken by adversity, who does not hanker after pleasures and who is free from attachment, fear and anger.[12] Such a self-realised person is always cheerful and he neither grieves nor desires.[13] To him a clod of earth, a stone, gold,[14] honour and dishonour[15] are all alike. Svāminārāyaṇa fully endorses this description and says that no object of the world can ever bind such a self-realised person (Jñānī)[16].

6. Jīvanmukta and Society

We have described the inner experience of Jīvanmukta. Now we shall describe his outer conduct. Outer conduct has a reference to his social intercourse. We shall form some idea of the social life of Jīvanmukta. The ideal of Svāminārāyaṇism is not negativism,[1] but performance of actions in a detached spirit.[2] Ideal is not Naiṣkarmya, but Niṣkām Karma. So much so that even the desire for mokṣa should not be entertained.[3]

The liberated man has no end to achieve. He has no axe of his own to grind. He works without any fear of further bondage. Work fetters a man only when it is performed with attachment. The jīvanmukta works without hope of gain and is not affected by success or failure. He simply acts for the good of the people. He works for social consolidation (Lokasaṅgraha). According to Svāminārāyaṇa, action is not eliminated for the liberated soul.[4] Svāminārāyaṇa maintains that the case of a self-realised person who renounces the world, adopts a life of total renunciation and lives in seclusion is a case of empty self-realisation.[5] A self-realised person who engages himself in the meditation of God and social service excels the person who lives a life of total renunciation in seclusion.[6] In the words of Dr. J.A. Yajnik, "the jīvanmukta passes his life either in worshipping and meditating upon God or keeps himself busy with activities which would help as many members of society as possible to realise the true end of their life. The latter is regarded by Śrī Svāminārāyaṇa as far more preferable to the former. He has, therefore, strongly recommended it."[7]

This social service is not thought to be incompatible with liberation by Svāminārāyaṇa. Even for one who has attained jīvanmukti selfless activity is necessary for the good of those who are still in bondage. The Jīvanmukta helps others in their spiritual quest for perfection. Svāminārāyaṇa has gone to the extent of saying that the saint who does not help humanity to attain spiritual freedom is to be considered as impotent (Asamartha).[8]

Like Christianity Svāminārāyaṇism lays a great deal of emphasis on social work and on humanistic ethics. The liberated man is the ideal of society and his life is worthy of imitation by people at large. In his own life of intense social service Svāminārāyaṇa had followed this ideal. This ideal is advocated by eminent modern Vedāntists like Svāmī Vivekananda.[9]

An important point regarding morality vis a vis the liberated (Jīvanmukta) requires to be considered. As we saw earlier, a self-realised man goes beyond the sense of egoity and attachment for wordly objects and he is, therefore, not bound by his actions.[10] Just as God is not bound by his good (śubha) or bad (Aśubha) actions, jīvanmukta is also not bound by his good or bad actions.[11] A question can legitimately be asked : does this mean that a self-realised man would do immoral actions without being responsible for them? Svāminārāyaṇa has given a categorical answer to this question. He has clearly said that it is impossible for a self-realised man to do an immoral act.[12] He would never do an immoral act.[13] Having discarded Adharma totally, he firmly remains established in Dharma.[14] He can never become immoral. The liberated, who was so far the servant of moral law, becomes master of it. As A.K. Lad has put it, the mokṣa is not a lapse into immorality, but a state of super-moral perfection.[15]

The conception of jīvanmukti has always remained controversial among the Vedāntins, even among the followers of Śaṅkara. Rāmānuja, Madhva, Vallabha, Nimbārka and other Vaiṣṇava Vedāntins have rejected the conception of jīvanmukti. They believe that there cannot be mokṣa so long as body exists. Absolute freedom and embodiment are not compatible. According to them Jīvanmukta is a self-contradictory conception. Svāminārāyaṇa does not agree with this view of Vaiṣṇava Acāryas. Svāminārāyaṇa believes that jīvanmukti is not a matter of argumentation but a matter of spiritual experience[16]. According to Svāminārāyaṇa, jīvanmukta is a person who has attained the state of liberation (siddhadaśā). A person who has acquired siddhadaśā sees God everywhere all around him in all movable and immovable objects.[17] Gītā says that a man of true knowledge sees God everywhere. But such persons of true knowledge are very rare.[18]

According to Svāminārāyaṇa jīvanmukti is a very important ideal in the spiritual life of an individual. It inspires the individual to transform his life here and now. Such an important ideal cannot be rejected. A.K. Lad has very aptly remarked that the conception of jivanmukti is a very valuable contribution of Indian Philosophy to the world thought and we cannot afford to abandon it just because it creates certain difficulties in our way of systematisation.[19]

REFERENCES

1. Concept of Jīvanmukti

1. V.G.L.S. 2; V.G.L.S. 7.
2. V.G.M.S. 45.
3. V.G.M.S. 66.
4. M. Yamunācārya, Rāmānuja's Teachings, p. 124 quoted in the concept of Liberation in Indian Philosophy by A.K. Lad (1967), p. 143.
5. V.G.F.S. 12.
6. V.L.S. 7.
7. V.K.S. 8; V.L.S. 13; V.G.L.S. 39.

2. Jñāni Mukta and Mahā Mukta

1. V.G.F.S. 39.
2. V.G.F.S. 39.
3. V.G.F.S. 39.
4. V.G.F.S. 39.
5. V.G.F.S. 39.
6. V.G.F.S. 39.
7. V.G.F.S. 39.
8. V.G.F.S. 39.
9. V.G.F.S. 39.
10. V.G.F.S. 39.

3. Nature of Mystical Experience

1. V.G.M.S. 13; V.G.M.S. 13.
2. V.A.S. 1.
3. V.S.S. 3.
4. V.S.S. 13.
5. V.G.F.S. 19.
6. *See above* V.G.M.S. 13; *See also* V.G.M.S. 62.
7. V.L.S. 7.
8. V.G.M.S. 62.
9. V.G.M.S. 62.
10. V.G.M.S. 62.
11. V.G.M.S. 62; *Also* V.G.M.S. 66.
12. V.G.M.S. 62.
13. V.G.M.S. 62.

14. V.G.L.S. 3.
15. V.K.S. 7; Gītā 6:30; Gītā 7:19.
16. Gītā 18:54.
17. Gītā 2.72.

4. Supernormal Powers

1. V.A.S. 1.
2. V.G.M.S. 62.
3. V.G.F.S. 72.
4. V.G.F.S. 68.
5. V.J.S. 5.
6. V.G.F.S. 68.
7. V.G.F.S. 68.
8. V.S.S. 2.
9. V.J.S. 5.
10. V.A.S. 1.

5. Jīvanmukta and Morality

1. V.P.S. 3; S.P. 116.
2. V.S.S. 12.
3. V.G.M.S. 30.
4. *See above* V.L.S. 7.
5. V.G.F.S. 78.
6. V.G.F.S. 78.
7. *ibid.*
8. V.S.S. 14.
9. V.G.M.S. 66.
10. V.S.S. 14.
11. V.S.S. 14.
12. Gītā 2:36
13. Gītā 18:54.
14. Gītā 14:24.
15. Gītā 12:18.
16. V.L.S. 10.

6. Jīvanmukta and Society

1. V.V.S. 17.
2. V.G.M.S. 65.
3. V.G.F.S. 43.

4. V.V.S. 17.
5. V.V.S. 17.
6. V.V.S. 17.
7. Philosophy of Śrī Svāminārāyaṇa, by Dr. J.A. Yajnik (1972), p. 115.
8. V.G.F.S. 31.
9. Vide, Practical Vedānta, by Svāmī Vivekānanda.
10. V.V.S. 14.
11. V.S.S. 11.
12. V.S.S. 14.
13. V.G.L.S. 26.
14. V.G.M.S. 66.
15. The Concept of Liberation in Indian Philosophy by A.K. Lad, (1967), p. 119.
16. V.G.M.S. 66.
17. V.K.S. 7.
18. Gītā 6:30; Gītā 7:18.
19. The Concept of Liberation in Indian Philosophy by A.K. Lad, p. 150.

PART FIVE
SOME COMPARISONS

CHAPTER 16

SOME COMPARISONS

1. Introductory Remark

We have come to the end of our studies. In the preceding pages we have attempted to narrate the philosophy of self as found in Svāminārāyaṇism. We, now, propose to compare Svāminārāyaṇa's philosophy of self with those of Śaṅkara, Rāmānuja, Madhva, Vallabha and Plato. We shall attempt to bring out points of agreement and disagreement between Svāminārāyaṇa and these philosophers.

2. Svāmīnārāyaṇa and Śaṅkara

On reading Vacanāmṛta, in view of the vehement criticism of the so called followers of Śaṅkarācārya, one is likely to carry an impression that there can never be any agreement between Svāminārāyaṇa and Śaṅkarācārya on any point. But such an impression would be far from correct. It is true that differences between Svāminārāyaṇa and Śaṅkara are many and more striking. But that does not mean that they do not and would not agree on any point. They do agree on certain points. We shall attempt to bring out certain points of agreement and disagreement between the two. First we shall note the points on which both Svāminārāyaṇa and Śaṅkara agree. The following are the points of their agreement.

1. Both believe in the authority of Vedas and also other orthodox scriptures like Upaniṣads, Bhāgavata, Purāṇas and Smṛti.
2. Both are opposed to Jainism.
3. According to both, selves (jīvas) and the world are beginningless.

4. According to Śaṅkara, every one is conscious of the existence of one's own self. No one thinks "I am not."[1] But although we know that the self is, we do not know what it is. According to Śaṅkara, self is both known and unknown.[2] Svāmināṛāyaṇa, would completely agree with this view of Śaṅkara. According to Svāmināṛāyaṇa, one can have knowledge of self only about its existence and not about its metaphysical nature. According to Svāmināṛāyaṇa, self is, to use the words of Dr. J.A. Yajnik, "mediately suggested rather than immediately known."[3] This means that according to both Svāmināṛāyaṇa and Śaṅkara, we can have knowledge about the existence of self, but we cannot have knowledge as to what it's nature actually is. In other words, according to both, we cannot have the knowledge of ontological character of self. Thus, according to both, self is both known-knowable and unknown-unknowable.

5. According to Śaṅkara, the superimposition of one's self on one's body is a glaring instance of one's beginningless ignorance. Svāmināṛāyaṇa also regards the identification of one's own self with one's body as a case of ignorance. This ignorance can be removed by absolute knowledge (Kevalajñāna) according to Śaṅkara and discriminatory knowledge (Vivekajñāna) according to Svāmināṛāyaṇa.

6. Both believe in the law of Karma.

7. Both believe in the efficacy of Knowledge of effect mokṣa (liberation). Of course, Svāmināṛāyaṇa's concept of Knowledge is different from that of Śaṅkara.

8. Both believe in the interminable nature of mokṣa. Once liberated is liberated for ever. According to both, once the state of liberation is attained, there is no return from it.

9. Both believe in liberation while embodied (jīvanamukti).

Thus, there are several points of which Svāminārāyaṇa is found to be one with Śaṅkara. In fact, if we keep aside, Śaṅkara's ultimate point of view and focus our attention only on what he has said from the empirical standpoint, we find that there is more agreement than disagreement between them. Even if we look into the individual self's empirical relation to God, Svāminārāyaṇa's view does not appear to be in conflict with that of Śaṅkara. According to both Svāminārāyaṇa and Śaṅkara, God is the highest object of worship for individual selves. According to both, God is the giver of fruits to individual selves according to their deeds.

Now, we shall attempt to bring out the salient points of disagreement between the two great philosophers. The differences between them are striking and fundamental.

1. Śaṅkara makes a distinction between Jīva and Ātman. According to Śaṅkara, Ātman is a metaphysical entity and Jīva is an empirical entity. In Śaṅkara's view, when Ātman is associated with antaḥkaraṇa (internal organ) it becomes Jīva. Svāminārāyaṇa does not admit any distinction between Jīva and Ātman. For him, Jīva, Ātman and Jīvātman are synonyms. According to Svāminārāyaṇa Jīva is the real subject of knowledge. Antaḥkaraṇa which is the outcome of matter[4] cannot be the subject of knowledge.

2. According to Śaṅkara, Brahman alone is the supreme reality. All finite selves are nothing but appearances of Brahman. The relation between the self and Brahman is that of identity. Self and Brahman are not different. They are one. According to Śaṅkara, the individual self is nothing but Brahman limited by the unreal adjuncts caused by Māyā. There is no reality in such a thing as an individual soul absolutely different from Brahman.[5] According to Svāminārāyaṇa, God (Puruṣottama) is the supreme reality. But individual selves are not appearances of God. Individual selves are as real as God. They are, according to Svāminārāyaṇa, eternally different from God. They are eternally co-existent with God.

3. According to Śaṅkara, Self is only one. There cannot by many selves. Any finite self is identical with Brahman. Plurality of selves is unreal. The appearance of plurality of selves is caused by Māyā. Svāminārāyaṇa refutes this monastic doctrine and says that selves are many. Manyness of selves is not an appearance, but a stark reality. Svāminārāyaṇa advocates the doctrine of plurality of selves. According to Svāminārāyaṇa, selves are not only different from God, but are different from one another also. Each self is distinct from the other. There is an infinite number of selves, each having its own distinct and inalienable individua- lity.

4. According to Śaṅkara, self is pure consciousness only. It is not a conscious subject or a knowing subject. If self is a mere knowing subject, it will not remain immutable, because knowing will involve change. But, real self is immutable. And, therefore, self is not a conscious subject but consciousness itself. Svāminārāyaṇa repels this position of Śaṅkara and says that self is not mere consciousness. Self is a spiritual substance in which consciousness inheres as an inseparable quality. According to Svāminārāyaṇa as the consciousness is a quality, knowing does not involve any change in the self which is the underlying substance of that quality.

5. From the above point of difference between Śaṅkara and Svāminārāyaṇa, another point of difference between them emerges. According to Śaṅkara, self itself is knowledge. Knowledge is the nature of Self. There is no Knowledge apart from self.

   Svāminārāyaṇa is in total disagreement with this position of Śaṅkara. According to him, Knowledge is the quality of self. Knowledge, by itself, independent of self, does not exist. It exists only as a quality of self. In the self Knowledge by itself is never possible. Knowledge is not possible without knowing subject. As pointed out by Dr. J.A. Yajnik, "Svāminārāyaṇa believes that

Knowledge is always of a reality, and belongs to reality, and therefore should not be regarded as a reality itself."[6]

6. According to Śaṅkara, as Brahman is the only reality, the self, the object of knowledge as well as the instruments of Knowledge are unreal. And therefore, all knowledge is false, false in its very inception. Svāminārāyaṇa is a thorough realist. According to him, self, the object of Knowledge as well as the instruments of knowledge are real. The objects are not created by perceiving mind. They are there and exist irrespective of perceiving mind. And therefore, according to Svāminārāyaṇa, all knowledge is real.

7. According to Śaṅkara, the self is ubiquitous (vibhu). According to Svāminārāyaṇa self is not ubiquitous. It is atomic (aṇu). According to Śaṅkara, self cannot be of the atomic size. The position of Śaṅkara on this point, as worked out by Dr. G.N. Joshi, is that "if the self is of the atomic size, the fact of sensation extending over the whole body cannot be accounted for".[7] The answer of Svāminārāyaṇa to the position of Śaṅkara is that the self pervades the whole body by means of its quality, namely, consciousness. He illustrates the point and explains that just as a lamp placed in the centre of the room, is seen to extend to the whole of the room, in the same way the consciousness of the self dwelling in the heart pervades the entire body.[8] Svāminārāyaṇa has clarified that it is consciousness, and not the self, which is ubiquitous.[9]

8. According to Śaṅkara, Brahman is non-active and the self being Brahman itself, is also non-active. According to Śaṅkara all action is unreal and false. Brahman is the only reality, one without the second, therefore agency cannot be attributed to Brahman. Now, self is Brahman and therefore agency cannot be attributed to self. According to Śaṅkara, self is never an agent (Kartā). Svāminārāyaṇa repudiates the Śaṅkarite doctrine of non-agency of self. According to Svāminārā-

yaṇa, self is an agent.[10] In his view, agency belongs to self as its inherent attribute. If agency is denied to self, then according to Svāminārāyaṇism, endeavours for attainment of liberation involving Bhakti and Upāsanā, would become impossible with the result that no self in bondage would ever be in a position to attain liberation.

9. According to Śaṅkara, the ultimate reality, Brahman, is formless and impersonal. According to Svāminārāyaṇa, the ultimate reality has form and personality. Svāminārāyaṇa calls his God Supreme Person (Puruṣottama) who always has a two-armed and two-legged divine personality like a human being. Svāmīnārāyaṇa advances various arguments against the doctrine of formlessness and impersonality of the ultimate reality as advocated by Śaṅkara. With great vehemence Svāminārāyaṇa seeks to establish that the ultimate reality possesses both form and personality. Svāminārāyaṇa says that if God is formless He cannot undertake any activity. Without form no activity is possible.

10. According to Śaṅkara, Conceptual knowledge of Brahman is not possible. The moment we attempt to describe Brahman in rational terms, It is brought down to the position of finite. According to Śaṅkara, as observed by S.R. Bhatt, "the Knowledge of Brahman is in the form of identity consciousness which means realising oneself as identical with Brahman."[11] Svāminārāyaṇa also believes that conceptual Knowledge of God is not possible. According to Svāminārāyaṇa, God is beyond the reach of either sense or reason.[12] But that does not mean that Knowledge of God is an impossibility. According to Svāminārāyaṇa, God can be known by intuition. One can have personal intuitive experience of God.[13] As Dr. J.A. Yajnik has worked out" the released soul definitely knows God."[14] But according to Svāminārāyaṇa, God cannot be completely known. No one can completely know God.[15] Greatness and

glory of God are inexhaustable and unfathomable. Therefore, complete knowledge of God is an impossibility. The self attains the Knowledge of God according to its receiving capacity. Of course, Svāminārāyaṇa has admitted the growth in the receiving capacity of the soul. According to Svāminārāyaṇa the more it knows the greatness and glory of God, the more its capacity to know God increases. Thus, we can see a sharp disagreement between the views of Śaṅkara and Svāminārāyaṇa on the point of Self's knowledge of God.

11. On the question of liberation both the philosophers adopt diametrically opposite attitudes. According to Śaṅkara, path of knowledge is the only path of liberation and all other paths are subordinate to it. For Śaṅkara ignorance of the soul that it is Brahman constitutes bondage and knowledge that it is Brahman constitutes liberation. According to Śaṅkara, Knowledge itself is liberation. Svāminārāyaṇa advocates path of devotion (Bhaktimārga). But according to Svāminārāyaṇa, devotion must be coupled with knowledge. For Svāminārāyaṇa Knowledge is essential for attaining liberation. But both interpret Knowledge in different ways. According to Śaṅkara, liberating Knowledge is the Knowledge of Self's identity with Brahman. According to Svāminārāyaṇa, liberating Knowledge is Knowledge of the essential nature of the five ultimate reals. For Svāminārāyaṇa mere knowledge are not enough for attaining liberation. According to Svāminārāyaṇa, God's grace is SINE QUA NON for attaining liberation.

With great vehemence Svāminārāyaṇa criticises the Advaita doctrine that Jīva (self) is Brahman (God). He openly shows his dislike for this Advaita doctrine.[16] According to Śaṅkara, the attainment of Knowledge that "I am Brahman" is liberation (mokṣa). Till this saving Knowledge is gained, Jīva remains tied upto with the chain of birth and death. Now, if jīva is Brahman, Brahman will also become subject to the cycle of birth and death. This will make Brahman subject to periodical births and deaths.[17] By saying that jīva is Brahman, Advaita Vedāntins falsify their own doctrine of liberation.[18]

12. According to Śaṅkara, the self in the state of liberation merges in Brahman and loses its individuality. On liberation the self becomes one with Brahman. Svāminārāyaṇa strongly repredicates this Advaita doctrine. He vehemently opposes this theory of Śaṅkara which entails obliteration of individual self as the ultimate goal of life. According to Svāminārāyaṇism, self effacement can never be the goal of life. In very clear terms Svāminārāyaṇa explains his doctrine of liberation and says that self is eternally distinct and different from God and retains its unique individuality in the state of liberation. Even in the state of liberation self remains distinct and different from God. Not only this. In the state of liberation the self attains similarity (sādharmya) with God. In the state of liberation the self attains a divine body (bhagavati tanu) similar to that of God and with that divine body it enjoys divine communion with God and eternally remains in the blissful service of God. Thus we find resemblances and difference between the views of Śaṅkara and Svāminārāyaṇa. By and large Indian thinkers have attempted to formulate doctrines regarding the relation of finite self with infinite Brahman (God) either in terms of identity or in terms of difference. Śaṅkara, as is well known, is the propounder of the ultimate identity between self and Brahman, while Svāminārāyaṇa is the advocate of eternal difference between them. It is worth nothing that when Svāminārāyaṇa criticises the Advaita doctrine of Śaṅkara in severe terms, he appears to be an ardent propounder of Dvaita Philosophy, a Philosophy of eternal difference. But when he interprets the monistic doctrines of scriptures, he appears to be a staunch advocate of monism. As pointed out by Dr. J.A. Yajnik, Svāminārāyaṇa systematically avoids the extremes of

Abstract Monism and unqualified Pluralism, and yet retains in its synthetic system the elements of truth contained in both of these extreme positions.[19] In other words, Svāminārāyaṇism stands for reconciling the truth of both Monism and Pluralism.[20]

3. Svāminārāyaṇa and Rāmānuja

It is well known that philosophy of Rāmānuja is Viśiṣṭādvaita. Svāminārāyaṇa also calls his philosophy Viśiṣṭādvaita.[1] After detailed analysis of the doctrine of Rāmānuja and Svāminārāyaṇa, Dr. J.A. Yajnik has pointed out that "Svāminārāyaṇism in essence is Viśiṣṭādvaitism."[2] In certain philosophical circles Svāminārāyaṇa's Philosophy is described as Neo-Viśiṣṭādvaita. S.G. Mudgal prefers to call it Akṣara Viśiṣṭādvaita.[3] Of whatever variety it may be, the fact remains that the philosophy of Svāminārāyaṇa is Viśiṣṭādvaita.

P.B. Vidyarthi has observed that "in the religious history of India, Rāmānuja seems to have made a strong case for a true conception of self."[4] On a proper study of Vacanāmṛta one would definitely feel that this observation of P.B. Vidyarthi would be equally applicable to Svāminārāyaṇa also. A very strong case, possibly stronger than that of Rāmānuja, has been made out by Svāminārāyaṇa for a true conception of self. The reason why Svāminārāyaṇa's case for self is stronger is this that certain significant points of Madhavācārya's philosophy of self, which are lacking in Rāmānuja's philosophy, have found place in Svāminārāyaṇa's philosophy.

It will be interesting to compare Rāmānuja's philosophy of self with that of Svāminārāyaṇa and attempt to bring out salient points of similarities between them. First we shall attempt to bring out some similarities between them. They are as follows:

1. Both believe that selves are infinite in number.
2. Both believe that selves are finite.
3. Both believe that selves are eternal.

4. Both believe that self is atomic in size.
5. Both believe that self is subtle and resides in the heart.
6. According to both self is of the nature of bliss.
7. Both believe that the self is doer (Kartā).
8. Both believe that the self is enjoyer (bhoktā).
9. Both believe that the self is the knower (jñātā).
10. Both believe that the self pervades the entire body.
11. Both believe that God resides in Jīva as antaryami.
12. Jīvas in themselves are pure but are bound on account of their beginningless association with Prakṛti in Rāmānuja and Māyā in Svāminārāyaṇa.
13. Both believe in Śarīrātmabhāva. That is, both believe that Jīva is the body of God and God is the soul of Jīva.
14. For both God is the Lord of Karmas, that is, He dispenses the fruits of actions to Jīvas according to their desert.
15. Both believe that Jīva should attain Knowledge which discriminates between body and self.
16. According to both, Jīva can attain liberation.
17. Both lay stress on devotion as a means of liberation. Both believe that liberation can be made possible by Upāsanā.
18. Both believe that for attaining liberation mercy (Kṛpā) of God is necessary.
19. Both believe in personal communion with God in the state of liberation, Rāmānuja in Vaikuṇṭha and Svāminārāyaṇa in Akṣaradhāman.
20. For both of them God is the object of worship. God is the ultimate goal of our religious aspiration, according to both.

21. Both believe in Svāmī-Sevaka Bhāva in the state of liberation.
22. Both are critical of the view of Śaṅkara pertaining to self.
23. Both keep One and Many.

So the above-mentioned are some of the similarities between the views of Svāminārāyaṇa and Rāmānuja on self. Now we shall attempt to bring out important differences between them in their views on self. It should be noted that the differences between them on this point are very important.

1. Although Rāmānuja accepts the reality of Jīvas (cit), he does not regard them as altogether different from Brahman, the ultimate reality. He rather believes Jīva as constituting part (aṁśa) of Brahman in the form of Its body. Svāminārāyaṇa regards self as absolutely and eternally different from God. He, in clear terms, says that Jiva is not a part of God's body. Jīva is a distinct entity eternally co-existing with God.
2. According to Rāmānuja, Jīva, Prakṛti and God form a unity. According to Svāminārāyaṇa, it is not so. According to him, realities are distinct and different.
3. According to Rāmānuja God is an absolute reality possessed of both matter (acit) and consciousness (cit) as His inseparable qualities. Svāminārāyaṇa does not believe in the material aspect of God. For him, God is altogether spiritual and divine.
4. According to Rāmānuja, individual self is an attribute or mode of Brahman and at the same time has an individuality of its own. Svāminārāyaṇa does not accept such a dual position. Svāminārāyaṇa is very clear in his standpoint that the self is neither an attribute nor a mode of God. It is eternally distinct and different from God. According to Svāminārāyaṇa self is co-existent with God in its own unique individuality.
5. Rāmānuja does not believe in the Jīvanmukti of Jīva, because he maintains that the very association of the

self with the body constitutes bondage. Svāminārāyaṇa believes in the Jīvanmukti, because he maintains that when discriminatory Knowledge is attained by Jīva, it becomes free from the consequences of its past actions (Prārabdha Karma).

6. Rāmānuja does not admit any distinction between selves in the state of liberation. For him in the state of liberation all selves are alike. Svāminārāyaṇa posits distinction between selves even in the state of liberation. According to Svāminārāyaṇa there are eternal differences between selves in the state of liberation. According to Svāminārāyaṇa no one can completely know God. As Dr. J.A. Yajnik has pointed out "infinite wealth of God's nature makes room for infinite differences in the degrees of His Knowledge possessed by different souls."[15] According to Svāminārāyaṇa the intrinsic differences between selves continue even in the state of release. As worked out by Dr. J.A. Yajnik, "even in the state of release self retains its distinct individuality and owns distinct experiences which are organised by it into a unity."[16]

4. Svāminārāyaṇa and Madhva

Philosophy of Madhvācārya is known as Dvaita. In this section we shall attempt to bring out some important points of agreement and disagreement between Svāminārāyaṇa and Madhvācārya. First we shall note some points of agreement between them.

1. Both are philosophers of difference (bheda).
2. Both are strongly opposed to Śaṅkara.
3. Both believe in independent (Svatantra) and dependent (Paratantra) realities.
4. For both of them an eternal reality can be eternally dependent on another eternal reality.
5. Both believe in plurality of selves. According to both, souls are infinite in number.

6. Both believe that souls are as eternal as God.
7. According to both eternal souls are eternally dependent on God for their existence and activity.
8. According to both God is the only independent reality.
9. According to both souls are of three kinds: Nitya Mukta (eternally liberated), Mukta (liberated) and Baddha (bound).
10. According to both devotion to God is the most essential condition of soul's release from bondage.
11. Both believe that grace of God is necessary for attaining liberation.
12. According to both, grace of God can be won only through intense devotion and complete surrender to Him.
13. Both believe that a soul's liberation is possible only by liberating Knowledge of real difference between the soul and God through His grace.
14. Both believe that the state of liberation is an everlasting state. Once liberation is attained there is no return from it.
15. According to both in the state of liberation soul is not merged in God but retains its individuality.
16. According to both even in the state of liberation souls remain distinct and different from God and also from one another.
17. According to both state of liberation is the state of blissful fellowship with God.
18. Both believe that when souls are released from bondage, neither ignorance nor misery exist for them.
19. Both believe that bliss constitutes real nature of self.
20. Both believe that in the state of released souls attain similarity with God.

21. Both believe that no two souls are alike as regards their enjoyment of bliss. According to them no two souls are alike in any manner.

22. Both are against the position which describes God as formless (nirākāra) or attributeless (nirguṇa).

23. Both believe that God is Knowable. But they also believe that God can never be completely Known.

24. Both believe in the concept of tāratamya. Both believe that there are gradations based on varying degrees of knowledge and bliss since beginningless time. This gradation, according to both, persists even in the state of liberation.

Now we shall note some important point of disagreement between Svāmināyaṇa and Madhvācārya.

1. Svāminārāyaṇa explains the absolute metaphysical dependence of self on God by the analogy of Śarīraśarīri Bhāva. As Dr. J.A. Yajnik has pointed out "Madhvācārya has abandoned the analogy of Śarīraśarīri Bhāva and restored to the analogy of Bimba-Pratibimbavāda".[1]

2. According to Madhvācārya, the bound (baddha) souls are of two kinds: Muktiyogya (eligible for liberation) and tamoyogya (ineligible for liberation). Tamoyogya souls will never be eligible for liberation. They are eternally damned to remain in bondage. For Svāminārāyaṇa all souls are eligible for liberation. No soul is ineligible for liberation. As C.D. Sharma has observed, "the doctrine of eternal damnation is peculiar to Madhva alone in the whole field of Indian Philosophy."[2]

3. Madhvācārya does not believe in the embodied release (jīvanmukti). Svāminārāyaṇa believes in embodied release.

4. Madhvācārya does not make any distinction between the body and soul of God. Svāminārāyaṇa makes such a distinction. According to Svāminārāyaṇa, Akṣara-

brahman, physical universe (Māyā), Īśvaras (demigods) and individual selves constitute God's body. R. Balasubramanian, in this context, has said that "It has to be borne in mind that when the jīva and the physical universe are viewed as the body of Brahman, the term "body" (Śarīra) has been used in a special sense with implications of far-reaching character."[3] R. Balasubramanian has explained the position like this: "When the absolute is viewed in the context of the soul-body relation as the support and controller not only of the physical universe, but also of all sentient beings, we get a new insight into God-man relation in which following points emerge:

First, the relation between God and man is very intimate; second, man does not exist in isolation from God, third, he does not exist independently of God; and fourth; the purpose of life envisaged by man cannot and should not be opposed to divine purpose. This insight would enable man to work with hope and strength, individually as well as collectively as a community, for the higher purpose of life as willed by the Supreme Being.[4] The implications worked out by Balasubramanian are acceptable to Svāminārāyaṇa whereas Madvācārya would not fully accept them because he does not believe in this type of body-soul relationship.

5. Svāminārāyaṇa and Vallabha

The philosophy associated with the name of Vallabhācārya is called Śuddhādvaita. The philosophical system of Vallabha is popularly known as Puṣṭi Mārga. Here we propose to indicate some important points of agreements and disagreements between Svāminārāyaṇa and Vallabha. First we shall try to see some points of similarities between them.

1. Both believe in the authority of Vedas.
2. Both have similar conception of God. Both believe God as a Supreme Person.
3. Both emphasise Saguṇa and Sākāra aspects of God.

4. Both believe that the Upaniṣadic texts which speak of God as attributeless do not deny all attributes ascribed to Him.
5. Both are expounders of Bhakti Cult.
6. Both accept Bhāgavata as expounding Bhakti Cult.
7. Both regard love of Gopis of Vṛndāvana as the highest kind of devotion. According to both Gopis are the ideal devotees of God.
8. Both are opposed to Advaita (non-dualist) philosophy of Śaṅkara.
9. Both believe in the concept of Akṣara. But their concepts have different connotations.
10. According to both selves are infinite in number.
11. According to both self is eternal.
12. According to both self is real and not appearance of God.
13. According to both self is atomic in size.
14. According to both although self is of atomic size, it pervades the entire body through its consciousness.
15. According to both, the self is self-luminous.
16. Both believe that souls are eternally different from one another.
17. Both believe that God resides in selves as antaryami (indweller).
18. Both believe that self is a free agent, but its free activity is dependent on God.
19. According to both there are two states of existence for selves: One, state of mundane existence and state of liberation.
20. According to both state of liberation is a permanent state from which there is no return.

21. For both of them means of attaining liberation are the same.
22. Both believe that grace of God is absolutely necessary for attaining liberation.
23. Both believe that by intense love of God it is possible to have a vision of God.
24. Both do not advocate self-mortification; but that does not mean they advocate self-indulgence.

Now we shall attempt to point out the salient points of disagreement between Svāmināŗāyaṇa and Vallabha.

1. Vallabha calls his philosophy Śuddhādvaita, whereas Svāmināŗāyaṇa calls his philosophy Viśiṣṭādvaita.
2. For Vallabha self is a part of God. According to Vallabha there is a real identity between the whole (God) and the part (self). Vallabha believes that self is identical with God in its essential nature. Svāmināŗāyaṇa does not believe in the doctrine of identity between self and God. Nor does Svāmināŗāyaṇa believe that self is a part of God. According to Svāmināŗāyaṇa, self has a unique individuality and is eternally different from God.
3. To put the above point differently, according to Vallabha, the selves are real manifestations of God. And therefore, God and self are essentially identical. Svāmināŗāyaṇa does not agree with this view of Vallabha. Svāmināŗāyaṇa is an expounder of the philosophy of difference (bheda). According to him, self is not a manifestation of God, but an eternally existing spiritual entity having a distinct individuality of its own. According to Svāmināŗāyaṇa self is eternally co-existing with God.
4. According to Vallabha, unlike Alexander, God conceals His bliss and becomes matter.[1] Svāmināŗāyaṇa does not agree with this position of Vallabha. According to Svāmināŗāyaṇa God neither becomes soul nor

becomes matter. In his view God, self and matter are eternally different from one another.

5. According to Vallabha, there are three kinds of souls: one, Pravāhi; two, Maryāda; and three, Puṣṭi. Pravāhi souls are those that do not think of liberation. Maryāda souls are those that study Vedas and attain liberation by Jñāna Mārga laid down in them. Puṣṭi souls are the chosen souls of God. They worship God out of intense love for Him.[2] Svāminārāyaṇa does not accept this classification of Vallabha. According to Svāminārāyaṇa, also, souls are of three kinds. But the kinds of souls of Svāminārāyaṇa are different from those of Vallabha. According to Svāminārāyaṇa, the three kinds of souls are like this: One, Nitya Mukta (eternally liberated); two, Mukta (liberated); and three, Baddha (bound) Nitya Mukta souls are those that never were bound. They are eternally in the liberated state. Mukta souls are those that once were bound, but attained liberation by their intense love for and grace of God. Baddha souls are those that have yet to attain their liberation. Thus, the basis of classification of souls in Svāminārāyaṇa's philosophy is different from the one found in Vallabha's philosophy. Both the philosophers have different basis for their classification of souls.

6. According to Vallabha, God has created the world for His sport (Līlā).[3] Svāminārāyaṇa, does not accept the doctrine of Līlā. According to him, the world is created by God[4] out of twenty four elements so that the souls may experience the objects of the world and ultimately turn away from them and endevour to be worthy of the grace of God for attaining liberation.[5] In other words, according to Svāminārāyaṇa, God has "created" the world to help the bound souls in their attainment of liberation.

7. Vallabha admits Rasika Mārga as the means of liberation. Svāminārāyaṇa is highly critical about it. According to Svāminārāyaṇa, Rasika Mārga tends to divert its follower into degeneration and depravity.[6]

8. According to Vallabha, liberation is due to true Knowledge of non-difference (abheda) of the world and jīvas from Brahman (God). Vallabha agrees with Śaṅkara on this point. Svāminārāyaṇa does not accept this position of Vallabha. According to Svāminārāyaṇa, knowledge of the essential nature of eternal realities is the true and saving Knowledge.

9. According to Vallabha, there are two kinds of Mokṣa (liberation) suited to the followers of two different paths: Maryāda Mārga and Puṣṭi Mārga. The followers of Maryāda Mārga who regard Akṣarabrahman as the highest reality get gradual release. The followers of Puṣṭi Mārga get immediate release.[7]

   According to Vallabha, the followers of Maryāda Mārga, after departing from the body, travel by the path of gods and reach Brahmaloka. The followers of Puṣṭi Mārga are first merged in Purṇa Puruṣottama, without travelling by the path of Gods. Then God out of Sheer grace brings them out and gives them a divine form and allows them to participate in His eternal sport (Nitya Rāsa Līlā or Rāsa Līlā). To participate in the Rāsalīlā of God with Him and enjoy Bhajnānanda is the highest stage of Mokṣa.[8] For Svāminārāyaṇa Mokṣa is of one kind only. He does not admit the classification of Mokṣa made by Vallabha. According to Svāminārāyaṇa, the devotee of God after leaving the body, goes to Akṣaradhāman where he gains a divine body and with that divine body he eternally enjoys the blissful communion and servitude of God.

10. According to Vallabha Jīvanamukti is impossible.[9] According to Svāminārāyaṇa, the self, while embodied can attain liberation. According to him Jīvanamukti is possible.[10]

6. Svāminārāyaṇa and Plato

Plato was a Greek Philosopher. In many aspects Philosophy of Plato resembles that of Svāminārāyaṇa. Herein we shall attempt to bring out the points of agreement and disagreement between these two philosophers in respect of their philosophies of Self. First we shall note the points of agreement between them.

1. Both Plato and Svāminārāyaṇa believe that self is a real entity.[1]

2. Both believe that soul is imperishable. According to both, soul is immortal and it never perishes.[2] Plato says that since the soul does not come into being, it must be imperishable. According to Plato, it is as impossible that it should be destroyed as that it should come into being.[3] Svāminārāyaṇa would completely agree with Plato.

3. Both believe in the plurality of Souls.[4] Both believe that souls are infinite in number.[5]

4. According to both Plato and Svāminārāyaṇa, the number of souls in existence always remain the same. No soul ever perishes and therefore, their number cannot grow less. Nor does their number increase.[6] Plato says that the increase in immortal souls must come from the mortal. But, from mortal immortal cannot come. Therefore, the number of souls remain constant.[7]

5. Plato believes that indestructible soul must reap the consequences of its deed, good or bad.[8] This is what is called Law of Karma in Indian Philosophy. Svāminārāyaṇa would completely agree with Plato on this point. Svāminārāyaṇa believes in Law of Karma. According to Svāminārāyaṇa, man attains happiness or unhappiness in accordance with his past deeds.[9]

6. According to Plato, as pointed out by Dr. J.A. Yajnik, the first principles are derived not from sense perception or logical reasoning, but from intuitive experience.[10] Svāminārāyaṇa completely agree with Plato on this point. According Svāminārāyaṇa, as put by Dr. J.A. Yajnik, "knowledge is rooted in the very being of self."[11]

7. According to Plato, man cannot have knowledge of metaphysical nature of his self. As observed by Dr. J.A. Yajnik, "Plato has shown in Phaedrus that Socrates remained to himself an unfathomable mystery, inspite of the fact that he devoted the whole of his life for understanding himself."[12] Svāminārāyaṇa is one with Plato on this point. Svāminārāyaṇa has clearly said that man cannot know the metaphysical nature of his self.[13] He has further said that man can know about beauty and ugliness, about childhood, youth and old age, and about immunerable other things, but he cannot know anything about his own self.[14]

8. Both Plato and Svāminārāyaṇa believe in the reincarnation (rebirth) of soul. According to Plato, death is nothing but separation of the soul from the body. For establishing reincarnation of soul, Plato argues like this. If the soul at death perishes and if there is no return journey, then the stock of souls must finally be exhausted and life on earth must ultimately come to an end. Creation of new souls is impossible. Since life on earth goes on for ever, it is apparent that soul incarnates.[15] Svāminārāyaṇa would completely endorse this view of Plato.

9. Plato says that so long as soul is not purified, it has to be incarnated in a cycle of birth and death as a penalty for the sins of previous lives.[16] But, according to Plato, if the soul is purified, it can escape the wheel of birth and death.[17] According to Plato, there would be final deliverance for the purified soul.[18] Svāminārāyaṇa also says the same thing. He says that so long as the soul does not attain liberation, it remains tied up with the wheel of birth and death.[19] According to Svāminārāyaṇa, when the soul becomes free from the entanglements of avidyā, it attains liberation.[20] What is becoming free from avidyā in Svāminārāyaṇism in the same as one becoming purified in Platonism. What Plato calls Final Deliverance, Svāminārāyaṇa calls Ātyantika

Mokṣa.[21] The similarity between the two expressions is very striking.

10. According to Plato, as pointed out by Radhakrishnan, the wise man turns away from the world of senses and keeps his inward and spiritual eye ever directed to the world of eternal idea. Such a wise man becomes freed from the bonds of sensualism and after death his released spirit slowly mounts up higher and higher until at last its finds its way to the home of eternal light.[22] Svāminārāyaṇa would completely agree with Plato on this point. One whom Plato calls Wise, Svāminārāyaṇa calls Jñāni (maṇ of metaphysical knowledge). According to Svāminārāyaṇa, a man of knowledge turns away from the objects of the world.[23] He turns inward and realises his self as extreme effulgence and in that effulgence beholds the divine personality of God.[24]

11. What Plato calls Good, Svāminārāyaṇa calls God. According to Plato, the vision of Good is possible.[25] A purified soul can have a vision of Good. According to Svāminārāyaṇa also vision of God is possible.[26] According to both, the experience of ultimate reality is possible. In the words of Radhakrishanan, "the experience is felt as profoundly as possible, where darkness is turned into light, sadness into joy, despair into assurance."[27] "However much we may quarrel about the implications of this kind of experience, we cannot question the actuality of the experience itself".[28] According to Svāminārāyaṇa, experience of God is not an experience in imagination. It is an experience in reality. Experience of God is as vivid as experience of any other object. Svāminārāyaṇa declares the truth of such experience on oath.[29]

12. According to Plato, when the soul is liberated and when it reaches the home of eternal light, it dwells with the True Being for ever.[30] In other words, on liberation the soul eternally enjoys the blissful commu-

nion with God. According to Svāminārāyaṇa, the devotee of God, after leaving the body, goes to Akṣaradhāman which is eternal abode of God. There he enjoys the bliss of eternal communion with God.

13. As Radhakrishnan has pointed out "In Simposium Plato gives us the doctrine of timeless existence attainable here and now by an escape from time and form."[31] This doctrine of Plato is akin to Svāminārāyaṇa's doctrine of Jīvanmukti (liberation while embodied). According to the doctrine of Jīvanmukti, the true devotee of God attains the state of liberation here and now in the embodied existence.

Now we shall attempt to bring out a few points of disagreement between the two philosophers. Thy are as under:

1. According to Plato, the soul has three parts.[32] These parts are knowledge (wisdom), honour (spirit) and appetite.[33] Svāminārāyaṇa would not and does not agree with the doctrine of parts in the soul. According to Svāminārāyaṇa, soul has no parts. In his view soul is partless (akhaṇḍa).[34] Svāminārāyaṇa would argue that if the soul had parts, it would be like a composite thing. And a composite thing can hardly be said to be everlasting. Parts would disintegrate and the soul would perish. So, Svāminārāyaṇa would contend that soul having parts cannot be an eternal, imperishable soul. To this argument of Svāminārāyaṇa, Plato would reply that parts were not like material parts. Parts are nothing more, so would Plato say, than three forms of desire. Each part has its own pleasure and desire. Svāminārāyaṇa would not be satisfied with this reply of Plato. It should be noted that such division of soul is not found either in Svāminārāyaṇism or in Indian Philosophy. Svāminārāyaṇa cannot conceive of any idea of soul having parts. For him soul is a whole.

2. According to Plato, all souls are alike. He says that we must not think of the soul, in her truest nature, as full of diversity and unlikeness and perpetually at variance

with itself.[35] Svāminārāyaṇa would not agree with this doctrine of Plato. According to Svāminārāyaṇa souls are not alike. No soul is similar to another. In his view souls are different from one another. Each soul is intrinsically different from the rest. And this difference continues even in the state of liberation. Not only this. Svāminārāyaṇa has admitted the possibility of progress of soul in the knowledge of God and in the enjoyment of bliss of communion with God.

3. According to Plato, the ultimate reality, the True Being, has neither colour nor shape. It cannot be touched. Reason alone can behold it, and all knowledge is knowledge thereof.[36] According to Svāminārāyaṇa, God, the supreme reality, has a two-armed and a two-legged personality like a human being. And soul can have vision of such a personality of God.

4. According to Plato, the vision of the God is possible for those who are prepared for it by intellectual discipline and hard thinking.[37] For Svāminārāyaṇa intellectual discipline is not enough for attaining vision of God. According to Svāminārāyaṇa, intense love for God along with the knowledge of His greatness and glory are essential for having a vision of God.

REFERENCES

2. Svāminārāyaṇa and Śaṅkara

1. V.S.B. 1.1.1.
2. Śaṅkara Bhāṣya, Kena Upaniṣad 1.3; Śaṅkara Tattvopadeśa 25; Śaṅkara Bhāṣya; Bṛhadāraṇyaka Upaniṣad 3,9, 26.
3. V.K.S. 1; J.A. Yajnik, The Philosophy of Śrī Svāminārāyaṇa, p. 108.
4. V.G.F.S. 2.
5. Śaṅkara, Commentary on Vedānta Sūtras, Translated by Thibaut, Volume II, 3.2.7, p. 174.
6. Dr. J.A. Yajnik, The Philosopy of Śrī Svāminārāyaṇa, p. 82.
7. Dr. G.N. Joshi, Ātman and Mokṣa (1965), p. 468.
8. See above V.G.L.S. 4 (610).

9. See above V.G.L.S. 4 (610).
10. V.G.F.S. 57.
11. S.R. Bhatt, Studies in Rāmānuja Vedānta (1975), p. 16.
12. V.P.S. 4.
13. V.G.M.S. 13.
14. Dr. V.A. Yajnik, The Philosophy of Śrī SvāmināRāyaṇa, p. 82.
15. V.G.L.S. 37.
16. V.L.S. 14.
17. V.G.M.S. 18.
18. V.G.M.S. 18.
19. Dr. J.A. Yajnik, The Philosophy of Śrī Svāmināräyaṇa, p. 132.
20. Dr. J.A. Yajnik, *Ibid.*, p. 131.

3. Svāmināräyaṇa and Rāmānuja

1. S.P. 121.
2. Dr. J.A. Yajnik, The philosophy of Śrī Svāmināräyaṇa p. 123.
3. S.G. Mudgal, Article entitled "Mokṣa in the systems of Śaṅkara, Madhva and Svāmināräyaṇa" in New Dimension in Vedānta Philosophy, Bicentinary Commemoration Volume (1981), p. 82.
4. P.B. Vidyarthi, Knowledge, Self and God in Rāmānuja, (1978), p. 105.
5. Dr. J.A. Yajnik, The Philosophy of Śrī Svāmināräyaṇa, p. 114.
6. Dr. J.A. Yajnik, *Ibid.* p. 114.

4. Svāmināräyaṇa and Madhva

1. Dr. J.A. Yajnik, The Philosophy of Śrī Svāmināräyaṇa, p. 126.
2. C.D. Sharma, Indian Philosophy, (1952), p. 538.
3. R. Balasubramanian, The Absolute as the Basis for a Moral Community (Svāmināräyaṇa lecture) p. 5.
4. R. Balasubramanian, *Ibid.*, p. 5.

5. Svāmināräyaṇa and Vallabha

1. J.N. Sinha, A History of Indian Philosophy, Volume II (1952), p. 718.
2. A.K. Lad, The Concept of Liberation in Indian Philosophy (1967), p. 174.
3. J.N. Sinha, A History of Indian Philosophy, Vol. II, p. 714.
4. V.P.S. 1.
5. V.P.S. 1.

6. V.G.M.S. 2, Quoted earlier.
7. A.K. Lad, The Concept of Liberation in Indian Philosophy, p. 175.
8. A.K. Lad. *Ibid.*, p. 175.
9. J.N. Sinha, A History of Indian Philosophy, Vol. II, p. 713.
10. V.G.L.S. 7.

6. Svāminārāyaṇa and Plato

1. F.M. Cornford, The Republic of Plato (1961), p. 305; V.G.F.S. 7.
2. F.M. Cornford, *Ibid.*, p. 335; V.S.S. 1; V.S.S. 12.
3. Arthur Smullyan and other Introduction to Philosophy (1967), p. 38.
4. F.M. Cornford, The Republic of Plato, p. 336; V.G.L.S. 37.
5. F.M. Cornford, *Ibid.*, p. 336; V.A.S. 5; *See also* V.G.F.S. 13 and V.G.L.S. 39.
6. F.M. Cornford, *Ibid.*, p. 336
7. F.M. Conford, *Ibid.*, p. 336; V.G.L.S. 10.
8. F.M. Conford, *Ibid.*, p. 340.
9. V.G.F.S. 34.
10. J.A. Yajink, The Philosophy of Śrī Svāminārāyaṇa, p. 24.
11. J.A. Yajnik, *Ibid.*, p.25.
12. J.A. Yajnik, *Ibid.*, p. 108.
13. V.K.S. 1.
14. V.G.F.S. 20.
15. F.M. Cornford, The Republic of Plato, p. 337.
16. F.M. Cornford, *Ibid.*, p. 340.
17. F.M. Cornford, *Ibid.*, p. 337.
18. F.M. Cornford. *Ibid.*, p. 341.
19. V.G.M.S. 10.
20. V.G.F.S. 12.
21. V.L.S. 7.
22. Radhakrishnan, An Idealist View of Life (1947), p. 122.
23. V.L.S. 10.
24. V.G.F.S. 20.
25. Plato, Republic, III.
16. V.G.M.S. 13.
17. Radhakrishnan, An Idealist View of Life, p. 93.

28. Radhakrishnan, *Ibid.,* p. 93.
29. V.G.M.S. 13.
30. F.M. Cornford, The Republic of Plato, p. 337.
31. Radhakrishnan, An Idealist View of Life, p. 304; V.G.M.S. 45; V.G.L.S. 2.
32. F.M. Cornford, The Republic of Plato, p. 126.
33. F.M. Cornford, *Ibid.,* p. 127.
34. V.G.F.S. 13.
35. F.M. Cornford, The Republic of Plato, p. 337.
36. Arthur Smullyan and Others, Introduction to Philosophy, p. 39.
37. Plato, Republic VII.

BIBLIOGRAPHY

1. A.K. Lad, The Concept of Liberation in Indian Philosophy (1967), Girdharlal Keshavdas, Chowk, Buranpur M.P.
2. A.N. Whitehead, Process and Reality (1929) Cambridge U.K.
3. Bhai Manilal Parekh, Śrī Svāminārāyaṇa (1936) Shri Bhagwat Dharma Mission House, Harmony House, Rajkot.
4. B.G. Desai, Ethics of Sikṣā Patrī (1970) M.S. University, Baroda
5. Bhagwad Gītā (1969), Gita Press, Gorkhpur.
6. G.N. Joshi, Ātman and Mokṣa (1965) Gujrat University, Ahmedabad.
7. H.T. Dave, Life and Philosophy of Śrī Svāminārāyaṇa (1974), Akṣarapuruṣottam Mandir, Shahibag, Ahmedabad.
8. J.A. Yajnik, The Philosophy of Śrī Svāminārāyaṇa (1972) L.D. Institute of Indology Ahmedabad.
9. New Dimension in Vedānta Philosophy Svāminārāyaṇa Bicentenary Commemoration Volume (1981) Akṣarpuruṣottam Mandir, Shahibag, Ahmedabad.
10. Plato, Republic of Plato, Translated by Francis Macdonald Cornford, The Clarendon Press, Oxford (1941).
11. Radhakrishnan, Indian Philosophy Part I and II (1977) George Allen and Union Limited, London.
12. Works of Śaṅkarācārya, Volume 16, Vani Vilas Press Shrirangam N.D.

13. Īśā dyaṣṭottaraśatopaniṣad, Edited by V.S. Panshikar, Nirnaya Sagar Press Bombay (1970).

14. Śaṅkarācārya, Bhāṣya on Bhagwad Gita, Nirnaya Sagar Press, Bombay ND.

15. Śaṅkarācārya, Brahmasūtra Bhāṣya, Edited by Mahadev Shastri Bakre, Nirnaya Sagar Press, Bombay (1909).

16. Svāminārāyaṇa, Vacanāmṛta, Akṣarpuruṣottam Mandir, Shahibag, Ahmedabad.

17. Svāminārāyaṇa, Śikṣā Patrī, Aksharapurushottam Mandir, Shahibag, Ahmedabad.

18. Śrīmad Bhāgavata, Sastu Sahitya, Bhadra, Ahmedabad.

19. Yogavāsiṣṭha, Sastu Sahitya, Bhadra, Ahmedabad.

20. Yoga Sūtra, Sastu Sahitya, Bhadra, Ahmedabad.

INDEX